Archaeology and the Modern World

Starting with voyages of discovery in the sixteenth and seventeenth centuries and continuing through to the present – when the material world is represented on the Internet – the author of *Archaeology and the Modern World* reveals a crucial dimension of historical archaeology that lies beyond words.

The focus is on two areas – the Chesapeake (Virginia and Maryland, USA) and the Cape region of Africa. Past colonial societies of these areas relied heavily on slave labour and there was little if any direct contact between them. Yet, as Martin Hall observes, there were marked similarities in the ways the people created and used the material around them. It is these comparisons that the author uses as a measure for evaluating the major theoretical traditions in historical archaeology.

Although structuralism, critical materialism and other theoretical perspectives have taken historical archaeology forward over the past 20 years, such interpretations are not able to do justice to the complexities of the past 500 years. Working through the rich texture of individual lives, specific landscapes and cityscapes, individual buildings and everyday objects, this work develops an approach that builds on earlier theory. Through this study, the early colonial world emerges as a set of unstable compromises, imbued with violence, in which material culture played a crucial mediating role.

Throughout this study the past is seen as vitally connected with the present. It becomes apparent that whether through the claims for recognition by Thomas Jefferson's African American descendants, through the terminal rituals of white South Africa in the demise of apartheid, or in the way in which the material evidence of the past is mobilized in the Balkan conflicts, the material world of past centuries is still with us and continues to shape the future.

Martin Hall is Professor of Historical Archaeology in the Centre for African Studies and Dean of Higher Education Development at the University of Cape Town as well as President of the World Archaeological Congress.

Archaeology and the Modern World

Colonial Transcripts in South Africa and the Chesapeake

Martin Hall

London and New York

First published 2000
by Routledge
11 New Fetter Lane, London EC4P 4EE

Simultaneously published in the USA and Canada
by Routledge
29 West 35th Street, New York, NY 10001

Routledge is an imprint of the Taylor & Francis Group

Typeset in Baskerville and Gill by Steven Gardiner Ltd
Printed and bound in Great Britain by Biddles Ltd, Guildford and King's Lynn

British Library Cataloguing in Publication Data
A catalogue record for this book is available
from the British Library

Library of Congress Cataloging in Publication Data
Hall, Martin, 1952–
      Archaeology and the modern world : colonial transcripts in South Africa and the
Chesapeake / Martin Hall.
         p.   cm.
      Includes bibliographical references and index.
      1. Material culture –South Africa – Cape of Good Hope.   2. Material
culture – Chesapeake Bay Region (Md. and Va.)   3. Cape of Good Hope (South
Africa) – Antiquities.   4. Chesapeake Bay Region (Md. and Va.) – Antiquities.
5. Archaeology and history – South Africa – Cape of Good Hope.   6. Archaeology and
history – Chesapeake Bay Region (Md. and Va.)   7. Cape of Good Hope (South
Africa) – History.   8. Chesapeake Bay Region (Md. and Va.) – History.   9. Slavery – South
Africa – Cape of Good Hope.   10. Slavery – Chesapeake Bay Region (Md. and Va.)   I. Title.
DT2025.H35 2000   00-032317
968.7'02 – dc21

ISBN   0 415 22965 0 (hbk)
ISBN   0 415 22966 9 (pbk)

For Brenda

Contents

List of figures

Acknowledgements

A great many people contributed to the making of this book. In particular, I would like to acknowledge the help of Yvonne Brink, Marley Brown II, David Bunn, Meg Conkey, Brenda Cooper, Glenda Cox, James Deetz, Ronette Engela, Carolyn Hamilton, Ian Hodder, Matthew Johnson, Jane Klose, Mark Leone, Antonia Malan, Ann Markell, John Parkington, Carmel Schrire, Emma Sealy, Nick Shepherd, Julian Thomas, Ruth Tringham, Fiona Wilson, Margot Winer and David Worth.

I thank Karen Press for permission to quote from her poem, *Krotoa's Story* (Buchu Books, Cape Town, 1990).

I am grateful to the following for copyright permission:

MuseumAfrica Johannesburg (Figure 2.1)
Cape Archives (Figures 2.2–2.5, 4.1, 5.2, 6.1, 6.2, 6.4 and 7.2)
District Six Museum, Cape Town (Figure 7.5)
Heidelberg Project (Figure 1.3)
Kongelike Bibliotek, Copenhagen (Figure 2.6)
Mauritshuis, The Hague (Figure 3.5)
National Gallery, London (Figures 3.1, 4.2 and 4.8)
South African Library, Cape Town (Figure 5.1)
Visoki Decani Monastery, Kosovo (Figure 8.1)
William Fehr Collection, Cape Town (Figures 3.3, 6.3 and 7.1)

Chapter 1

Material conditions

This book is about the relationship between 'things' and 'words' – the material world and the ways in which people express themselves verbally and describe their experiences.

A wonderful passage from the Peruvian writer Isabel Allende's *The House of the Spirits* captures this relationship. The patriarch Esteban Trueba wants a classical style for his new mansion:

> ... two or three heroic floors, rows of white columns, and a majestic staircase that would make a half-turn on itself and wind up in a hall of white marble, enormous, well lit windows, and the overall appearance of order and peace, beauty and civilization, that was typical of foreign peoples and would be in tune with his new life. His house would be the reflection of himself, his family, and the prestige he planned to give the surname that his father had stained.

But Clara, Esteban Trueba's wife, fights back with 'protuberances and incrustations', the same weapon of expression:

> Every time a new guest arrived, she would have another room built in another part of the house, and if the spirits told her that there was a hidden treasure or an unburied body in the foundation, she would have a wall knocked down, until the mansion was transformed into an enchanted labyrinth that was impossible to clean and that defied any number of state and city laws.
>
> (Allende 1986: 114–5)

In her magical–realist imagination, in which things are never quite what they seem, Allende causes the relationship between Esteban and Clara to materialize in the physical world that they create around them. They give meaning to their actions in their columns, staircases and labyrinthian corridors and, in turn, the house and the things in it become a means of expression in their relationship, and in their relationship with others. In one sense, *The House of the*

Spirits is an archaeological novel, moving between settings filled with objects that often seem to have lives of their own.

Allende is also engaged with the larger themes of South America's history – colonialism and its brutal consequences, imperialism, and the ways in which global issues play out in the life histories of individuals. Here again, her fiction finds resonance with the 'archaeology of the modern world' (Orser and Fagan 1995) – the era that begins with European voyages of colonial discovery and conquest in the fifteenth century and continues to the present day. This historical archaeology has long been concerned with landscapes, houses and the 'small things' of everyday life, and also with the ways in which such material things circulated in the global networks that colonial settlement brought.

Julian Thomas has argued that the existence of objects – whether houses or teaspoons – cannot be taken for granted. The discovery of the meanings of things comes from a play between language and observation – the 'conditions of materialisation' – and that such discovery is the defining purpose of archaeology (Thomas 2000). Such 'conditions of materialisation' are as apposite to the present as they are to the past. Today, global distributions of images and large-scale movements of people render the construction of local identities ever more complex and salient (Appadurai 1996; Castells 1996, 1997, 1998; Hall, S. 1990). This can be illustrated by means of one contemporary example of the connection between global media flows, issues of local identity and competing claims for possession of the material evidence of history.

Between 1995 and 1996 in the USA, some 100 southern church buildings were damaged or destroyed by burning, and about forty of these were places of worship for African American congregations. These acts of rage played out through arson – surely one of the most dramatic uses of the material world for expression – received extensive coverage and national political attention (see e.g. Dougherty 1996). This high media profile had, in turn, many further consequences, one of which was the formation of 'a collective of journalists, writers, artists, church-based racial justice advocates, communicators and entrepreneurs'. This group founded a Web site, 'The Black World Today' (TBWT 2000), in direct response to 'the terrible epidemic of Black church burnings'; 'the racial animus that fueled most of the fires gave impetus to the launch of this site'. TBWT aims to provide 'an online global Black community . . . the single most important destination on the information superhighway, the one 'must stop' in cyberspace for Blacks the world over . . .'. In the non-linear stringing of hypertext associations that is characteristic of the Web and contemporary digital media, TBWT in turn promoted the launch of Sankofa University, a virtual resource for the promotion of Black history and an awareness of the Black diaspora, and named for the Akan concept of looking backwards in history for inspiration in the future (TBWT 1997). This completed the connection between the present and the origins of the African diaspora in the slave trade that began with European colonial settlement.

This example is one of very many that could have been used to show the ineluctable connection between particular and specific events given material form (racial hatred expressed by torching the local church) and the global circulation of opinions and images. Such global circulation has been conceptualized by Arjun Appadurai (following Rosenau 1990) as a set of 'cascades' – action sequences that have a 'global turbulence' and a bewildering variety. Global images such as these fold into local events with the result that 'the local political imagination is increasingly subject to the flow of large events (cascades) over time' (Appadurai 1996: 156). This is part of what Appadurai has called 'the production of locality' – the material construction of identity 'under conditions of anxiety and entropy, social wear and flux, ecological uncertainty and cosmic volatility, and the always present quirkyness of kinsmen, enemies, spirits, and quarks of all sorts' (Appadurai 1996: 181).

The chapters that follow focus this enquiry into materiality on two early localities that were produced as a consequence of the global interests of European trading companies (Figure 1.1). The Dutch East India Company was founded in 1602 with the purpose of exploiting the rich trade of the East Indies. The gruelling voyage south through the Atlantic and then around Africa to the East required a port for refreshment and refurbishment, and Table Bay, close to the southernmost tip of Africa, fulfilled this requirement. A small outpost was set up in 1652 and, over the next 150 years, the frontier of farming settlement pushed ever further inland. The second locality followed from the formation of another chartered enterprise – the London Company of 1604 – that rode on the same tide of enthusiasm for trade to the far ends of the earth. Its express purpose was the settlement of Virginia, and in 1607 the fortified post of Jamestown was established on the James River, upstream from Chesapeake Bay. As with the Cape, colonial settlement expanded over the years that followed, as woodlands were cleared for plantations.

An inventory of these two colonies in the middle years of the eighteenth century reveals 'conditions of materialisation' in which there were marked similarities in structure, and contrasts in its expression. A Virginia plantation owner on the James River would probably have despised the baroque-inspired culture of the Cape as peasant-like and unrefined, while a Cape notable cultivating vineyards on the Liesbeek River would no doubt have derided the Chesapeake's gentry as effete and affected, and their architecture as bland and unimaginative. But both Virginia and the Cape's gentry were obsessed with order in the design of their houses, the visible demonstration of wealth and status and the subservience of slaves and servants marked out for all to see. Such circumstances of comparison are ideal for revealing the complex ways in which localities were created within global systems of distribution.

But neither the Dutch Cape nor the British colonial Chesapeake make sense in isolation, and such specific cases need to be situated within the global

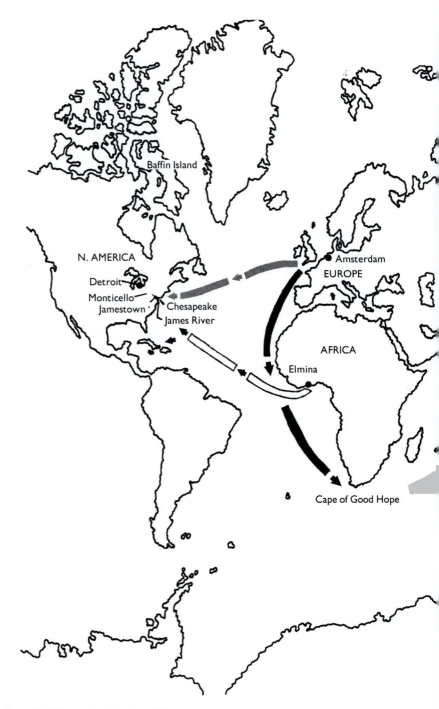

Figure 1.1 The early colonial world.

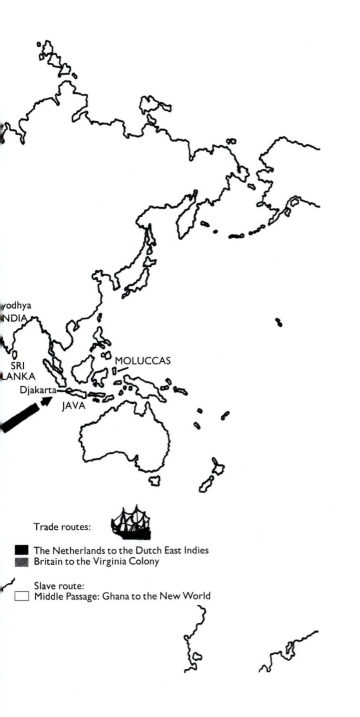

yodhya
NDIA

SRI
LANKA

Djakarta

JAVA

MOLUCCAS

Trade routes:

The Netherlands to the Dutch East Indies
Britain to the Virginia Colony

Slave route:
Middle Passage: Ghana to the New World

circulation of words and things, and the networks of interests that connected them. Consequently, the following chapters will visit the landscapes of early modern England, Baffin Island at the point of its discovery by a British expedition, Dutch Batavia and the Sri Lankan Kingdom of Kandy. Similarly – and because our understanding of the past can never be detached from our concerns in the present – giving meaning to these first manifestations of a world system requires a contemporary frame of reference, and is enriched by moving backwards and forwards through the centuries. These connections show how the colonial Cape and Chesapeake are represented, and reproduced as heritage, in the contemporary world, and the manner in which the 'production of locality' continues to draw on the power of the material world.

A second example from the contemporary world, matching the case of the southern church burnings, shows how the past is constituted within the present. Thomas Jefferson's Monticello was built between 1770 and 1775 as the central focus of an extensive estate, and is today an international heritage site and a long-standing focus of archaeological research. Jefferson's history embodies the paradox of American concepts of civil liberty, for how could the author of the Declaration of Independence – 'we hold these truths to be self evident, that all men are created equal ...' – also own well over 100 slaves (Morgan 1975)? This paradox is inscribed in Monticello's soil – in the foundations of the master's mansion and in the adjacent Mulberry Row, where excavations have revealed the archaeology of Jefferson's slave quarters (Kelso 1986). Two centuries after Jefferson lived there, his tradition is curated by the Monticello Association of Descendants of Thomas Jefferson, an 800-strong, all-white group that owns the house and grounds. Their image of the United States' third president is well represented by their manicured Web site (Monticello Association 2000). Together with a massive panoply of historiography, museums, monuments and images, the Monticello Association is keeper of a part of the national heritage. Jefferson's official descendants have their standing certified in formal archives and written certificates, and uphold a moral order personified in their founding patriarch.

But there have always been other stories. Oral traditions recall that Jefferson fathered a son – Thomas Woodson – in a liaison with one of his household slaves, Sally Hemings. First claimed openly by political opponents during Jefferson's presidency, this other lineage has always been held as fact by Sally Hemings' family. Now organized as the Thomas Woodson Family Association, this alternative lineage comprises some 200 African American descendants – part of an estimated 1,400 living Woodson heirs (Duke 1993; Murray 1997).

The Jefferson–Woodson controversy is an instance of group identities forming around differing claims to tradition. It also represents the potential of narrow group issues to achieve a far wider significance in the ascription of race, and the play of contemporary media in the construction of identity. In April 1993, the Monticello Association felt able to invite Robert H. Cooley

III – retired Virginia judge and direct descendant of Sally Hemings – to a dinner to mark the 250 years that had passed since Jefferson's birth (Duke 1993). But 2 years later, James Ivory's popular blockbuster *Jefferson in Paris* was released, the film presenting the affair with Hemings as uncontested fact. Subsequently, attitudes hardened with, for instance, the secretary of the all-white Monticello Association refusing to be photographed with black Jefferson claimants: 'I can talk about it, but I don't know if I can be seen with these people' (Murray 1997).

At the heart of the issue is a contest for possession beyond the words of either the written certificates of Jefferson's white descendants or the remembered words of his African American heirs. For the house itself, resplendent with portico, dome and symmetrical façade, is the essential monument to the American dream. Beyond the house is the cemetery, last resting place for Jefferson and his white family, and under the exclusive control of the Monticello Association, which has the right to bury its dead there today. Contesting claims were referred to the deity of science. If DNA testing could prove that Thomas Woodson's family indeed continued Jefferson's genetic line, they would be allowed their place in his burial ground (Murray 1997). Comparison of Y-chromosomal haplotypes from male-line descendants of Jefferson's paternal uncle, male-line descendants of Thomas Woodson, and male-line descendants of Eston Hemings Jefferson, Sally Hemings fourth and youngest son, showed that it was unlikely that Thomas Jefferson was Thomas Woodson's father. But the study also showed that the third president was very probably the father of Sally Hemings' youngest boy Eston, suggesting that the liaison continued for a substantial period after Jefferson and Hemings returned from Paris (Foster *et al.* 1998).

The material world, then, remains as important in the construction of locality as it was in the earliest global explorations. The physical loss – and rebuilding – of the South's churches is as central to the construction of identity as is the possibility of burial in Monticello's cemetery. Similarly, pilgrimage to Ghana's slave coast has been a vital act of reconnection for many African Americans. There is no digital substitute for the bare darkness of Elmina's slave dungeon, or the touch of cold stone at the point where innumerable slave ancestors were forced aboard Dutch West India Company ships. Representations in our contemporary world are as underwritten by materiality as they were in the past.

This connection between ideas of identity and the tangible presence of the past in the contemporary world can be illustrated by a particularly striking example of the connection between global media flows, issues of local identity and competing, violent, claims for possession of the material evidence of history. The rise to prominence of India's Bharatiya Janata Party (BJP) in 1990 began with a sacred pilgrimage through the continent to Ayodhya, birthplace of the god-king Rama. This Rath Yatra was a media event in which aspirations for religious revival – Hindutva – were focused on the outrage that Rama's birthplace had, for the last four centuries, been the site of a mosque (Malkani 1998). Appeals for the demolition of this mosque – the Babri Masjid – and the construction of a temple for Lord Rama were based on interpretations and counter-interpretations of archaeological evidence (Mandal 1993). Two years later – on 6 December 1992 – the mosque was torn apart, stone by stone, by a crowd fired with religious fervour; an event that received huge media coverage. Thousands of people died in the subsequent riots between Hindu and Muslim communities across India.

Once in power in New Delhi, the Bharatiya Janata Party was committed to Hindutva in the spirit of Lord Rama, asserting Indian sovereignty with a series of nuclear tests that caused a worldwide political crisis. Meanwhile, Hindu revivalism was promoted throughout the world, and particularly through the Web. An example is the electronic journal *Hinduism Today*, based at the Himalayan Academy on the Hawaiian island of Kauai (Hinduism Online 2000):

> The world's oldest religion is donning shining new clothes. The age-old Hindu philosophy passed from mouth to mouth in tiny villages across India is now going high-tech ... bringing ... every aspect of Sanatana Dharma to millions of Internet users across the world.
>
> (Melwani 1998)

In New Delhi, the Vishwa Hindu Parishad (World Hindu Council) challenged BJP political expediency by announcing that massive columns for a reconstructed temple – replicas claimed to be based on authoritative archaeological evidence – were being assembled in secret workshops in preparation for transport to Ayodhya; a campaign that rested on its appeal to a global media (Miglani 1998).

The example of Ayodhya shows how global media (broadcast coverage of the Rath Yatra and mosque destruction, and Internet sites), the political manipulation of the past (the Bharatiya Janata Party's use of Hindu tradition), the materiality of the archive (the vital importance of the Temple site, the visceral action of the mosque's destruction, and the appeal of the announcement of its secret reconstruction) and violence (the thousands of deaths that followed the assault on Babri Masjid) are all part of a common nexus. Both Arjun Appadurai and Manuel Castells have argued that it is the connection between global media, large-scale movements of people and the contestation of interests and identities on a local scale that renders the late capitalist world so singularly unstable (Appadurai 1996; Castells 1996, 1997, 1998). And, just as diasporic Hindus assert an ethnic identity through claims to Rama's birthplace, so other ethnic identities are asserted through recourse to the past: Croats who have long lived in South America or the US; Algerian 'guest workers' in Germany; Chinese in Indonesia or Australia; white South Africans in Seattle, California or New Zealand.

News media present the politics of Ayodhya as an expression of an inevitable clash of ancient and essential titans – Hindu India versus Muslim
India. The BJP and many Hindu Web sites do the same, essentializing
Hindutva as the expression of age-old ethnic identities that must always
move towards a pure form of their expression. But historical analysis shows
how Hindu and Muslim India were colonial constructs – the colonial bureaucratic simplification of thousands of local identities for the purposes of administration and control (Appadurai 1996). And more probing journalism has
shown that, before the arrival of the Rath Yatra in 1990, the town of
Ayodhya accommodated many faiths, temples and mosques, and was rela-
tively untroubled by the domes of the Babri Masjid over the place where
Rama was rumoured to have been born (Nandini Rao, personal communication). Six years after the destruction of Babri Masjid, local Hindus and
Muslims were attending one another's weddings in Ayodhya, and blaming
the riots on the political agitation of outsiders (Iijima 1998).

One danger in focusing on this constant interplay between past and present,
well illustrated by the misconception that the destruction of Ayodhya's Babri
Masjid was inevitable, is the assumption of primordialism. It is claimed that
identity in the contemporary world is the consequence of age-old behaviours
that have somehow been inherited through the generations. Such assumptions
are deeply rooted, and continually sustained in contemporary media:
Shakespeare's Montagues and Capulets, revived in futuristic setting in
Hollywood's *Romeo and Juliet*; the medieval horror of Africa, canonized by
Joseph Conrad in *Heart of Darkness* (1971) and sustaining the assumption of
the inevitability of genocide in Rwanda; the assumption that today's
conflicts in Eastern Europe are the consequence of medieval tribal configurations (Appadurai 1996). Julian Thomas (2000) shows how such assumptions
of an unchanging humanity underlie influential strands in contemporary
archaeological theory, and argues that this is not a sound approach to understanding the past. We need to find out what people thought about the world –
to understand them as agents. To assume that people in the past were like us
in order to facilitate interpretation by empathy leads to a circularity in interpretation that renders historical inquiry self-serving.

In historical archaeology, such agency is triply inscribed. First, there is the
original actor, whether slave or governor, whose material and verbal expression has created the archaeological record. Secondly, there is the witness to
such acts of historical production, whether court scribe, enumerator, diarist
or travel writer. Sometimes, original agent and witness are one and the same.
On other occasions, the witness seeks a detachment and claims an objectivity
in recounting the circumstances of history. And thirdly, there are the interpreters – the authors of theoretical works, precedent archaeological and
historical texts, and myself, as author of the chapters that follow. The

consequence is a multi-stranded rope that links together a complex network of sources and connects the present with the past.

In this book, I rely heavily on a small group of witnesses whose texts are combinations of travel writing, ethnography, literary construction, propaganda and derivation from earlier sources. Such work has been described by Kenneth Parker as

> a hybrid form ... that belongs neither exclusively to the inventions of fiction nor to the 'facts' of science, neither to the public world of 'official discourse' nor to the private one of diary or autobiography, but contains and displays elements of all of these.
>
> (Parker 1995: 201)

The value of these writers to my study lies partly in what they saw around them (or read) and wrote about, and partly in their own positions and prejudices. As I hope to show, their ambiguities are invaluable indicators of the way in which their material world hung together. I feel ambivalent towards them and their texts, at once acknowledging them as fellow travellers, but also recognizing them as the enthusiastic agents of oppressive regimes. Because they play such an important part in the chapters that follow, they deserve to be introduced properly.

The eighteenth-century Cape is represented through the written accounts of three men, contemporary ethnographers, writing about southern Africa as a strange and curious place, and seeking to gain recognition through their claims of first-hand experience. Pieter Kolbe's *Present State of the Cape of Good Hope* was first published in 1719 (Figure 1.2). Kolbe was born in Germany in 1675 and worked as a tutor until he was sent by a patron to make astronomical observations at the Cape, where he lived between 1705 and 1713. He became embroiled in the complex politics of the Cape, first losing favour with the powerful Governor W. A. van der Stel and then regaining his position when the governor was recalled to the Netherlands in disgrace. Kolbe ended his career at the Cape as Secretary for the Dutch East India Company for the district of Stellenbosch and Drakenstein (1711–13), returning to Europe to write his ethnography, which first appeared in German, then followed by Dutch (1727), English (1731) and French (1742) editions (Beyers 1977).

Kolbe's account became one of the major print sources on southern Africa, and was referenced or plagiarized by most subsequent writers. One who regarded it highly was François Valentyn, who had this to say about it: 'Various authors have written concerning the Cape of Good Hope, each in his own manner, but no one better than Heer Pieter Colben'. However, perhaps jealous of his own ambitions as an authoritative writer, Valentyn felt constrained to add that Kolbe was 'too prolix concerning some unimportant matters, so that a Folio grew out of it, and indeed somewhat too concise con-

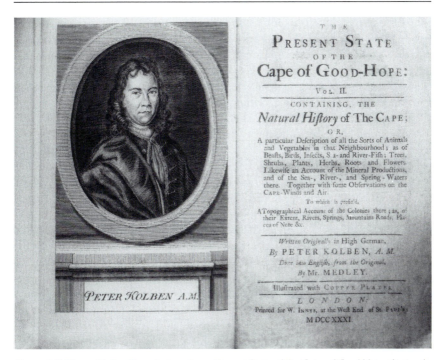

Figure 1.2 Pieter Kolbe. Frontispiece from *Present State of the Cape of Good Hope*, first published in 1719.

cerning some important ones . . .' (Valentyn 1973: 127). Valentyn set about correcting these errors in his own writing.

Nine years older than Kolbe, Valentyn had left the Netherlands a qualified minister of religion at the age of nineteen and had spent two long periods in Dutch East India Company service in the Moluccas before returning finally to Dordrecht in 1714. Like Kolbe, Valentyn was at home in the upper levels of the colonial order, and was obsessed with writing an authoritative account of his experiences. The *Oud en Nieuw Oost-Indien*, on which he worked after 1714, was intended as a compilation of facts, prints and maps about each settlement in the Dutch East Indies, presented to honour the Company and the Netherlands (Serton 1971). Valentyn visited the Cape in 1685, 1695, 1705 and 1714 on his way between Dordrecht and the East, spending 6 months ashore in all.

The third contemporary ethnographer of the Cape is Otto Mentzel, whose *Geographical and Topographical Description of the Cape of Good Hope* was first published between 1785 and 1787. Mentzel had been born in Prussia in 1709 and enlisted with the Dutch East India Company in a capacity that was largely a sinecure, arriving at the Cape in July 1733. He worked as tutor to a number of well-placed families, including that of Rudolf Siegfried Allemann, whose biography he was to publish in 1784 (Mentzel 1919). Intending to settle at the Cape as a freeburgher, Mentzel was returned to Europe in 1741 when the ship he was visiting sailed from Table Bay suddenly without the opportunity of putting him ashore (de Kock 1968). For the next 40 years, Menzel worked in the Prussian civil service, reading accounts of the Cape but not writing himself until old age. Consequently, his *Geographical and Topographical Description* (Mentzel 1921, 1925, 1944) absorbed earlier sources such as Kolbe, whom he despised. Robert Shell eulogizes Mentzel's writing:

> Mentzel could lay claim to being the Herodotus of the early Cape. He used many original documents of the Dutch East India Company, some of which are now 'lost', for example, the 1713 census. Mentzel also interviewed the colonists widely. He had no scientific background; consequently, his work is full of people, not the flora, fauna, and astronomy that occupied his contemporaries. Many of his animadversions about the demography of the early Cape are open to question, but he approached all topics with scholarly zeal and vigor, correcting with Prussian precision his predecessors' errors. He traveled widely in the Cape and poked into all sorts of corners of Cape society, which practice gives his work a vivid tone absent from many of his contemporaries' work.
>
> (Shell 1994: 457)

Others may be more skeptical of an account notable for its prejudice and inconsistency. But in any event, Otto Mentzel's texts are a major source for the historical archaeology presented here.

The Chesapeake, in contrast, is represented in these chapters by only one writer, although he was sufficiently prolific to produce a considerable amount of work in diverse genres. William Byrd II was a Virginia plantation owner who had gained his position by means of his inheritance. His father – a first generation tobacco farmer on the James River, had sent his son to school in England, and then on to read law and learn trade in the Netherlands and London (Wright 1966). Byrd returned to Virginia on the old man's death, where he established himself as a scion of Virginia politics and cultural life, maintaining active social connections in London and at the aristocratic estates of England. One of his first actions in adapting his father's more modest house, Westover, to a grandiose riverside mansion was to build a library. This he put to good use, producing a substantial corpus of writing that has given him the reputation of being the major Southern colonial writer before Thomas Jefferson (Bain 1987). These texts include the known fragments of a private diary, a voluminous correspondence and several travel accounts. Together, they reveal both the public transcript of the confident patriarch, and the private anxieties of a man coming to terms with his position in the world. In Byrd's own words, in a letter to his contemporary, the Earl of Orrery:

Like one of the Patriarchs, I have my Flocks and my Herds, my Bond-men and Bond-women, and every Soart of Trade amongst my own Servants, so that I live in a kind of Independence of everyone but Providence . . . However this Soart of Life is without expence, yet is attended with a great deal of trouble. I must take care to keep all my people to their Duty, to set all the Springs in motion and to make every one draw his equal Share to carry the Machine forward.

(Byrd 1924)

Tyree Guyton, an artist working in Detroit's East Side, composes with discarded objects that range from old shoes and bicycles to abandoned houses (Figure 1.3). Between 1986 and 1998, he transformed two deprived and derelict city blocks into a work of art that has been compared with Marcel Duchamp, Disney and rat-infested junk. Guyton uses 'small things' to give a new perspective on underclass life. 'Soles of the Most High', a tree hung with discarded shoes, recalls Guyton's grandfather's recollections of southern lynchings in his childhood – as a small boy, all he could see was the soles of dead men's shoes. The OJ (Obstruction of Justice) House is an abandoned shell, now adorned with painted trash and used for children's art classes. A house notorious as a crack den has been painted with large polka dots (Heidelberg Project 2000).

Guyton's work is an apt metaphor for the concept of historical archaeology that will be developed in this book. The Heidelberg Project – named for the street where Guyton was brought up and now works – exposes the way in which innumerable, ordinary, objects comprise an environment rich in meanings, an integrated array from an old shoe to a whole building and the landscape in which people live and express themselves. The immediacy of the neighborhood is coterminous with far-wider issues of authority and resistance, with the ambiguities of power and the imminence of violence.

Guyton's trash-adorned streetscapes draw to themselves the dissenting voices of the city. For some, this is a community arts project that counters the effects of unemployment, poverty and drug abuse: 'the Heidelberg Project has transformed a hard-core inner city neighborhood where people were afraid to walk, even in daytime, into one in which neighbors take pride and where visitors are many and welcome' (Heidelberg Project 2000). For others, it is a blight on property values: 'I want it to be gone yesterday. You can't force me to accept rat-infested junk as art, when it's jeopardizing the well-being of the community' (Councilwoman Kay Everett, in McConnell 1998).

The persistent force of the Heidelberg Project can be understood as an exemplar of the importance of material culture in our lives (the 'small things' around us), and in terms of local and individual action within the global circulation of ideas (the *Boston Globe*, art galleries and critics, *Newsweek* and the Internet). As an ongoing play of power and resistance, the Project captures

Figure 1.3 Tyree Guyton's Dotty-Wotty House, Heidelberg Project, Detroit (http://www.heidelberg.org).

the anxieties and violence of inner-city life – claiming back no-go areas for residents, living in the face of drug abuse and violent crime, anxieties about rights of ownership and accumulation of property.

Tyree Guyton's exploration of trash is also appropriate to historical archae-ology: Europe's colonial expansion, essentially concerned with the acquisition of materials from the periphery of its world and the creation of places to disperse or sell its products, has resulted in the scatter of more debris across the face of the globe than any other phase in more than 2 million years of human history. Consequently, the artefactual density that accumulated between 14 August 1415, when a Portuguese fleet captured Ceuta on the North African coast and began an inexorable radiation from five small countries across five large continents, and 28 June 1914, when a Serbian nationalist precipitated the end of the 'Age of Empire' (Hobsbawm 1987), was probably greater than the material record of all previous Palaeolithic, Bronze and Iron Ages combined.

Chapter 2

Colonial discourse

Kolbe, Valentyn and Mentzel sailed into Table Bay under the shadow of the same mountain, read other and each other's accounts and recorded both continuity and change in the unfolding colonization of Africa's tip. Similarly, William Byrd incorporated previous and contemporary accounts of the Chesapeake, gossip, travelogues, political scandal and contemplations about his health and bodily functions. Such writing constitutes what Paul Carter has called 'a travelling epistemology', the translation of experience into texts that is 'a process of symbolizing, a process of bringing invisible things into focus on the horizontal lines of the written page' (Carter 1988: 31). This production of journals and books completes a circle with the material world, as words become artefacts in their reproduction and distribution, a 'print-capitalism' that serves to fix consciousness (Anderson 1991).

In the chapters that follow I attempt to develop a consistent theoretical approach to understanding the 'material conditions' of the world that these men knew, and about which they wrote. This approach seeks to capture the particular quality of being, at one and the same time, in a global system of the distribution of knowledge and in local circumstances in which the mundane brutalities of colonial dispossession and resistance were played out in individual lives. In this, I depend on a theoretical approach that incorporates a set of key concepts.

Archaeology has experienced a plethora of theory. Indeed, so much so that some archaeologists have rejected theoretical models completely, arguing that the evidence of the past should 'speak for itself'. Although I would argue, along with many others, that it is not possible to have any practice without theory, it is certainly important to 'listen to the data'. In the chapters that follow I try to do this by fitting propositions against documents, artefact assemblages, and other sources of evidence, by looking at what these sources reveal about one another, and by modifying theoretical propositions in order to develop a better understanding of what was happening in the past.

What are the theoretical tools available to an archaeologist for writing the story of the modern world? One of the striking things about the theoretical approaches that have been applied in archaeological interpretation is that very few of them are archaeological. Archaeology certainly has its own theory – the adoption of the principles of uniformitarianism and stratigraphy from geology and their modification for archaeological purposes is a good example. But most interpretations of archaeological evidence depend on a body of theory that belongs to the social and historical sciences in general.

Some have seen this as indicating intellectual poverty. But a more convincing reason for archaeology's apparent theoretical dependence is that the study of the past is a unitary endeavour shared by many different areas of study. Most contemporary academic disciplines are inventions of the nineteenth century – somewhat arbitrary divisions of a broad intellectual field. Archaeology is history and history is archaeology. To study archaeology is to study the sociology of past communities. Both artefacts and literary texts make use of images; those who read their meaning did not respect the disciplinary boundaries of the practitioners who would one day seek to understand their minds. Rather than demonstrating intellectual poverty, such eclecticism illustrates a potential for new, exciting and versatile interpretations that lead us closer to understanding what was going on in the past and, through this process, understanding ourselves better in the present.

A seminal concept for the chapters that follow is Foucault's 'statement', developed further in James Scott's idea of the 'transcript'. I see the transcript as a web of relations that entwine both objects and words. Transcripts are the basic building blocks of my historical archaeology, because they are the means of connecting material assemblages (the key subject matter of archaeology) with texts (the key sources with which historians work). One of the most prevalent shortcomings in historical archaeology as a discipline has been the failure to marry words and things. Much historical archaeology is either the consequence of parallel history writing, in which material culture and written sources are treated as separate and rarely interact, or the now notorious 'handmaiden to history' approach in which the archaeologist is little more than an illustrator for history textbooks. In the chapters that follow I show that, together, Foucault's and Scott's theoretical insights help to build a new, transdisciplinary kind of evidence.

It is important to stress that transcripts are not static entities, merely new ways of describing assemblages of data that are fixed and unchanging. Foucault, particularly in his fortuitously titled *Archaeology of Knowledge* (1972), is careful to show how statements have ever-shifting meaning, leading to multiple readings and ambiguities. Similarly, Scott's transcripts are made of dialogues and the constant, shifting play of power relations. For both statements and transcripts, it is this quality of polyvalency and ambiguity that make them rich sites of cultural meaning. This quality of ambiguity is particularly important in the way in which I see material culture. Throughout the chapters that follow, I try to develop an approach to 'things' that see them, not as artefacts lined up and categorized on the laboratory bench preparatory to their summary description, but as rich sources of meaning that gain power in their polyvalency. This quality enables the past constantly to be reinterpreted in the light of the present, and is a reason why history and historical archaeology are important today. I will develop this connection in the chapters that follow, showing how, in both the Chesapeake and in Southern Africa, there is nothing static or dead about the past.

Both Foucault and Scott, whether writing about regimes of imprisonment and punishment in early capitalist Europe or about peasant societies in Asia, use the founding concepts of the statement and the transcript to build a wider understanding of social interaction and the way in which history is constructed. In their work, as in other studies, a key idea is that of 'discourse'. For Foucault, a discourse is a series of statements giving a regularity to social practice. Discourse is evident in patterns and trends at a larger scale than individual action. In Scott's work, transcripts play against one another. Public transcripts are the overt statements made by those who control resources and hold positions of authority. Hidden transcripts are, to adopt a title of one of Scott's studies, 'the weapons of the weak' – the day-by-day resistance of ordinary people against the imperatives of those in positions of authority (Scott 1985). This play between public transcripts and hidden transcripts also constitutes the discourse of history as it unfolds.

Another way of conceptualizing discourse is as the embodiment of power, not in the narrow sense, but in the broader way explored by Anthony Giddens (1984) and others. Appropriately, Foucault has described power as the 'microphysics' of discourse, and Scott's work is full of examples of the way in which claims to authority are made real by attempts to exercise power, and attempts at resistance that depend on the power that resides in everyday actions.

Thinking about transcripts as articulated into discourses allows us to tackle one of the more difficult problems in seeking an archaeology of the modern world. This is the question of scale. Archaeology is necessarily particularistic, getting involved in the rich detail of artefact assemblages and collections of documents. But at the same time an archaeology of the modern world must address the fact that objects, images and people circulated across oceans and through continents. A man such as Zacharias Wagenaer, whose life is explored further in this book, could be born in the Netherlands, start his career in Brazil, establish his reputation in Japan, and hold his last position at the Cape. He left his mark at each of these localities; paintings and drawings of Dutch settlement in Brazil, the promotion of the porcelain trade in Japan, and the construction of a new Castle at the Cape. Wagenaer needs to be understood both as an agent in the localized transcripts of each of these places, and as a player in the wider discourse of Dutch colonization of the Atlantic and Asian worlds. By focusing both on local transcripts and on global discourses, an archaeology of the modern world can do justice to a variety of scales.

Thinking about discourses in this way helps to develop an approach to comparison that yields the rich insights that come from working across the different registers of the archaeological record. Comparison has had a bad press in archaeology theory writing over recent years. Comparison was central to the 'new archaeology' of the 1960s, with its emphasis on scientific method. This, and the implication that there are general laws of human behaviour that can interpret the past, has been treated at best with suspicion by postmodern theorists. But, despite this, the regularities of the archaeo-logical record remain seductive. Why is it that the public transcript of archi-tecture in both Virginia and the Cape emphasized symmetry and regularity, despite the fact that the men who designed and built these houses had no contact with each other and despised one another's aesthetic and cultural traditions? Why did the assemblages of animal bones from the places where slaves lived in the Chesapeake and the wine lands of South Africa show similar patterns, suggesting parallelism in forms of day-by-day resistance to owners and overseers?

These, and many other examples, show that the transcripts of colonial set-tlement were repeated many times over in widely different parts of the world. Such regularities are surely revealing, and offer a rich payload in inter-pretation. The approach that I have followed depends neither on generalized laws of human behaviour, whether these be the positivist propositions of the 'new archaeology', or the world views of structuralism, or arguments for the particularistic interpretations of 'experiential archaeology'. My point is rather that an archaeology of the modern world must recognize that the merchant capitalism that drove exploration and colonial settlement by a small group of Western European countries had at its base a set of economic imperatives that in turn generated similarities of form. The concept of colonial discourse allows us to recognize the importance of this underlying structure – the global scale – while interpreting the richly textured, local man-ifestations of the exercise of power and resistance. The gentry of the Cape and the Chesapeake may never have known one another, and their slaves may never have realized that others were living in similar conditions 6 months away by sea.

However, both colonies shared an underlying set of economic imperatives. By plying backwards and forwards between the local and the global, an archaeology of the modern world can make a rich contribution to understand-ing how the interplay of words and objects gave reality to expressions of power and resistance.

Transcripts, the microphysics of power and discourse, are powerful analyti-cal concepts. But alone they are insufficient to allow a full interpretation of the archaeology of the modern world. The added dimensions required are those of gender and, because the colonial settlements of the Cape and the Chesapeake were supported by the extensive practice of slavery, of race.

The image of the Virginia countryside was well captured by Rhys Isaac in his seminal work on the colony in the eighteenth century (Isaac 1982), and his portrayal in words can serve equally well for the Cape's colonial countryside. Isaac described a landscape comprised of the mansions of wealthy patriarchs, connected to one another by networks of consanguinity and affinity that structured the distribution of the people and property. Patriarchy was played out through elaborate traditions of performance. Eighteenth-century gentry in the colonial Cape visited one another, ate and drank together and admired and envied one another's houses. Their contemporaries in the Chesapeake vied for power and position and competed for prominence in the size and magnificence of their houses, strung along the banks of the colony's major rivers. Here, we see public transcripts at work in their fullest sense, meshing together verbal representation and material culture in a rich kaleidoscope of power. But a key issue for this book is the search for that which lay behind these stage fronts. To what extent is it possible to find Scott's hidden transcripts of resistance? Where are the material traces of servants and slaves? Can we recognize in material culture claims to identity by people who would never figure in the formal records that constitute written history?

The claim that historical archaeology is 'democratic history' – a counterbalance to the record of 'great men' that constitutes the historical record – has frequently been made. It is unsound for two reasons. First, the practice of history has long moved on, offering the archaeologist a rich tradition of social study that has used documentary sources to probe most effectively into the lives of the colonial underclass. Secondly, anyone who has searched for these hidden voices through the archaeological record will have found them frustratingly illusive. What seems at first sight to be the material trace of the ordinary person all too often turns out to be the debris of those with power and influence. Slaves were owned. They owned little of their own and by and large left as faint a trace in the material record as they did in the written documentation.

It is in this area that the work of Gayatri Chakravorty Spivak has been particularly important. Spivak has shown how the 'subaltern voice' affects the form of public transcripts without necessarily being directly evident in itself. Spivak's concepts dovetail well with Scott and Foucault's ideas of the discourse of power. We can reasonably assume that a public transcript has a purpose. The substantial investment of effort and money that went into the construction of patriarchal façades in the Chesapeake and the Cape was motivated, in part, by the needs of powerful men to assert, reassert, and assert again their position in society because they felt it to be threatened. The source of the threat may now be difficult, or impossible, to see directly in the archaeological or the historical record. But the potency of the danger to those in power is reflected in the impression that their reactions have made on the record of the past. Foucault has taught us that power is used for a purpose. From this it follows that the performance of power has an audience, and that the form of the performance implies the nature of those to whom it was directed. I have found this approach very helpful in outlining the impress on history by women, and by the slaves and servants who were too low in the colonial hierarchy to have left a historical archaeology that they could have called their own.

Race is implicated in all of these interactions and makes their interpretation even more complex. Both the British settlers in the Chesapeake and the Dutch East India Company colonists in the Cape found indigenous populations. These were incorporated, expropriated and largely destroyed by the onslaught of colonial settlement. At the Cape the Khoikhoi – pastoralist communities who had lived in the southernmost part of Africa for some 2,000 years before European settlement – were not only dispossessed of their land and placed in a form of bondage only slightly removed from formal slavery, but also came to signify the lowest form of humanity. Men of letters speculated as to whether or not the Khoikhoi (whom they called Hottentots) were human, travellers revelled in descriptions of native customs that were designed to titillate readers back home, and settlers made the Khoikhoi daily victims of a barrage of violence. In a now-celebrated circulation of this colonial image of domination, one woman was exported to Europe, displayed naked in public and, at her death, stripped of her flesh so that her body parts could be displayed in the Musée de l'Homme in Paris (Figure 2.1). This alone connects the early years of colonial settlement with the present; at the time of writing, the museum continues to deny rites of reburial in South Africa to this woman despite the intervention of Nelson Mandela, surely the world's most celebrated avatar of the principles of freedom.

And then there was slavery. The Chesapeake was linked to Africa through the lives of bondsmen and bondswomen who were exported from the west coast of the continent to the eastern seaboard of North America against their will, and in chains. By the early years of the eighteenth century, slavery was well established as the economic underpinning of the major Chesapeake plantations. It is not possible to interpret the lives of Chesapeake patriarchs without understanding the way in which they defined themselves against the 'other', daily presented to them as the slaves whom they owned. At the Cape, despite its location in Africa, a significant proportion of slaves came from the East, from Bengal, Indonesia and other parts of the colonial world. As with the Chesapeake the lives and customs of slaves formed a crucial referent point for colonial settlers as they defined their own identity.

A particularly complex interaction occurred when race intersected with gender. Women played complex and differentiated roles according to whether they represented the ideals of European womanhood, or the dark pit of a seductive slave population. One-time slave women, incorporated into colonial society through their marriage to settlers, could see their status change radically in their lifetimes, mapped out in the fortunes of their children and grandchildren. Again these levels of complexity illustrate the utility of the idea of the transcript. The complex play of these dimensions of

Figure 2.1 Love and Beauty – Sartjee the Hottentot Venus (London, 1810). A contemporary depiction of a Khoikhoi woman – Sarah Bartman – who was exported to Europe and exhibited in London and Paris in the early nineteenth century (MuseumAfrica, Johannesburg, MA 55/541).

race and gender ensured a constant interaction between the material world and the documentary sources that are its verbal counterpart.

The last of the key concepts that has helped framed the analysis in the pages that follow is Homi Bhabha's 'third space'. Third space is a zone of uncertainty and ambiguity. It is best captured by Bhabha's now-classic study of an interaction between colonizer and colonized beneath a tree outside Delhi (Bhabha 1985). Here we see the formative process of colonial domination happening at its most immediate level. Eager to assert authority, the British missionary circulates the English Bible among the assembled natives. But the natives are not compliant. They question, challenge and keep the possibility of settlement and conformity hanging in the air. This in turn forces a continuing circulation of the material image of civility as the colonial settler again and again tries to reinforce the message. Transporting Bhabha's definitive example into an imagined archaeological realm, the Indians are airbrushed from the picture. They have become the hidden voices, the transcript of resistance that has not left a direct trace in the material record. But the record of domination remains – the anxious, repetitive voice of the colonizer insisting on being heard, and the material object of civility – the book – that makes the claims of domination real. The challenge for an archaeology of the modern world is to read a performance like this and to interpret it in its fullest sense.

How can Foucault's concept of the 'statement' be used in the specific context of historical archaeology? Foucault elaborates in the following way:

> Instead of being something said once and for all – and lost in the past like the result of a battle, a geological catastrophe, or the death of a king – the statement, as it emerges in its materiality, appears with a status, enters various networks and various fields of use, is subjected to transferences or modifications, is integrated into operations and strategies in which its identity is maintained or effaced.
>
> (Foucault 1972: 105)

A statement is a relation with a domain of objects, whether those objects be spoken words, written texts or material artifacts. Discourse is formed from a sequence of such statements, and in turn gives regularities to statements. Through this approach diverse, synchronic, sources can be articulated – for example, descriptions of the Cape by Otto Mentzel, critical assessments of Mentzel's position within Cape society, and material sources of evidence for his world, whether from surviving buildings or from archaeological excavations. These statements can then be articulated again along the thread of history – the palimpsest of 80 years of prior colonial settlement that made up the Cape Town that Mentzel knew, and the historical foundation to which he was contributing for those who would follow him.

This discursive approach also provides the basis for comparison. In setting the springs in motion that would keep the patriarchal estate moving forward, William Byrd II was obsessed with symmetry, whether in the façade of his mansion or in the recesses of his privy (Hall 1992a). His architectural preferences were shared by contemporary estate owners up and down the James River. At much the same time, slave-owning wheat and wine farmers far away in the Cape were beginning to build mansions with ebullient front gables that combined baroque motifs in molded plaster (Figure 2.2).

Figure 2.2 Bourgogne, Berg River Valley, with gable dated to 1791 (photographed by Arthur Elliott: Cape Archives).

Virginia's gentry understressed ornamentation, seeking a stark simplicity of design (Kimball 1966). The Cape's gentry vied with one another in extravagance of design, ornamenting the backs of houses, outbuildings, dovecotes and chicken houses (Fransen and Cook 1980). Nevertheless, as in Virginia, the dominant theme in the mansions of the Cape gentry is order. Façades are always regular, with a central doorway balanced by equal numbers of windows on either side. In two-storey buildings, vertical axes are always maintained. Front gables are always directly above the door and ornamentation, however elaborate, is always symmetrical around the central axis. Just as tidewater mansions replaced an ad hoc impermanent architecture (Carson *et al.* 1981), so the organic *langhuis* of the Cape, with rooms added as front, back or side extensions as convenience dictated, was replaced by a form of building in which the entire, ordered concept was worked out before construction began. In both tidewater Virginia and the Cape of Good Hope, the eighteenth-century gentry were thinking order with houses.

Historical archaeology has been strongly influenced by structuralism (a relationship that is explored further in the chapters that follow), the limitations of which are immediately apparent from the basic precepts of a Foucauldian interpretation. Structuralists insist that the gentry of Virginia and the Cape shared a common 'world order' and, indeed, the commonality of underlying architectural principles is striking. However, this notion does not take us further forward in understanding the history of the two regions, and the manner in which the actions of individual men and women were entwined in the global systems of production, distribution and consumption that were the hallmark of the eighteenth century. The structuralist approach also fails to account for the significance of the differences between the elite architecture of the Chesapeake and the Cape. If they had observed one another's domestic architecture, the two groups would not have recognized a common world order at all, and would probably have heaped on one another the jingoistic venom that characterized Anglo-Dutch relations across the English channel (Schama 1988).

However, if tidewater Virginia and the Cape of Good Hope are seen as the sites of discourses, then the insights to be gained from comparison are considerable. Remembering Foucault's insistence that the regularities of statements are to be attributed to the form of the discourse, eighteenth-century Virginia and the Cape can be interrogated purposefully. And now the salient observation must be the fact of slavery (Figure 2.3). Although Virginia lacked the urban slavery of Cape Town, the political economy of the countryside was structured similarly in both areas. As with Virginia, the Cape had a small group of large-scale slave owners, whose daily contact with the slaves was mediated by overseers (*knechts* in the Cape), and a substantial group of smaller, yeoman farmers. Although the details of economy were different (the principal crops on Cape estates were grapes and wheat, in contrast with tobacco and, later, a more diversified agricultural economy in Virginia) the relationships between slaves, overseers and owners had much in common – overbearing paternalism, coloured by the paranoic fear of insurrection, dominated daily life in both Virginia and the Cape. The statements emerging from these widely separated places are similar because the discourses of which the statements form a part are similar. In turn, the discourses are similar because they are both part of the wider discourse of the expansion of European merchant capital.

Foucault emphasizes that statements have a history of changing significance, leading to displacements from one domain to another, and again this

Figure 2.3 Slaves in Cape Town, drawn by Johannes Rach in 1762 (Cape Archives, M166).

can be seen in the case of the gable. Eighteenth-century Reformed churches at the Cape were often built with gables, using the subservience of slaves as an allegory for the power of religion, as usually slaves were not permitted baptism into a religion which was used to mark the distinction between the civilized and the uncivilized. Pioneer Moravian missionaries, who in the verbal texts of their catechism were averse to slavery, could adopt the symbol of the gable on their churches to represent the authority of their religion to displaced remnants of the indigenous population who were settling at the missions precisely to avoid a form of slavery. Later still, ornate baroque gables were used by disaffected Dutch farmers who, while forced to sign an oath of loyalty to the British crown, wished to reject British rule in a way that could not be proved seditious (Hall 1992a). Elements of the material world, such as baroque gables at the Cape, can thus have multiple meanings. In that they are signs that participate simultaneously in different domains, such material elements have the potential to be 'overdetermined': laden with meaning. Since they, by definition, cannot be verbally defined by those who use them, material symbols have the potential to reveal the world beyond documentary evidence and oral tradition.

Central to the notion of discourse is the concept of power and its 'microphysics', discipline (Foucault 1979: 139). Foucault sees discipline as originating in the distribution of individuals in space, a domain in which location and division serve to establish control, and is best known for his studies of hospitals, prisons and other forms of institutional plays of power. But the concept is equally applicable to contexts such as the eighteenth-century Cape

and Chesapeake. 'Discipline is an art of rank, a technique for the transformation of arrangements. It individualizes bodies by a location that does not give
them a fixed position, but distributes them and circulates them in a network
of relations' (Foucault 1979: 146). And again: 'in organizing "cells",
"places" and "ranks", the disciplines create complex spaces that are at once
architectural, functional and hierarchical. It is spaces that provide fixed
positions and permit circulation; they carve out individual segments and
establish operational links; they mark places and indicate values; they
guarantee the obedience of individuals, but also a better economy of time
and gesture' (Foucault 1979: 148).

This is the point at which it is useful to add James Scott's concept of the
'transcript'. The strength of Scott's work is its emphasis on the mundane –
the everyday world of ordinary people and the significance of objects and
actions that are generally seen as historically insignificant. Scott stresses the
importance of everyday actions:

> the prosaic but constant struggle between the peasantry and those who
> seek to extract labor, food, taxes, rents, and interest from them ... the
> ordinary weapons of relatively powerless groups: foot dragging, dissimu-
> lation, false compliance, pilfering, feigned ignorance, slander, arson,
> sabotage and so forth.
>
> (Scott 1985: 29)

Peasants are not necessarily deceived by the ideologies that landlords
construct to justify their actions, while in turn landlords may be well aware
that their tenants conspire to create a view of the world which morally
justifies their resistance. This perspective allows Scott to distinguish between
the 'public transcript' ('the open interaction between subordinates and those
who dominate') and the 'hidden transcript', 'the critique of power spoken
behind the back of the dominant' (Scott 1990: xii, 2).

The concepts of power and discourse, and of transcripts, are developed
further, and applied to the particular circumstances of the Cape and
Chesapeake, in later chapters. The particular challenge for historical archaeology lies in the intersection of two axes – the play between local and global
action and knowledge, and the rich meanings that stem from the play
between verbal and material expression. Neither structuralism nor particular-
ism (represented by phenomenological interpretations) can do justice to the
complexity of the past, or to the play between the past and the present. The
concepts of power and discourse, in contrast, can show how the material
world was constantly implicated in identity and the expression of power,
whether the domain was everyday life on the farm, the conscious expression
of identity, or the grand schemes of house form, garden design and the layout
of towns and cities. Both the Chesapeake and the Cape were rich in examples
of such plays of power.

Power takes many forms, resulting in varying forms of agency that include the ever-present dimensions of gender, class and race, and the contradictions set up by their intersections. Again, Isabel Allende's fiction serves to introduce the point. Clara and Esteban's 'House of the Spirits' is an expression of gender – the undermining of the classical façade by an 'enchanted labyrinth that was impossible to clean'. At the same time the house, and particularly Esteban's estate of Tres Marías, also expressed the relationship between the governing class and the people who were soon to rise in rebellion against the established order, while the saga of the generations runs through a society defined by the history of slavery and race (Allende 1986). The rich narrative quality of *The House of the Spirits* – its discourse – is founded in the complex intersections of gender, class and race.

William Byrd's explicit recognition of his status as a patriarch – his power and responsibility for his flocks, herds, bondsmen and bondswomen – heralds an unusual combination of self-awareness and naivety in his writing which makes it particularly useful for the study in the chapters that follow. Heidi Hartmann's now-classic definition of patriarchy clearly applies to the world that Byrd inherited and built around himself: 'relations between men, which have a material base, and which, though hierarchical, establish or create interdependence and solidarity among men that enable them to dominate women' (Hartmann 1981). The great mansions of the Chesapeake expressed the material base of patriarchal power in Virginia, and were nodal points connected as much by marriage alliances as by paths through the woodlands (Isaac 1982).

The contemporary Cape was similarly ordered by public displays of patriarchal claims to authority. As with many colonial settlements, an orthogonal town plan made a claim for order and regularity in the teeth of the chaos and barbarism of the native landscape (Hall 1992b). Such public, orderly, systems related men to other men in systems of differentiated status (Figure 2.4). Not surprisingly, men were often represented by their houses. Valentyn (1971: 79) used the spatial grammar of the Cape to draw a plan in words, describing first the 'four broad, straight streets' and then the houses by their associations with men – 'those of Henrik Hommen, Richter, and another ... the row of Brommert's houses ... the houses of Heer Blesius'. Men moved about easily in this grid, calling on one another and carrying out the business of politics, trade and administration.

The essence of this sort of power lay in its performance, and the association between claims to authority and its material expression have long been recognized. Thomas Aquinas, whose writing marked the beginning of the early modern world, believed that 'building cities is the duty of kings': 'The most powerful nations and the most illustrious kings acquired no better glory than comes of founding new cities, or associating their names to cities already founded by others' (*De regimine principum* II.i: Kostof 1991:110–11). The Dukes of Savoy took such injunctions very seriously, making Turin the first

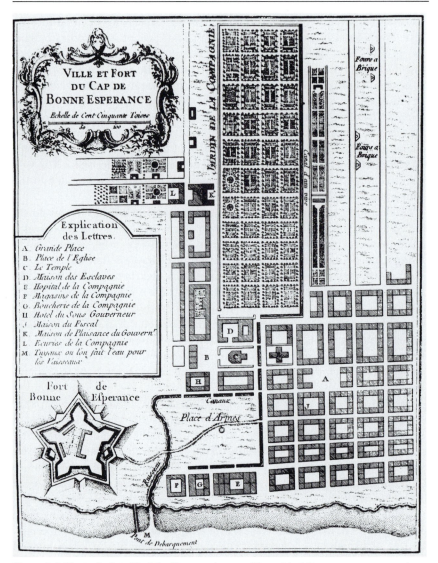

Figure 2.4 The orderly grid of the Cape settlement. The grid of the street system continues into the geometric layout of the Company's garden. Map dated 1764, and drawn by Jacques Bellin for his *Petit Atlas Maritime*.

geometrically regular urban citadel (Pollack 1991), and a model for many colonial settlements, including the Dutch East India Company's Castle at Table Bay. The streets of Turin were a theatre in which dynastic rights and claims were formalized as triumphant entries into the city, mock battles and comedy/ballets. In 1663, for example, Carlo Emanuele II married a French princess. Evening festivities were marked by fireworks exploding over an artificial mountain constructed in a city square:

> From the piano nobile level of the palace the guests watched the fireworks exploding over the mountain that occupied the square in front of Palazzo di Città. This mountain – topped with the bull of Mars representing both the duke and the city of Turin – was an element present in many Savoy family wedding celebrations (1620, 1650); it burst into flames at the conclusion of the display, ignited by a dove with burning wings, representing the bride, which crashed into the bull from the top of the palace ... The naturalistic display of mountain, dove, and bull destroyed by flames was countered by the geometrical display of sweets and out-of-season fruit (a recognized Torinese whim to this day) in the salone of the palace. There the royal guests enjoyed the visual bravura of the pyramids of fruit and watched with glee the 'sacco di detta tavola', the sack of the table, and the 'scalata alla piramide fruttata', the scaling of the pyramid ...
>
> (Pollack 1991: 161–2)

Life in other cities may have been more restrained, but the demonstration of power through performance was often important. Roger Leech (1999) has shown how Bristol was a site for processions that demonstrated power and status in the middle years of the eighteenth century. A century earlier, the ever-resourceful John Evelyn had seen in London's Great Fire a magnificent opportunity for reconstructing the capital as a theatre of majesty. His proposal, presented to Charles II in November 1666, insisted on the three principles of beauty, commodiousness and magnificence. All utilitarian buildings and services, whether bakeries, graveyards or warehouses, were to be banished to the perimeter, leaving the waterfront unencumbered, and a stage for the public demonstration of power (Kostof 1991). Such principles of urban design had a direct influence on the design of Annapolis and Williamsburg – the colonial theatre of power in which William Byrd played a leading role.

Streets, then, were the site for formal public events where male dominance, and the status of men relative to one another, was asserted in ceremonies rich in their materiality (Figure 2.5). Here is Mentzel's account of a funeral procession at the Cape:

> There may be as many as 16 hired bearers who are each provided with black crape bands, button holes, white gloves and a citron ... The bier and the coffin are covered with a white cloth and over it is placed a pall of black cloth with silk fringes. The sexton usually acts as undertaker and marshals the funeral procession. He walks in front of the coffin, which is carried out of the house of death on the shoulders of the bearers, but, after proceeding some fifty paces, the coffin is lowered and a short halt is

Figure 2.5 Order in death: the funeral of Baron van Oudtshoorn, Cape Town, 1773 (Cape Archives, M172).

made to permit the formation of an orderly procession of mourners according to the precedence list that had been decided upon. The mourners follow slowly two-by-two.

(Mentzel 1925: 123)

'Women', Mentzel stressed, 'do not attend funerals'.

Rank, precedence and gender all came together in church. Separate pews were reserved for the Governor and his sons and for his wife and daughters. Upper Merchants, members of Council, military officials and ordinary burghers sat between the columns of the church or around the walls, while the women were seated in the centre, 'upon their own chairs that are drawn up in regular rows one behind the other by the verger and his assistants before the service ... arranged in a definite sequence of precedence' (Mentzel 1921: 123–5). Men often argued out the implications of their wives and daughters' church seating. During the first British administration at the Cape, for example, two elders argued so bitterly about the placing of a single chair that the matter had to be sent to the highest authority for resolution. The ferocity that the issue generated is captured in the tenor of the complaint made by Church Warden Brink to the Acting Governor:

> I ... removed the chair of the deceased, and placed that of my wife in its room, but this [brought] the unexpected consequence upon me, that Mr Rhenius inconsiderately, caused Mrs Karnspeck's chair to be replaced, sending that of my wife home, and threatening me again in a message by the Sexton, that, if I dared to put my wife's chair in the aforesaid place again, he would break it in to pieces.
>
> (Brink 1801)

But, whether in Virginia, at the Cape or in Isabel Allende's South America, the playing out of relations of patriarchy was far more complex than a simple system of male and female domains, and their coincidence with public and private worlds (Davidoff and Hall 1987). For a start, it is notable that almost all accounts of eighteenth-century Virginia and the Cape under Dutch rule were written by men, all implicated in one way or another in the patriarchal regimes that they were describing. Valentyn was openly partisan in a factional fight for control of the Cape's economy, Kolbe and Mentzel were in the service of the Dutch East India Company and Byrd was the scion of one of Virginia's leading plantation families. They were, in other words, actors in the public transcripts of domination that they were describing.

Here, Scott's concept of the 'hidden transcript' is particularly useful. Denied an overt position of enunciation, women at first seem either silent or invisible – shut inside the houses, or displayed passively on chairs in the nave of the church. All overt voices are male – the dominant transcript – and they seem to be part of a straightforward system in which men control the public world of the streets and landscape, while women are confined without opposition to the private domain of the drawing room or to orderly displays of subservience, such as the nave of the church. At first, the dominance of the male, public transcript may seem complete. But, as Spivak (1985) has insisted, the female subject exists beyond this mere absence of texts. Indeed, the fact that everyone insists on speaking for her means that she 'is rewritten continuously as the object of patriarchy or of imperialism' (Young 1990: 164). Thus women's presence is continuously rewritten through its very denial in the male transcripts of domination.

To make a space for this 'other voice' – the non-verbal experiences or yet-to-be-discovered accounts of women that contributed to the 'hidden transcripts' of the colonial Cape and Virginia – it is necessary to try and unravel contemporary, male accounts. Here, key indicators are contradictions and ambiguities, flaws and inconsistencies in the public transcript. In this perspective, anecdotes and fragments of information that seem trivial in the grand narrative of colonialism take on new meaning as imprints of 'subaltern voices' on the fabric of the historical record.

Men at the Cape expected women to follow a rigid regime in the public world. Mentzel reported that, for women as well as men, social distinctions were sharply graded:

> Pomp and circumstance play a leading rôle in determining rules of etiquette ... The time that must elapse before a lady of higher rank may call upon or return the call of a lady a step below her in official precedence; the time of announcement and the hour of calling; the duration of the visit and the time of departure; all these and a hundred and one other important trifles are rigidly fixed by convention and closely observed.
>
> (Mentzel 1925: 107)

But accounts such as these are expectations, as much as descriptions, of what really happened. Recent feminist studies of early modern England, for example, have shown that the complex interplay of class with gender often put women in authority over men, causing ambiguity in contemporary, male-authored advocacies of social and familial order (Amussen 1988: 1). Amy Louise Erickson (1993) has approached the same issue from the perspective of legal practice, comparing property laws with women's everyday experience of inheritance, marriage and widowhood. She concludes that, although it is commonly assumed that the doctrines of coverture in marriage (the notion that the husband is a single legal person that incorporates the wife) and primogeniture in inheritance were effectively applied, ensuring a patriarchal structure, both had a considerably diminished impact in practice.

A similar discordance between male theory and actual practice was evident at the Cape. In her study of probate records for eighteenth- and early nineteenth-century Cape Town, Antonia Malan has confirmed that a significant number of women owned extensive property and possessions, and exercised considerable influence in running semi-legal commerce in the port town from the front rooms of their houses (Malan 1990, 1993). Traces of the ownership of houses, and the routes by which property was passed to successive generations, similarly reveal that women exercised considerable authority and influence in the Cape countryside – this aspect of local colonial history will be discussed in detail in Chapter 5.

One small but significant incident reveals the extent to which women could unsettle male authority. In December 1782, the Cape's patriarchal establishment was much exercised by the case of Sophia Boesses and what to do about it. Boesses gained instant notoriety by attempting to elope with a young soldier stationed at the Cape. But the incident gained particular significance because Boesses was none other than 'Mevrouw van Oudtshoorn', the 61-year-old widow of Pieter Baron van Rheede van Oudtshoorn, and that the events were recounted as a crisis of public order by the owner of one of the largest Cape wine estates in correspondence with a former governor. In a transformation of identity, Sophia Boesses shrugged off her reputation as 'a pious lady, the pearl and paragon of the Cape church', donned male clothes and 'walked swiftly' across the town at night to rendezvous with her 20-year-old lover from Luxembourg and a Catholic priest. However, it had been noted that Sophia had tried to withdraw her inheritance from safe keeping, and suspicious Company officials were watching her. The lieutenant and the priest fled, and the thwarted bride was returned home under restraint. The scandal lay not in the difference of age (marriage to a wealthy widow was the gateway to prosperity for many a Cape patriarch) but the inversion of the male public order – dressing in a man's overcoat, going about the streets at night, claiming control over an inheritance and the right to marry. Sophia Boesses continued to demand her lieutenant, but she was placed under guardianship and symbolically expelled from society; it was recorded that 'her chair has been removed from the church' (Schutte 1982: 373).

A second example returns to the institutional domain – the heartland of Foucauldian analysis of discourse. The Cape's hospital was in Valentyn's eyes a 'noble edifice', with high gables matching the church on the other side of the Heerengracht and a symmetrical plan. Indeed, the hospital shared other characteristics with the public order celebrated in the church, with a similar ground plan, prayers every evening and 'edifying sermons' on Sundays. The general wards served patients irrespective of their condition:

> Patients suffering from different diseases lie close together, hence the air is fouled by various odours due to perspiration, to the presence of many patients suffering from dysentery or diarrhea, to those who had taken emetics or purgatives, to the use of sanitary chambers, and to the train-oil burning in the lamps . . .
>
> (Mentzel 1921: 113)

Venereal patients, however, were treated differently. Contemporary views associated venereal disease with sex and sin – with the polluting dangers in intimate contact with women. It had long been believed that syphilis resulted from the introduction of poison into the body. For example, Cataneus wrote in 1504 that venereal disease was 'a morbid condition originating in a total infection of the substance of the blood linked with a poison contained in the menstrues' (quoted by Quétel 1990: 25–6). A variety of treatments was promoted, but the most prevalent involved the use of mercury in plasters, frictions and fumigations, all with the idea of drawing out the poison (Quétel 1990). Treatment was allied with punishment. On admission, venereal patients were segregated from other patients, put on half-pay and charged a medical fee (unlike other inmates, who were maintained on full pay for a month). Any man in the hospital was liable to be punished for sexual delinquency while under the medical regime. Absence for a night could result in a punishment known as the 'Dutch Garden' (a specific reference to feminine qualities) in which the miscreant was 'placed between three half-pikes and beaten with thin Spanish canes' (Mentzel 1921: 13). Beliefs in self-cures expressed a similar ambiguity about gender. Mentzel noted that he had 'heard from several who have been infected with this disease, that they cured themselves merely by eating a piece of meat or fat of a hippopotamus, and by drinking the melted fat' (Mentzel 1944: 256). The hippopotamus, known in South Africa as the sea cow, was widely believed to be hermaphrodite. In Kolbe's words, hippopotamus meat was 'much coveted' and 'a most agreable Present', 'reckon'd an excellent Thing against a Surfiet and a Redundancy of Humours in the Body'. Kolbe reported that 'some are of Opinion, the Sea-Cow is an Hermaphrodite, acting one While the Male, and another the Female', although he hastened to add that 'I Know not what Grounds they have for this Opinion: Nor can I say any Thing in Support of it' (Kolbe 1968, II: 132).

Male patriarchal authority was at its most disturbed, however, when the ambiguities of gender coincided with the ambiguities of race. In setting up as a free farmer at the Cape, the acquisition of a wife was crucial, as in the rest of the Dutch colonial world (Stoler 1991). Mentzel provided an idealized prescription – the public transcript again – in which

> many of the new colonists brought out their wives and children, and the single men soon ventured into matrimony. It is a great disadvantage to be without a helpmate: house-keeping requires female as well as male management, and when the man is at work he cannot attend to the cooking, washing, baking, milking the cows or churning the butter.
>
> (Mentzel 1921: 53)

But in practice it was more difficult than this, for women were in short supply. In 1679, of 142 free adults, 87 were men and 55 women. But the garrison (from which new freeburghers were mostly drawn) was almost entirely male, and by 1717, when the total free population had grown to about 2,000, there were considerably fewer adult women to adult men. During the eighteenth century, the ratio settled down to about three men for every two women (Guelke 1989).

One solution to this shortage was to bring orphan girls from Amsterdam, but this proved unsuccessful. An alternative was to turn to a more manipulable source of women – slaves. Some authors – including Mentzel – tried to pass off miscegenation as the pardonable consequence of youthful folly. But other passages reveal contemporary male paranoia about black female lasciviousness. Here, for instance, is Kolbe on the subject of sex at the Cape:

> The European Women in the Cape-Colonies are generally modest, but no Flinchers from Conjugal Delights. They are excellent Breeders. In most Houses in the Colonies are seen from Six to a Dozen Children and upwards; brave Lads and Lasses, with Limbs and Countenances strongly declarative of the Ardour with which they were begotten. The Negro-Women at the Cape are very lascivious Creatures. As they are exclud'd there from Working, and indulg'd in an idle Life, for about Six Weeks before and Six Weeks after Travail, they are the most intemperate Wretches upon Earth in the Article, and greedily swallow, and enflame themselves with, all the Provocatives they can come at, until they are got with Child.
>
> (Kolbe 1968: 340)

Thus the intersection of the requirements of class and gender created a need for a differentiation between women, introducing race as a central aspect of Cape colonial society, and of colonialism in South Africa. This process has been well theorized by Ann Stoler, who shows how colonial communities were structured and conceived around asymmetries of race, class and gender, rather than around balanced and mechanical systems of control. European women in the colonies experienced social divisions differently from European men. European women, in the face of the perceived dangers of miscegenation, were charged with carrying colonial identity and with promoting white solidarity: 'active agents of imperial culture in their own right' (Stoler 1991). But at the same time they were themselves subordinate in colonial hierarchies, and subject to patriarchal control that intruded into all aspects of their lives.

William Byrd – self-aware as he often seems in his pronouncements about his position in the world – revealed in his writing as many ambiguities about his own sexuality, and his relations with women, as any other writer of the period. His 'Secret Diary', as it has become known, combines a record of the mundane with a jumble of inconsequential associations and jagged edges: prayer, food, politics, slavery, lust, rejection, food, drink, prayer, masturbation, reflection. Here, for example, is the entry for 21 April 1710:

> I rose at 5 o'clock and read two chapters in Hebrew and some Greek in Homer. I said my prayers and ate milk for breakfast. I had abundance of people come to see me. About 8 o'clock I went to see the President and then went to court. I settled some accounts first. Two of the negroes were tried and convicted for treason. I wrote a letter to England and then went to court again. About 3 o'clock I returned to my chambers again and found above a girl who I persuaded to go with me into my chambers

but she would not. I ate some cake and cheese and then to Mr Bland's where I ate some boiled beef. Then I went to the Presidents where we were merry till 11 o'clock. Then I stole away. I said a short prayer but not-withstanding committed uncleanness in bed. I had good health, bad thoughts, and good humor, thanks be to God Almighty.

(Wright and Tinling 1941)

The particular value of Byrd's writing lies in the opportunity it gives to set specific incidences of the public transcript of the patriarch-in-the-world against private anxieties – the intersection of class, race and gender. In 1728, Byrd was appointed to a commission to resolve a boundary dispute between the colonies of Virginia and North Carolina. The argument had arisen because the earlier boundary between the two colonies had been inexact, place names had been forgotten and revenues and rights over a strip of land some 15 miles wide were in dispute. By order of the Crown, both colonies appointed commissioners and surveyors to mark out the line accurately. Byrd kept the official journal of the expedition, and subsequently wrote two texts: his *History of the Dividing Line betwixt Virginia and North Carolina Run in the Year of our Lord 1728*, and the manuscript now known as *The Secret History of the Line* (Wright 1966; Lockridge 1987).

Most readings of the *Secret History* and the *History of the Dividing Line* assume that they are sequential: a formal (and now lost) expedition journal, trans-formed into a satirical account for largely private amusement, transformed again into an epic account designed for publication (although never published). There is certainly a strength in this interpretation. In the *Secret History*, the commissioners and surveyors are given appropriate pseudonyms: Byrd himself is 'Steddy', and the other Virginian commissioners are 'Firebrand' (Richard Fitzwilliam) and 'Meanwell' (William Dandridge). Their counterparts from North Carolina are 'Jumble' (Christopher Gale, the Chief Justice of the colony), 'Shoebrush' (John Lovick), 'Plausible' (Edward Moseley) and 'Puzzlecause' (William Little). The expedition is recounted as a hilarious cavalcade from coast to mountains, although there is also a serious attempt to hold 'backwoods lawlessness and civilized standards of law and order in some sort of realistic balance ...' (Arner 1975: 112). This, Robert Arner argues, is achieved by the juxtapositioning of Firebrand and Steddy, thus casting Byrd himself as the epitome of civilization. In the *History of the Dividing Line*, the code names have been deleted and the satire has been generalized and directed to North Carolina as a collective, rather than at indi-viduals. The work has been expanded, with the addition of a comic history of Virginia by way of introduction, greater detail of natural history designed for a readership in England, and the inclusion of advocacy of the expansion of colonial settlement. The central issue remains the conflict between order and chaos: now represented as the Christian society of Virginia versus the 'Lubberland' of North Carolina (Bain 1987).

But the *Secret History* and the *History of the Dividing Line* can also be taken together, rather than sequentially. In this reading, the chronology of authorship is irrelevant, because Byrd must have written one with the knowledge of the other. Furthermore, although the theme of order versus chaos runs through both texts, it is cast in fundamentally different ways; tropes that complement each other, rather than standing in a relationship of revision.

In his *History of the Dividing Line*, written for his public, Byrd makes the connection between landscape and sexuality in a detached, academic tone. For instance, he tells the 'Indian secret' that bear meat is an aphrodisiac, making the man who eats it 'exceedingly impertinent to his poor wife' (Wright 1966: 278). Here Byrd is the ethnographer, standing back from his subject and describing the flora and fauna for the edification of his readers. In contrast, the *Secret History* is a bawdy, debauched adventure. As Kenneth Lockridge has noted,

> in the Secret History, much of the mastery is the shared mastery of men over women. Byrd reveals that he never let a country wench go by without speculation on her sexual possibilities, which he plainly assumed any of the men might have appropriated had they attempted with a modicum of grace.
>
> (Lockridge 1987: 132)

Byrd's recollections of 11 March 1728 illustrate the point. The text of the *History of the Dividing Line* is ethnographic:

> We had encamped so early that we found time in the evening to walk near half a mile into the woods. There we came upon a family of mulattoes that called themselves free, though by the shyness of the master of the house, who took care to keep least in sight, their freedom seemed a little doubtful. It is certain that many slaves shelter themselves in this obscure part of the world, nor will any of their righteous neighbors discover them.
>
> (Wright 1966: 186)

Given the suggestion that the 'mulattoes' were runaway slaves, and that Byrd was a substantial slave owner himself, this passage is notably insincere. A more credible account of the same event occurs in the *Secret History*:

> Shoebrush and I took a walk into the woods and called at a cottage where a dark angel surprised us with her charms. Her complexion was a deep copper, so that her fine shape and regular features made her appear like a statue in bronze done by a masterly hand. Shoebrush was smitten at the first glance and examined all her neat proportions with a critical exactness. She struggled just enough to make her admirer more eager, so

that if I had not been there, he would have been in danger of carrying his
joke a little too far.

(Wright 1966: 60)

Byrd claims to have kept his own reputation – to have saved the girl's virtue by
his presence – but the untamed landscape, the 'dark angel' and sexual excitement are tightly linked.

Similar connections are made in many more passages in the *Secret History*,
and are highlighted by their sanitization in the *History of the Dividing Line*. The
equivalence Byrd gave to conquering the landscape and sexual dominance is
made particularly clear in the September 24th entry in the *Secret History*:
'Our shooters killed four more wild turkeys. Meanwell and Captain Stith
pretended to go a-hunting, but their game was eight fresh-colored wenches,
which were not hard to hunt down. The neighbors supplied us with pretty
good cheese and very fat mutton' (Wright 1966: 98). Wild turkeys and fresh-
colored wenches were common game for the colonial patriarch.

One further analytical device helps in assembling examples of ambiguity
and contradiction such as these in a way that reveals the play between public
and hidden transcripts, and the ever-present subordinate voices that are
denied a place in contemporary accounts and in the public constructions of
the colonial countryside. Bhabha's concept of the 'third space' illuminates
the zone of ambivalence and anxiety generic to colonialism. Symptoms of the
third space at work are the constant repetition of the emblems of domination,
and consequent and continual depletion of their effectivity. The result is
uncertainty: 'the meaning and symbols of culture have no primordial unity
or fixity; that even the same signs can be appropriated, translated, rehistori-
cized and read anew' (Bhabha 1994: 37).

Bhabha's exemplar of this characteristic is that of colonial control and resistance in early nineteenth-century India. He shows how the Bible (an item of
material culture for the purposes of the argument here) was both the insignia
of colonial authority and the signifier of colonial discipline and concepts of
civility. Consequently, it was essential to British colonial authorities that
Indian subjects should accept both the authority of the Bible and its physical
weight and presence in paper and leather binding as evidence of their accep-
tance of their subjugation. But Bhabha shows that there was much more to it
than simple 'implicit meaning', both for colonist and colonized. For the
British, the materiality of the book made their claim to authority seem real,
and the imperative to distribute the Bible gave form to an otherwise intangible
claim of authority. The purpose of seeing their Bible circulating from hand to
hand between their Indian subjects seated under the tree outside Delhi – and
under innumerable other trees throughout colonial India – was to stabilize
what Bhabha terms an 'agonistic space'.

There was, though, a fatal flaw in this dream of effective domination. The
'English book' was a claim to a natural and universal standard of civility, but

the need to insist on its circulation simultaneously attested the prevalence of its barbaric opposite, a contradiction that is given emphasis by the materiality of the heavy, leather-bound volume. The more the book circulated – the longer it is passed between those gathered under the tree – the more the unspoken opposites against which the emblem of the book stood were asserted and made real. Repetition was essential – the colonial official must insist that the book continues to circulate until its authority is accepted – but this very repetition served to undermine the emblematic authority of the artefact: 'the colonial presence is always ambivalent, split between its appearance as original and authoritative and its articulation as repetition and difference' (Bhabha 1985: 93).

This approach to reading the traces of colonialism opens up a different way of understanding the material culture of domination and resistance. Rather than understanding material culture only as the imposition of an order from above, such things can also be seen as remnants of the repetitive insistence on difference and, in this repetition, evidence of the anxiety of those with power to regulate the spaces and places of their authority. In this, these manifestations of the generic 'English book' are also the impressions of the 'hidden transcripts' of resistance, Scott's (1985, 1990) mundane forms of obstruction to authority, such as passing the Bible from hand to hand around the tree for an interminable amount of time.

Such performances of relations of power are explored in more detail in later chapters. By looking closely at the complex web of relationships between the families who lived in the Cape's grand manor houses, the influence of women is evident, pulling many strings behind the façades of patriarchy. The ambiguities of such contradictions between the assertions of the public transcript and the realities of everyday life can be discerned in men's attitudes to nature, gardens and the unreliability of the body itself. Similarly, the ways in which men such as Kolbe, Valentyn, Mentzel and Byrd wrote about the colonized landscape and its inhabitants shows repetition and anxiety – the 'third space' in which the impress of the unseen but constantly present subaltern voice is evident. Again, there is continuity between scales of perception, with interpretations of the world-at-large mapped out in corporeal observations and mythologies.

The central idea in this chapter has been that of instability. The discourse of colonialism in southern Africa, the Chesapeake and elsewhere was a movement between the public transcript of those in power and the hidden transcript of those resisting authority and domination. Here, as elsewhere in the colonial world, we have seen Foucault's microphysics of power in constant play.

In their public transcripts slave owners may have argued that slavery was part of a natural order of the world and that women should know their place.

In their public fronts, whether in the verbal records that have survived them as the raw material of history, or whether in the façades of their houses, patriarchs asserted their right of domination and the obligations of subservience. However, they lived in constant fear of insurrection. Whether or not frequent slave uprisings were a historical reality, many slave owners certainly believed such rebellion to be a constant possibility. Violence alone did not suffice. To own a slave was to own the potential agent of one's own demise. Through the mundane acts of resistance, the ordinary actions of people low in the social order to frustrate and slow down the daily round of life, we see the hidden transcripts that James Scott has revealed so eloquently. However elaborately staged, the public performances of power were constantly art risk of being undermined.

Women challenged male patriarchal power in complex ways adding a further source of instability to this rich web of statements. Women's sexuality was ambiguous, the subject of male desire but a source of fear of the surrender of power. This source of instability found expression in a wide variety of forms, including a fear of contagion that matched the terror of the slave uprising, and practices of separation and protection that found expression in architectural forms such as the hospital. The instability that stemmed from the intersection of gender in the daily recreation of patriarchy was given additional complexity by race. Early colonies in places such as the Cape were, initially, overwhelmingly male. Colonial administrators had the challenge of ensuring a viable garrison and domestic units that could underpin household economies. The obvious, and sometimes the only, solution was the deracination of slave women and colonized subjects to produce a new generation of enculturated indigenes. But this in turn set up further instabilities along the access of gender as women were graded by perceptions of racial purity and married through ambitions of status. We will see in later chapters how these structural instabilities in colonial patriarchy gave women a degree of power that is often not recognized.

William Byrd has served us well as an exemplar of the colonial patriarch. Through his energy and, his literary ability, and his use of words to explore his own psyche, Byrd has done history an enormous favour. Unlike most other people of his time, who have left only fragmentary imprints of their lives even if they held high office, Byrd has left us public transcripts in his writing and his architecture, and a private record of his innermost thoughts. Again, the overriding impression is of instability. The more William Byrd seems to have asserted the public face of power, the more his private uncertainties seemed to have haunted him.

Not surprisingly, since everything in this colonial discourse seems to have swirled around in a myriad set of meanings, the interpretation given to material culture was constantly unstable. This material instability is well captured in the shifting significance of the gable in the architecture of the Cape. Standing proud in the façade of a patriarchal mansion, this was

Figure 2.6 Tupi Woman and Child, Albert Eckhout, 1641 (Kongelike Bibliotek, Copenhagen).

a symbol of hospitality, asserting the standing of a house's owner and recognizing the like status of the owners of similar houses. But for slaves the same gable was an image of domination – the authority of the master and the daily round of subservience as the gabled slave bell called bondsmen and bondswomen to the vineyards and fields. The gable has continued to support such varied and unstable meanings with the passage of time. As we will see later, it stood for Afrikaner nationalism and the civility claimed for the old Cape in the face of insurrectionary movements of the twentieth century. Today the gable of the Cape house adorns the labels of wine bottles and tourist literature, luring visitors to a rich history. Similarly the great houses of the Chesapeake invite participation in a bygone era of gentility. The discourse of colonialism continues its plays of meaning in our contemporary world linking together over 300 years of history.

Both the richness and ambiguity of this material world can be summarized in an image from the early years of colonial settlement. Albert Eckhout accompanied the first Dutch expedition to Brazil as a court painter, his work intended as part of a royal curiosity cabinet (Thomsen 1938). His paintings appeal through their apparent realism, and capture the different dimensions of colonial settlement in a single canvas – the expansive sweep of the colonial landscape that forms the backdrop, and the detailed representation of the bodies of new colonial subjects in the portraiture of the foreground. But first impressions are deceptive. As with the work of contemporary traveller-ethnographers, Eckhout's subjects conform to European expectations. They are people who have been invented prior to encounter – the lowest order as cannibals, reproducing the long-established genre of the 'wild man', and more civilized tribes looking and behaving far more like Europeans (Mason 1990).

There is also ambiguity behind these confident strokes. The Tupi woman's sensitive facial features and voluptuous body, emphasized by the silken loin cloth, invite sexual possession (Figure 2.6). This possibility is driven home by the painting's emblematic referral to Jacob Cat's well-known homily of the woman whose pot has been broken by being dipped too frequently in the well; whose virtue has been lost through dalliance (Leighton 1862: 43) – a parable widely repeated in the seventeenth-century Netherlands (Schama 1988). In the foreground of the painting is a bright-eyed, bloated toad: a long established symbol for the devil.

Chapter 3

Regimes of order

This chapter addresses two key issues. The first is the way in which assertions of power and status are made using material objects. A good deal of evidence for this has already been presented in the previous chapter – the sets of artefacts such as the mansions of slave owners lining the James River and the fine houses that still are seen by many as characteristic of the Cape winelands. This chapter digs deeper in this area, central to any archaeology of the modern world. Second is the issue of scale, crucial in any attempt to understand both the rich detail of individual agency and also the implications of an economic and cultural system that girded the world. Again, Zacharias Wagenaer and William Byrd can stand as instances of this particular quality of historical archaeology. How do we understand Wagenaer, who traversed in his career the perimeter of the known world while, at each stop, making a detailed but intense impact on the local cultural environment? How do we understand Byrd, who was at one and the same time a cosmopolitan who moved between the Governor's Court in Virginia and the aristocratic houses of London, and also the lord of a local cultural landscape that centred on his mansion of Westover?

Another way of foregrounding the importance of these related issues is to consider the question of agency. Without reconciling the issue of scale, one cannot make a connection between acts of individual agency and the world system within which people worked and lived. And, without understanding the relationship between power, status, and the sets of artefacts that made up the material world, one cannot develop an archaeology that is more than illustrative. In other words, an archaeology that does not work within the integrative framework of discourse runs the risk of merely being an illustrator's practice.

Asking these questions leads to a critique of two broad traditions in the interpretation of the archaeology of the modern world that have become important theoretical trends. Both are insufficient in addressing the key issues that have been identified here. But both have contributed a rich tradition of interpretive insight. The first is structuralism. This is a particularly strong strand in historical archaeology, and is best represented in the work of James

Deetz, examined in some detail later in this chapter. Structuralism is also found in many other variants, in some cases explicit and other cases masquerading as an empirical, non-theoretical approach to understanding the past. As used in archaeology, structuralism rests on the concept of the 'world view'. This postulates that people, in a collective sense, share an innate tendency to order the world in regular ways that can be analysed as binary sets of oppositions: up/down, cold/hot, left/right, male/female. Structuralism has been particularly attractive to archaeologists, because it presents a way of reading the minds of people in the past from material residues that they have left behind them. But structuralism fails because it is unable to explain change – and therefore history – within its own set of theoretical propositions. As we will see, structuralist interpretations fall back on poorly thought-out notions of historical change that are inconsistent and contradictory. Essentially, a structuralist world is a world without history.

The second of these major approaches is phenomenology. Here, the proposition is that the past is, inevitably, a subjective experience. In polar opposition to the law-like generalizations that were sought by the 'new archaeology', experiential archaeology sees empathy as the way of understanding the past. The key is personal experience, and the reading of the landscape, and of all material culture, in relation to one's own feeling. Phenomenology recognizes that all histories that we construct have a major element of subjectivity – they are what we want to see, and they incorporate an essential connection between the past and the present. However, as with structuralism, phenomenology must fail as an approach to understanding the archaeology of the modern world. This is because phenomenology depends centrally on the romantic projection of present, personalized experience into the past. Such an experiential archaeology assumes that the past and the present are connected by a common humanity. People in the past were essentially like us. But this is a dangerous assumption. Although it is clear that any reading of the past is subjective, it is necessary to subject that subjectivity to vigorous interrogation, rather than relying on an immersion of the ego in the evocative remnants of a past age.

One other feature characterizes both structuralism and phenomenology. Although they would be uneasy bedfellows, both seek closure. Theirs is an ordered world. Structuralist world-views predispose people to certain patterns of behaviour and a historical record that is not dissimilar to the orderly collections of an archaeological laboratory. Phenomenology seeks a closure between the past and the present – an almost spiritual unity that completes the circle. I take a different view. Certainly, understanding colonialism depends on a theorized structure of social forces; but it also depends on appreciating the potency of ambiguity, confusion and uncertainty, and the daily reality of violence.

How are the theoretical tools that have been outlined to be used to construct an alternative approach? This chapter starts at the exotic court of Dutch

Brazil in the early seventeenth century – the world of Eckhout and his paintings of voluptuous women against the backdrop of colonial plantations. Here, an entourage of naturalists and artists was brought together to bring everything into a regime of order that would have pleased a structuralist. In their attempt, though, they revealed the sort of uncertainties, and the microphysics of power, that were the discourse of colonialism at work. From this, we move to the rich, inter-oceanic trade and the way in which value was given to exotic possessions in marking out position and status.

Circulating alongside such rare and valuable goods were preconceptions of the world. These were ideas of what the natives of yet-to-be-colonized lands would look like and how they would respond to the landfall of the first exploratory expeditions. Again, colonial systems of order – the orthogonal grids of settlements and towns – sought to bring regularity to this chaos, whether in the Cape or in the Chesapeake. Such public transcripts invoked dissent that ranged from satire, through disobedience and punishment, to outright insurrection. By seeing colonial societies as unstable compromises in a constant struggle between the dominant and the subservient, we begin to get a richer understanding of what the discourse of colonialism was really about.

In 1576 Captain Martin Frobisher set sail from Britain – the first of three annual voyages in search of the north-west passage to the fabled riches of the East. He was accompanied by George Beste, chronicler to the expeditions and keen observer of the world of commodities that was opening up as a result of the new possibilities of navigation. With the lucidity that came from living out a period of change, Beste made a direct connection between exploration and the acquisition of fine things to mark out standing and position – silks, fine fabrics and other possessions:

> Whatsoever sundry sorte of corne, grayne, and meates former yeares have had, we not only have all the same in farre greater abundance, but thereunto are added thousandes of new things simple and compound, never heretofore seene or heard of. And as for coverture to defende the bodye, the matter is growen to such excellencie of architecture and building, to such finenesse of cloth and silkes of all sortes and colours; that man studieth no more to multiplye the encrease thereof; so much as to devise fashions, to make it serve more for ornament, than for necessarie uses. And the chiefest cause of all these effects (next after ye divine Providence) is the searching wit of man ...
>
> (Collinson 1867)

Onboard Martin Frobisher's *Gabriell* there was a formal hierarchy of status, and throughout his account of the voyage George Beste was careful to distinguish between the 'gentlemen' and the 'men of all sorts', with people such as

Master, Mate, Pilot and Master Gunner standing between these extremes. When the crew first landed on Baffin Island, these distinctions continued to be carefully observed as the act of possession was appropriately signified. The men were mustered under the Queen's standard:

> Our general with his best company of gentlemen, souldiers and saylers, to the number of seaventie persons in all, marched with aunciente displayde uppon the continent of the Southerlande where, commandying a trumpet to sounde a call for every man to repayre to the auncient, he declared to the whole company, how much the cause imported, for the service of hir majestie, our countrey, our credites, and the safetie of our own lives, and therefore required every man to be conformable to order and to be directed by those he shoulde assigne.
>
> (Collinson 1867: 134)

The positions of the captains of the three ships ceremonially reaffirmed, the whole company knelt in prayer. Then, rank and precedence divinely affirmed, the parade struggled across the arctic landscape:

> and so, in as good sorte as the place suffered, we marched towardes the tops of the mountains, which were no lesse painful in clyming, than dangerous in descending, by reason of their steepenesse and ise.
>
> (Collinson 1867: 135)

Beste's account of Frobisher's landing on Baffin Island well illustrates the two aspects of the discourse of colonialism that will themselves be explored further in this chapter. First are the ways in which assertions of power – status, and the authority to command others – are made overt in the realm of objects. These are the 'conditions of materialization' in the early landscape of colonialism, the complex play of gender and status in seeking the control of new territories. The repetition of the regime of order – the assertion of andro-genous power by marching across the ice in hierarchical order, beneath the Queen's flag – had as its purpose the discovery of new ornaments – things beyond 'necessary use' – that could give substance to the fine differences of standing in society. At the same time, such demonstrations of authority were examples of the very phenomena that they sought to reproduce.

Second, there is again the question of scale. On the one hand, materialization of the sort described in Beste's expeditionary account is a precise, localized development of meaning – the use of the flag to recall and reinforce obligations of social order, in one place and in a short and defined span of time. But, at the same time, the meanings salient in this very specific event depend on a global regime of order – the Queen's claim to sovereignty in the world. How can these frames of meaning – so different in scale – be reconciled?

Another encounter recorded by Beste fleshes out the issue further. Bringing his flagship, the *Gabriell*, to anchor off Baffin Island, Frobisher found evidence of fire, and saw an Inuit band from the top of a hill. After a bout of bartering, in which animal skins were exchanged for trinkets, five ordinary sailors disobeyed Frobisher's orders and attempted to trade privately, undermining both ship's discipline and the interests of the sponsors of the voyage: '. . . our mariners, contrarie to theyr captaines dyrection, began more easily to trust them, and five of oure men going ashoare, were by them intercepted with theyr boate, and were never since hearde of to this daye againe' (Collinson 1867: 73). In compensation, Frobisher decided to capture an Inuit and sail home with him as a prize; 'a sufficient witnesse of the captaines farre and tedious travell towards the unknowne partes of the worlde', even though his 'language was neyther knowne nor understoode of anye'.

Taken from the periphery of the known world back to England, the prize died without any verbal comprehension between him and his tormentors. Nevertheless, the Inuit's body was still of value. Frobisher had a series of death masks made – as well as portraits in native dress, in English clothes, and naked – and took some of these back to Baffin Island on his second voyage and showed them to a new hostage, provoking responses in words and gestures that the captain felt able to interpret as information about his missing crew, although the men were never found (Greenblatt 1991: 112). In this chain of small incidents the silenced body of the captive was transformed into a set of artefacts and circulated between the edge of the early modern world and its core, where these now-material things were valued for their rarity and exoticism. The map of this incident – part of the emerging discourse colonial possession – was both the full extent of the known world, and the body of a single captive. What Stephen Greenblatt (1991) has termed the 'representational machine' operates simultaneously in several domains.

This problem – how to interpret and understand both the immediate, perso-nalised meanings of things and their wider roles in systems of production and circulation – is general to all archaeology, but has added significance for an archaeology of the modern world, in which the particular has constantly to be referred to the general to be interpreted. For example, colonial estate owners in the eighteenth-century Cape and Chesapeake brought individual stylistic embellishments to their domestic architecture, making each façade unique. But at the same time, they were also referring to local colonial tradi-tions and also broad concepts of baroque and neoclassical design which link together Virginia, British India and London, and the Cape, Batavia and Amsterdam. The local can only be understood within the global, and the global 'representational machine' only exists in its local expressions.

There have been two broad traditions in recent interpretations of the archaeology of the modern world, and neither of them deals adequately with the problem of the simultaneous relationship of dependency between large-scale systems and individual agency. The one tradition has tended towards generalization, submerging individual agency beneath large-scale patterns of behaviour. The second has been particularistic, reading off the histories of individual households or events. Their implications can be brought out through a comparison of two texts. James Deetz's influential *In Small Things Forgotten*, first published in 1977, and reissued in an expanded and revised edition in 1996, is the paragon of structuralist readings in historical archaeology. Christopher Tilley's *A Phenomenology of Landscape: Places, Paths and Monuments*, published in 1994, is not concerned directly with the archaeology of the modern world. This book, however, eloquently represents a broad movement towards particularistic interpretations of the past.

Deetz's interest is 'that sector of our physical environment that we modify through culturally determined behavior' (Deetz 1996: 35), the complete 'cultural landscape', which can be defined as 'the entire range of terrain from the house lot, the smallest and the most frequently studied, through gardens and field systems to truly large units of analysis, entire regions that bear the imprint of a shared set of values'. For Deetz, as with all structuralists, the forms of such cultural landscapes are expressions of an underlying, universal mind: 'a grammar, in linguistics, is a set of rules for the formulation of utterances in such a way as to be mutually accepted by all speakers of the language'. This grammar is likely to be subliminal – beneath the awareness of the individual agent:

> a grammar can be thought of as a set of rules for the creation of artefacts mutually accepted by the members of the culture producing them. Such rules definitely exist, even if they cannot be explicitly stated by their users.
> (Deetz 1996: 154)

Deetz's reading of European settlement of the eastern seaboard of North America portrays cultural history from first colonial settlement to the War of Independence as the succession of three such world-views, constructed from such structuralist grammars, and represented in ceramics, gravestones, building styles, refuse disposal and the other minutiae of daily life (Deetz 1977, 1993, 1996). The first – from earliest settlement until about 1660, was 'essentially that of old England ... the establishment of the rural English tradition on New World soil' (Deetz 1996: 59). The second marked an ever-slowing divergence away from English culture, a natural process for successive generations who had had no direct contact with England. This worldview was marked by regionally diverse folk cultures, marked by isolation and conservatism, and held by rural communities little affected by changes in the towns and cities. The third worldview, a mid-eighteenth-century transition anticipated in the work of men such as William Byrd, was marked by 're-Anglicanization' – the Georgian order – 'mechanical where the older was organic, balanced where the older had been asymmetrical, individualized where the older had been corporate ...' (Deetz 1996: 63).

In addition, there was a fourth 'African American mindset' which 'had the strength and integrity to resist the full impact of this transformation' (Deetz 1996: 186), and which was represented by a different underlying cultural grammar: 12-ft building units, rather than the Anglo-American 16-ft standard; a 'corporate spirit' resulting in different arrangements of buildings within a settlement; different foodways; and different ways of using colonial material culture. This African American archaeology is set apart from the European American experience in order to attain

> a better appreciation of the way in which various facets of a cultural whole are related and integrated than if they were related piecemeal to those of another, different cultural configuration, particularly if the latter is that of the dominant group.
>
> (Deetz 1996: xi)

Deetz sees the small and fragile ships that followed Frobisher in plying the Atlantic in the seventeenth century as encapsulating new cultural orders that would define the new colonies; English immigrants who 'brought with them a blueprint – in their minds – for recreating the culture they had left behind' and slaves who 'brought with them, against enormous odds, traditions from their West African homelands which would endure in a new and hostile environment'. Together, he argues, these mindsets would 'combine in complex ways through both resistance and accommodation to form a new culture, one not seen before and one that would become a vital component of our modern society' (Deetz 1996: 58).

Tilley is also concerned with the relationship between material objects and language, but from a very different perspective to Deetz and other structuralists. For Tilley, the material world is part of language. In accordance with Saussurian principles, meaning is seen to be resident in a system of relationships between signs, and not in the signs themselves. Language, conceived in this way, is the paradigm for understanding all other aspects of social life. Therefore an assemblage of objects is a meaningful significative system (Tilley 1989). This leads Tilley to phenomenology and the concept of a 'social space':

> a social space, rather than being uniform and forever the same, is constituted by differential densities of human experience, attachment and involvement. It is above all contextually constituted, providing particular settings for involvement and the creation of meanings ... Spaces are intimately related to the formation of biographies and social relationships.
>
> (Tilley 1994: 10–11)

In this approach, landscape is much more than representation – it is rather the site of the construction of meaning in language and in material things. Landscape – and the material and linguistic world that it contains, is closely related to myth and derives its meanings only from people who use it, and who create it through their use. As a result, meanings are intimately connected with memories, and are highly personalized. Tilley's methodology is consistent with his theory. Because social spaces are personal biographies, they can only be understood through ethnography and through empathy. Tilley's approach is to 'read' the 'bones' of the land – its physical structure – which can be assumed to have been substantially the same as in the past. This reading is achieved through the experiencing of walking – the 'perpetually shifting human visual experience of place and landscape':

> Things in front of or behind you, within reach or without, things to the left and right of your body, above and below, these most basic of personal spatial experiences, are shared with prehistoric populations in our common biological humanity. They provide tools with which to think and to work.
>
> (Tilley 1994: 74)

This approach to understanding the material world is the opposite of Deetz's structuralism. Where Deetz has world-views, shared by many thousands of people, transported between continents and beneath the level of individual comprehension, Tilley has social spaces that only exist in personal experience, and in the memory of previous personal experiences, passed through time as myth. Such knowledge is both specific and explicit, and cannot be detached from its specific, physical anchors to the earth. Neither approach, however, is adequate in seeking to understand the complex encounters of early colonial expansion.

Deetz, in common with many structuralist analyses, tends towards ahistorical interpretations, reading off fundamental differences of cultural expression that remained intact for generations. Thus, for example, Anglo-American house form can be traced back to a fundamental 16-ft unit of measurement (Glassie 1975), while African American house form recreates, generation after generation, a 12-ft unit of measurement that can be traced back to slave origins in West Africa (Deetz 1996, following Vlach 1986). When faced with the problem of explaining change from within a theoretical approach that emphasizes changelessness, Deetz grafts on a very different model of cultural process, assuming influence, cultural flow and merging, and suggesting a metaphor of infection (Appadurai 1996). For example, when the evidence shows two world-views coexisting side by side, they are seen to flow into one another:

> the new, academic architectural form was not without its impact on the earlier, vernacular tradition. One style did not simply replace the other,

and houses of the older type continued to be built until the end of the eighteenth century or later. In time, the earlier tradition took on aspects of the new. Sometimes this modification was more thorough than a simple transfer of discrete elements. In its simplest form, an attempt as made to create a Georgianized façade for an otherwise pre-Georgian building, almost as if the owners desired to present a more contemporary face to the world while retaining their comfortable older house behind it.

(Deetz 1996: 158)

But how could this be, if the two traditions of building were the consequence of ingrained, subliminal structures of paired oppositions that had been passed down through the generations?

For his part, Tilley tends towards a conflation of observer and observed – a romantic identification that, equally, denies the possibility of historical change. His preference is clearly for the 'non-capitalist' and the 'non-Western'. Among other things, 'non-Western and pre-capitalist' spaces are sanctified, sensuous and ritual and rhythmic in social action, while 'Western' spaces are desanctified, controlled and temporally linear. Pre-capitalist spaces are 'within a qualitatively different landscape invested with mythological understandings and ritual knowledges intimately linked with bodily routines and practices' (Tilley 1994: 22). Places in pre-capitalist landscapes draw on the qualities of the earth to define their meaning:

> people routinely draw on their stocks of knowledge of the landscape and the locales in which they act to give meaning, assurance and significance to their lives. The place acts dialectically so as to create the people who are of that place. These qualities of locales and landscapes give rise to a feeling of belonging and rootedness and a familiarity, which is not born just out of knowledge, but of *concern* that provides ontological security. They give rise to a power to act and a power to relate that is both liberating and productive.

(Tilley 1994: 26)

Tilley's approach is part of what Julian Thomas has termed a coalescence of humanistic archaeology. There is an emphasis on the individual over the social and on the importance of experience – 'something of a craze for experiential archaeologies which assume that past people's encounters with landscapes and architecture would have been much the same as our own' (Thomas 2000).

Neither approach is adequate in seeking to understand the complexities of the European global order, of which Frobisher's expedition was an early instance. Frobisher's genius was the ability to think both the impossible, lands available for exploration and seizure beyond known horizons, and the calculated and specific – the Inuit as hostage and the value of his death mask, and other things 'beyond necessary uses'. A structuralist world-view sacrifices agency in search of a unified and comprehensive system of description. Experiential archaeology abandons global context for the sake of the specific 'social space'. In contrast to both approaches, an archaeology that does justice to the complex discourses of colonialism must think like Frobisher, holding both specific circumstance and global context in the analytical frame at the same time.

'Thinking like Frobisher' also involves translating the fear, uncertainty and violence of colonial encounters – the ambiguities of the 'third space'. A striking feature of both structuralist interpretations and experiential approaches is their quest for closure. Deetz's approach is to seek symmetrical, logical world-views that can be broken down in a continuing sequence of binary oppositions, ultimately explaining all aspects of culture, including the form and function of material culture. Tilley seeks symbiosis with his subject through empathetic understanding – the liberation that comes from escaping into a non-Western, non-capitalist past. The result, in both of the studies examined in detail here and in many others like them, is a deracination in which the violence of competing claims and histories of domination become sanitized. *In Small Things Forgotten* leads the reader through an early-colonial America which is largely benign and civilized. *A Phenomenology of Landscape* takes us though a largely desirable world, rather than places of violent conflict and stinking ossuaries. Neither would have been worlds that their contemporaries recognized.

Something of all of this was captured by Hans Holbein in his lifesize portrait of Jean de Dinteville and Georges de Selve. *The Ambassadors* (1533), captures the smallest detail of the rich fabric of the men's clothing, their jewelry, and the collection of objects on the shelves between them (Figure 3.1). This is the new materialism of Beste's 'things beyond necessary use', a point famously made by John Berger in his discussion of the genre of oil painting: 'Oil painting did to appearances what capital did to social relations. It reduced everything to the equality of objects. Everything became exchangeable because everything became a commodity. All reality was mechanically measured by its materiality' (Berger 1972). The objects in the painting represent both the ambassadors' personal achievements, and the achievements of global trade. The upper shelf carries a collection of astronomical and mathematical instruments, signifying the mapping and measurement of the world. On the lower shelf are instruments of culture and learning and a globe lying so that it shows De Dinteville's family seat, but also the northern and western parts of Africa (Ganz 1950). Here, then, is the simultaneous consciousness of the world system that made such individual achievement and wealth possible.

There is a conundrum, though – the distorted human skull suspended obliquely in the lower foreground, playing with the rules of perspective. Berger points out that its different optical representation prevents this

Figure 3.1 The Ambassadors, Hans Holbein, 1533 (National Gallery, London).

death's head from losing its metaphysical implication – by not conforming to the perspective of the rest of the picture, the skull cannot become an alienable object like everything else (Berger 1972). Similarly, if the portrait is looked at extremely obliquely so that the skull appears true to life, then the ambassadors themselves appear grotesquely deformed, as if in a distorting mirror. The consequence is an apparent moral ambiguity about the values of the new, global materialism of which his subjects are agents, an uncertainty, we can assume, that was shared by Jean de Dinteville, who commissioned the painting – the gnawing, morbid uncertainty of the 'third space'.

In 1637, Prince Johan Maurits van Nassau-Siegen arrived in Brazil from Amsterdam with an entourage that included botanists, astronomers and artists. Maurits was obsessed with possession. In his colonial capital of

Mauritstad, he established a botanical garden into which he attempted to gather every species of plant and animal:

> He also brought thither every kind of bird and animal that he could find; and since the local moradores knew his taste and inclination, each one brought him whatever rare bird or beast he could find in the back-lands. There he brought parrots, macaws, jacifs, canindes, wading-birds, pheasants, guinea-fowl, ducks, swans, peacocks, turkeys, a great quantity of barnyard-fowls, and so many doves that they could not be counted. There he kept tigers, ounces, cissuarana, ant-bears, apes, quati, squirrel-monkeys, Indian boars, goats from Cape Verde, sheep from Angola, cutia, pagua, tapirs, wild boars, a great multitude of rabbits – and in short there was not a curious thing in Brazil which he did not have...
>
> (Fr. Manuel Calado, in Boxer 1957: 116)

When Maurits returned to the Netherlands, he turned his palace into a private museum of his Brazilian collections and, years later, sent a 'curiosity cabinet' to Louis XIV in the hope that its contents would be used as models in the Gobelins tapestry factory (Smith 1938; Benisovich 1943).

Early colonial acts of possession such as these capture the lure that the material world held for those hungry for wealth and power. George Beste could see the rich potential of the unusual, sought out through bold ingenuity. Prince Maurits could see that such potential would be lost if such wealth in things could not be contained, illustrated, and described in words – and then returned from the furthest periphery of the world to be displayed through art and artifice.

Although varying in their circumstances and specific history, both British and Dutch expeditions can be seen as part of a single system. This has been conceptualized by the *Annales* school of historical writing: Fernand Braudel's *weltwirtschaft*, and Immanuel Wallerstein's 'world-economy' (Braudel 1981, 1982, 1984; Wallerstein 1974, 1980). Its origins are in the 'long fifteenth century' (1450–1650); the transformation from feudalism, and the voyages of discovery that brought the Americas, Africa and the East within a regular network of European trade. A central feature is the contrast between the core area and the outer reaches of the network, divided in turn between peripheries and external areas. Peripheries were both sources of products and markets for the re-export of manufactured commodities such as cotton textiles: eastern Europe and the Americas rapidly became important peripheries to the north-western European core. External areas also served as important sources of commodities, but were lesser markets for re-export and trade in European manufactured goods. Important external areas were the Indian Ocean rim and the East Indies, the Muslim Mediterranean and the African coasts. Here, currency played a minor role as exchange tended to be bilateral and conducted in commodities that were inversely valued: silver for spices, or cattle for tobacco (Wallerstein 1974). By 1600, economic control of this new, global, economy was firmly located in north-western Europe: Holland and Zeeland, London, the Home Counties and East Anglia, and north and western France.

Wallerstein's approach is explicitly an attempt to work with the largest possible units of measurement and description, and the model has been criticised for casting exchange rather than production as the driving force of capitalist expansion (Brenner 1977). It is certainly true that there were innumerable forms of localized production. The particular form of the slave economy on the wheat and wine estates at the Cape was different from the slave economy of the Chesapeake plantations such as William Byrd's, and both were distinct from the mode of production of Dutch Indonesian spices. But it is also true that many of the actors involved saw themselves as part of a world system and were influenced by this in their behaviour (Taylor 1981; see also Frank 1978). In many cases, they came to know very different parts of the world system intimately during their own lives. Byrd moved between core and periphery: schooling in England, a James River patriarch on the death of his father, and then back to England again for a sustained period to fight for his economic and political interests (Lockridge 1987; Wright and Tinling 1941). In contrast, Zacharias Wagenaer moved around the outer reaches of the world system, starting as a painter in Prince Maurits's Brazilian entourage, seeing service in Japan (where he was responsible for establishing the Dutch East India Company's lucrative trade in Japanese porcelain), and ending his career as the Company's commander at the Cape, where his major task was to begin the construction of the new Castle (Spohr 1967). Others – more often than not nameless – were moved from continent to continent with little choice, or by direct and often brutal coercion: soldiers and common employees of the great European trading companies, driven to colonial service by necessity or trickery, or the tens of thousands of slaves who endured the middle passage from West Africa to the American colonies, or who were shipped from India, Indonesia and other parts of the East to servitude at the Cape (Patterson 1982; Shell 1994).

Looking at the early colonial world through this dual perspective of global system and local knowledge also has the virtue of focusing on the distribution and consumption of commodities – central to understanding the social meanings of material culture (Douglas and Isherwood 1978; Miller 1987; Brewer and Porter 1993). George Beste's fashions that served 'more for ornament, than for necessarie uses' were the direct consequence of late fifteenth and early-sixteenth-century voyages of discovery: Diaz's rounding of the Cape in 1487, Columbus's landfall in the West Indies in 1492, da Gama's voyage via the Cape to India in 1498, Cabral's voyage to Brazil in 1500, the capture of Malacca in 1511 and Magellan's circumnavigation of the globe.

Although the weight of historiography has emphasized the needs of raw materials for production as the force driving Europe's expansion to new peripheries, others have stressed the role of the 'rich trades' – the search for Beste's 'thousandes of new things simple and compound, never heretofore seene or heard of'. For instance, Jonathan Israel has challenged the long-standing view that Dutch economic primacy was based overwhelmingly on the Baltic carrying-trade, fishing and specialized agriculture (e.g. by Braudel 1984; Huizinga 1968 and Geyl 1964). While nodding to the obvious importance of such bulk trade, Israel sees control of the rich trades as crucial: silk, pepper and spices carried to Moscow, from which furs, leather and caviar were taken back to Europe; luxury goods sold to the land-owning nobility of the Baltic states; Netherlands manufactured textiles shipped to the Mediterranean; gold, ivory, gum and sugar imported from plantations on the periphery of the world economy. Thus the Netherlands became an entrepôt for rare, valuable and exotic goods – a 'world reservoir of commodities' (Israel 1989: 73). Commercial success was based on linking geographically separate areas; goods common in the one were rare in the other, and in their movement between the core and the outer reaches of the world system they acquired value as indicators of status and power.

Chinese porcelain can stand as an example of this process – particularly appropriate given that ceramic assemblages are the ubiquitous signature of the archaeology of colonialism. Interest in fine porcelain from the east was whetted by the auction of the cargo of the captured Portuguese ship *San Jago* in Amsterdam in 1602 and by the popularity among the European elite of tea drinking: some enthusiasts advocated up to 200 cups per day. Spurred by the profits that the porcelain trade offered, the Dutch established an outpost on the Chinese mainland at Canton, from where they negotiated designs for the European market from the Imperial kilns at Ch'ing-tê-Chên. Cargoes were shipped back to Batavia, distributed around the eastern offices in Dutch ships and packed beneath tea, raw silk and spices for the long voyage back to Europe. On the quayside in Amsterdam, porcelain was auctioned in large lots to merchants, who re-exported fine wares to the nobility of the Mediterranean, the Baltic states and western Europe. Some consignments were reloaded for the Mediterranean and were redistributed again from warehouses on Curaçao's *Handelskade*. By the middle years of the eighteenth century, people signified their status by displays of porcelain throughout the core and periphery of the world economic system (Jorg 1982; Kerr 1986; Savage 1963; Volker 1959, 1971; Woodward 1974).

Israel's argument for the central importance of the rich trades in the foundation of the modern world economy places the overseas trading companies on centre stage and accounts for the marked competitiveness for connections with peripheral and external areas. The London Company established the fortified post of Jamestown on the James River, upstream from Chesapeake Bay, in 1607. The early colony thrived on tobacco cultivation and the immigration of large numbers of indentured labourers – by 1671, the population of Virginia was reported as 45,000 (Hasseltine and Smiley 1960). In turn, these colonial communities became important markets for European manufactured goods, establishing the ligaments of trade and distribution upon which the Byrd family's prosperity was based, and the means by which patriarchs such as William Byrd II marked out their position in the world. In the East, British trading interests were in fierce competition with those of the Dutch. The Dutch East India Company – which Zacharias Wagenaer served for most of his career – had a monopoly east of the Cape of Good Hope and west of the Straits of Magellan, and an administrative centre at Batavia (the modern-day Indonesian city of Djakarta). Outward bound fleets left the Netherlands in September, December and April. After a voyage of some 6 months, cargoes were trans-shipped at Batavia for trade in Japan, China and the Persian Gulf. Return fleets left Batavia in December and February.

The first ligaments to connect this global system of circulating commodities and ideas, princes, sailors and slaves, were the prior conceptions that formed a perception of local conditions before the first boat ever splashed ashore. The Dutch came to the Cape with their heads full of images of Africa – a mêlée of Medieval church imagery, fantastic stories about the edges of the known world and travellers' tales, told, retold, reworked and exaggerated beyond recognition. In consequence, they had no doubt that the Khoikhoi – the indigenous nomadic herders of the Cape whom the Dutch called Hottentots – were at best semi-human freaks (Figure 3.2). In J. M. Coetzee's words,

> in the early records one finds a repertoire of remarkable facts about the Hottentots repeated again and again: their implosives ('turkey-gobbling'), their eating of unwashed intestines, their use of animal fat to smear their bodies, their habit of wrapping dried entrails around their necks, peculiarities of the pudenda of their women, their inability to conceive of God, their incorrigible indolence.
>
> (Coetzee 1988)

For their part, the Khoikhoi had known about explorers and traders from Europe for more than half a century. The tribes that visited Table Bay as part of a regular round of seasonal movement were part of an interlinked network of herders that spread from the south-west coast deep into the interior of southern Africa, where they met settled agriculturists at another frontier (Elphick 1985; Hall 1987). These mutual perceptions shaped the 'construction of locality', and set the ground for the construction of a unique place within a familiar, global system.

The settlement at Table Bay was laid out as a grid of perpendiculars enclosing the Company's garden – crucial for provisioning the fleet – freehold plots, residential erven (areas of land) and streets: Olifantstraat,

HOE ZY DE VISSCHEN VANGEN

Figure 3.2 Dutch encounters with Khoikhoi at the Cape of Good Hope from Pieter Kolbe's *Present State of the Cape of Good Hope.*

Heerestraat and 'the street along the sea shore', eventually to become known as Strand Street (Cairns 1974). This design had been the work of Pieter Potter, the Company's surveyor at the Cape; late in 1660 the Commander at the Cape, in leaving the fort for a day or two, had instructed that Potter was 'to be kept conscientiously at his work of making maps' (Thom 1958: 293). The nucleus of the settlement was a large, open square to the west of the Fort; a layout in common with innumerable port towns from different parts of the Dutch colonial world, and familiar to history from the Greek and Roman worlds, from Medieval European *bastides*, from Spanish settlement in South America and from town designs of other colonial powers as they stamped their authority on Europe's new peripheries (Braunfels 1988; Fraser 1990; Kostof 1991).

How had this general 'mental template' of the correct layout for a colonial settlement been cut into the scrubby vegetation and sandy soils beneath Table Mountain? In common with other colonial authorities, the Dutch East India Company had definite notions of orderliness and the manner in which it was appropriate to mark its authority in bricks, mortar and the layout of settlements. By Resolution of Council of Seventeen in Amsterdam on 25 March 1651, it was instructed that the first building at the Cape should be a wood-and-sod four-bastioned fort, following standard Dutch military engineering principles (Leibbrandt 1896: 28–30; see also Guelke 1974). But when it came to laying out the town a few years later, bureaucratic attention in the Netherlands had turned elsewhere; the Cape was too unimportant a settlement to warrant specific attention, and the Commander had been told by his superiors that 'we give no precise instructions' (Leibbrandt 1896: 28–30). As with the layout of Spanish colonial towns in South America a century earlier, where the rules for settlement design were codified by Philip II after many towns were already established (Fraser 1990), the Company's officials at the tip of Africa were expected to know the right thing to do.

The particular way in which this concept of orderliness was applied showed the play between this global concept of an orderly settlement, and local circumstances and inclinations. By the winter of 1659, there had been a cluster of houses and other buildings around the fort; a community that the Company officials at the Cape had begun to recognize as 'town burghers', in distinction to the farmers who had settled out of sight, along the Liesbeek River. It was clearly time to lay out a proper town. But the Commander and his officials had specific and pressing requirements of their newly recognized townsfolk. Provisioning the Dutch fleets was the Cape settlement's *raison d'être*, and although the officials in the fort felt able to allow the town burghers the right to sell 'divers shop-goods and chandler's wares' (provided that these provisions were bought wholesale from the Company's stores, and for cash), the Liesbeek farms were still too poorly developed to be reliable in meeting the fleets' needs. Consequently, the Commander placed a condition on rights in the new town; each burgher was ordered to keep a minimum of six sows and a boar in order to ensure an adequate and dependable supply of salted pork.

The layout of plots within the Cape settlement's orthogonal grid had to take account of this specific, local requirement: 'each [freeman] shall be granted as much freehold land as he considers necessary for carrots and other garden produce' (Thom 1958: 126–8). In practice, individual herds proved impractical and in April 1660 the town burghers were allowed to keep a common herd. Nevertheless, documents specifying the first eight erven were signed on 20 September 1660. Cape Town's underlying grid of streets, then (still evident today) was the consequence of a global form of settlement design mediated by local circumstance – the need to supply Dutch fleets in the mid-seventeenth century (Hall 1992b).

Similar, local, expediency governed the next major building project at the new settlement. By the time Zacharias Wagenaer arrived at the Cape to take command, the first wood-and-sod fort by Table Bay was dilapidated and unfit for its purpose. Wagenaer was instructed to build a new castle of stone, and duly laid the foundation stone in 1666 (Figure 3.3). The design was very familiar – a standard pentagon plan that had been used for over a century in both the new colonial periphery and in Europe's cities (Hall *et al.* 1990a). As with the orthogonal grid of streets, this was a consequence of a worldwide concept of the manner in which fortifications should be laid out in the Dutch colonial world. But, again, a closer look shows how both vague and impractical orders had been modified to fit local conditions. Rather than instructing that the new stone fortification be erected on the site of the old fort, Wagenaer had a site cleared 500 paces to the north. This, in turn, threw off the alignment of the street grid, leaving an open space that was a hazard of open ditches and winter mud in place of what, in principle, should have been the symbolic focus of the town. The moat – years in completion – was never more than a symbolic gesture to the principles of fortification. The result is a building that has an unmistakably similar imprint to fortifications as widely dispersed as Cape Town, Djakarta, Recife and New York but is, at the same time, a consequence of the individual circumstances, interpretations, opportunities and mistakes that give each a unique, local, character.

A similar play between global ideas and their local manifestations lay behind the layout of the Chesapeake's early towns. Francis Nicholson took up his appointment as Governor of the colony of Maryland in 1693 and set about transforming the small settlement of Anne-Arundel town, renaming it Annapolis (in honour of the Queen's sister). Three years later, Nicholson moved south as Governor of Virginia, and immediately started the design of the new town of Williamsburg (in honour of King William). He was succeeded, in 1710, by Alexander Spotswood, who further embellished the new town's architecture.

Nicholson designed Annapolis around the concept of the dual authority of church and state, taking advantage of topography to add emphasis and

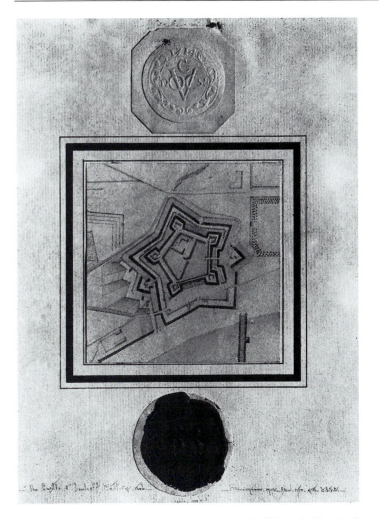

Figure 3.3 Plan of the new Castle at the Cape, with VOC seals. The Castle was built from 1666 onwards (William Fehr Collection, Castle, GH81/6).

monumentality (Figure 3.4). St Anne's Episcopal Church and the State House were built on twin hills, surrounded by circular drives. Streets radiating outwards from Church Circle and State Circle ensured that vistas from all sides would contain one or another of the town's monumental buildings as a focal point. Nicholson's dream for his new city was three dimensional, seeking more emphasis than could be offered by the stamp of the more common orthogonal grid. In Mark Leone's words, Annapolis was 'a baroque vision of the world that managed the principles of optics for political purposes' (Leone 1988: 243).

Figure 3.4 Governor Nicholson's Annapolis.

In the event, though, the Governor's vision was slow to come to realization. By 1697 there were only some forty houses built, and a decade later the project provided ready grist for Ebenezer Cooke's satirical pen:

> A city situate on a plain
> Where scarce a house will keep out rain;
> The buildings framed with cypress rare
> Resemble much our Southwick fair;
> But strangers there will scarcely meet
> With market place, exchange, or street;
> And if the truth I may report,
> It's not so large as Tottenham Court.
>
> (Anderson 1984: 15)

In the middle of the following century, visitors could still comment that Nicholson's original ideas were unfulfilled. Here is Thomas Pownall, writing in 1754: 'the town is far from being compleat, nor do the traces of such a plan appear in what is built; it makes a very irregular appearance, and is in size and form but a very poor town' (quoted by Anderson 1984: 17).

Nicholson, though, did not long have to endure the disillusionment of a glorious plan foundered on the shore of practicalities, for the Crown moved him south, and to new opportunities to celebrate royal patronage. Virginia's capital had been the notoriously unhealthy Jamestown. The new site, Middle Plantation, was an outpost consisting of a few widely scattered houses, church, tavern and the College of William and Mary, founded in 1695. As in Annapolis, Nicholson laid out Williamsburg to emphasize its monumental buildings, although the flatter site necessitated a different solution. The central axis was 'the Main Street' (later renamed Duke of Gloucester Street): a broad, open avenue nearly a mile in length with the College of William and Mary at one end and the Capitol building at the other. The Main Street intersected Market Square, later the site for the James City County Courthouse. To the west of Market Square, the town was laid out as a square incorporating Bruton Parish Church, which had been standing since before 1683. The Governor's Palace (on which work began in 1706) was built at the head of a wide avenue running north from the Church.

But – again – such exercises of authority were not without their detractors. Some years earlier, one of Nicholson's enemies offered his own point of view. In his *History and Present State of Virginia*, published in 1705, Robert Beverley wrote of the Governor:

> Soon after his Accession to the Government, he caused the Assembly, and Courts of Judicature, to be remov'd from James-Town, where there were good Accommodations for People, to Middle-Plantation, where there were none. There he flatter'd himself with the fond Imagination, of being the Founder of a new City. He mark'd out the Streets in many Places, so as that they might represent the Figure of a W, in Memory of his late Majesty King William, after whose Name the Town was call'd Williamsburg. There he procur'd a stately Fabrick to be erected, which he placed opposite to the College, and graced it with the magnificent Name of the Capitol. This imaginary City is yet advanced no further, than only to have a few Publick Houses, and a Store-House, more than were built upon the Place before. And by the Frequency of Publick Meetings, and the Misfortune of his Residence, the Students are interrupted in their Study, and make less Advances than formerly.
>
> (Beverley 1968)

As with the settlement at the Cape, the designs of Williamsburg and Annapolis reflect widely held views about what a dignified and monumental city should look like, modified by the local contingencies of resources, perceptions and individual ambitions. And behind the façades of order was the ever-present violence of dispossession and the coercion of slavery. The laying of the Castle's foundation stone was celebrated by a poem, inscribed in the Company's journal (Leibbrandt 1901: 1700):

> Thus more and more the kingdoms are extended,
> Thus more and more are black and yellow spread.
> Thus from the ground a wall of stone is raised,
> On which the thundering brass can no impression make.
> For Hottentots the walls are always earthen,
> But now we come with stone to boast before all men,
> And terrify not only Europeans, but also
> Asians, Americans and savage Africans.
> Thus holy Christendom is glorified,
> Establishing its seat amidst the savage heathens,
> We praise the great director and say with one another,
> Augustus' dominion nor conquering Alexander,
> Nor Caesar's mighty genius has ever had the glory
> To lay a cornerstone at earth's extremest end!
> (Unknown author 1666, in Gray 1989)

This outward-looking belligerence was matched by an internal regime of violence. In 1657 nine men and their families, released from Company service, had been allowed to farm along the Liesbeek River on the far side of Devil's Peak, building rudimentary structures of timber, mud and thatch. This was the nucleus of the freeburgher community that, over the following century, was to disperse far into the interior (Guelke 1974, 1989). In the following year, the first two shiploads of slaves had arrived: 228 captured by the Company at Dahomey, and 174 (mostly children) taken from a Portuguese slaver en route from Angola to Brazil (Armstrong and Worden 1989). By 1663, then, all the main elements of Cape colonial society were in place – Company officials, free farmers and slaves.

This – like so many other colonial settlements – was a visceral environment of drunkenness, sweat, blood and violence in which regulation was enforced and resisted. The Cape settlement was, above all else, a port city. There was little profit in legitimate support for the Company's monopoly, and soon there were illicit taphouses everywhere (Thom 1958; Guelke 1974). Alcohol softened some of the brutalities for an indentured and enslaved labour force that was required to hew stone, bake bricks, carry firewood, dig ditches, tend the herds and weed the Company's Garden. The fort's officers and soldiers tried to control this labour force in a number of ways, and keelhauling, flogging, branding or other bodily mutilation would follow even the most elliptical suggestion of insubordination. Not surprisingly, few had much enthusiasm for this life. In 1660, fifty freemen and Company servants had slipped on board the ships of the return fleet headed for Amsterdam – more than a quarter of the non-slave population of the Cape. Only thirteen had been found and put back on shore. The year before, Company employees, together with fifteen slaves, had planned an abortive insurrection, during which they had hoped to burn the fort, seize a ship from the Bay and sail away to an unspecified destination (Thom 1958); anywhere but the Cape of Good Hope.

These desperate attempts to get away highlight the effects of distance, and the way in which the regularity of the grid and the geometry of the fortifications stood in conscious opposition to the perception of the wild and disorderly continent that stretched away to the north. Indeed, those who attempted to escape the heavy hand of Company regulation could have a hard time; as did Jan Blanx when, with three companions, he deserted from the fort in September 1652. Equipped with four biscuits, some fish, four swords, two pistols and a dog, the mutineers were chased by a pair of rhinoceroses through the brushwood of the Cape Flats, loosing a sword. The dog was near-fatally wounded when it tried to savage a porcupine, and all that the party could find to eat were some shellfish and some chicks from a bird's nest (Thom 1952: 68). On the far side of False Bay they turned back, preferring the colony's rough justice to the harshness of Africa beyond the Liesbeek River. The Commander had every detail of the experience recorded in the Cape's log, adding the force of words to the physical presence of the new colony.

The superimposition of scales – the global system of colonialism played out in a myriad local circumstances – has always this imminence of violence. Whether an expedition such as Frobisher's landing on Baffin Island, Holbein's contemplation of de Dinteville and de Selve's world, the colonial settlement on America's eastern seaboard, or Jan Blanx and his companions looking nervously back behind them as they fled the scruffy Dutch settlement at the Cape, colonial encounters were about dispossession and occupation by force, and the imposition of power. Understanding the 'conditions of material-ization' in an archaeology of the modern world requires an understanding of violence. And this is most evident in the ultimate logic of global themes that were constantly played in local theatres of action – the imposition of the colonial order on the human body itself.

Here again, Foucault's work on discipline and punishment is of central importance. Foucault has shown how the body of a guilty person carried the 'legibility' of the sentence. Torture and forms of execution often matched the crime – tongues of blasphemers were pierced, the impure were burned, the right hands of murderers were cut off. Public executions were ceremonies in which power was manifested – the 'unrestrained presence of the sovereign'.

> This enables us to understand some of the characteristics of the liturgy of torture and execution – above all, the importance of a ritual that was to

deploy its pomp in public. Nothing was to be hidden in the triumph of the law. Its episodes were traditionally the same and yet the sentences never failed to list them, so important were they in the penal mechanism: processions, halts at crossroads and church doors, the public reading of the sentence, kneeling, declarations of repentance for the offence to God and to the king.

(Foucault 1979: 49–50)

Public torture and execution aimed to make an example through excess, and through direct inscription on the body of the guilty.

Public torture and execution were common in the eighteenth-century colonial world, and the inscription of sovereign order on the body of the guilty was a common sight. Robert Shell (1994) has calculated that, at the Cape, on average one slave was executed in public every month through the period of Dutch rule. The decaying corpses were left hanging as a public example. Here is Otto Mentzel's description of one such execution.

A murderer is broken on the wheel; the same punishment is meted out for the crime of arson. They are stretched upon a double wooden cross and tightly lashed to it, and their arms and legs are broken by blows from a heavy iron club. In some cases the coup de grace is then administered by a blow on the chest with the same instrument; if this is not done, the wretched man may be stretched by chains on a wheel, notwithstanding his broken limbs, and linger on in agony until death releases him, some 24 hours later. A more lingering death is the lot of him who is condemned to transfixion, a form of crucifixion whereby death may not take place until two or three days have elapsed.

(Mentzel 1925)

It is often said that New York has the most logical of urban designs – any address can be identified from the intersection of streets and avenues. New York's orthogonal street grid has a relentlessness that stretches many miles but the Big Apple's layout is only the best known, and largest, of many similar cities. Seventeenth-century Dutch Mauritstadt was constructed at much the same time as Manhattan's New Amsterdam. The small, scruffy settlement on the Hudson River was nothing in comparison to the Dutch East India Company's capital of Djakarta, also organized as a grid. Cape Town, a small outlier in the Dutch East India Company's world, followed the same pattern of intersecting streets. Beyond these there were many more again – colonial towns in southern Africa and Australia (sometimes named after the same colonial administrators), new towns in Europe and old colonial towns in Spanish South America. Although the orthogonal grid is only one of many possible urban layouts, it is a ubiquitous feature of towns and cities throughout the world.

This way of organizing the city can be seen as the imposition of a geometric grid of order on the disorderly landscape. The Dutch settlement at the Cape of Good Hope was laid out across sand dunes scattered with shell middens that recalled countless nomadic visits by pre-colonial communities. Mauritstadt's founder was challenged by the alien urban geography of the earlier Portuguese settlement but nevertheless managed to stamp the grid-like street arrangement as the template for his colonial capital. The Dutch East India Company built on a massive scale to hold back the tidal floods and ensure that Batavia was an appropriate jewel of the East. Such orthogonal town plans represented both a global system of signification and a set of familiar, local references. The early colonial administrator moving between outposts, and feeling the disorientation of a long sea voyage at the mercy of the elements, would step ashore to a familiar system of street names and a town layout that took little effort to read. Similarly, the interrelation of public spaces – bastions, garrisons, places of worship and areas of differing social status – were related to one another by a limited set of urban planning solutions. City layouts are excellent examples of artefacts that were read simultaneously at a local and a global scale.

It would be futile to try and describe such a system of signification in terms of the phenomenological experience of the individual. Such an approach would not show how such an individual would read these different regimes of order. A structuralist interpretation, however, seems at first glance more attractive. A street grid can easily be described as a system of binary opposi-tions. A system that can be both easily mapped and clearly replicated seems an obvious example of a mental template expressed in material culture. History, however, does not lie in such a generalization. Indeed, a historical archaeology that would read the urban artefacts of South American conquis-tadores in the same frame as settler pioneers of the Australian outback would be profoundly ahistorical. Rather than relying on the regularity of the world-view or on the extreme subjectivity of phenomenology, the richness of an archaeology of the modern world lies in the inconsistencies, unresolved issues and the imprint of resistance that makes the local far more than a camera-obscura image of the global.

Cape Town's urban grid had to accommodate disorderly free farmers in the face of whose daily, foot-dragging opposition despairing Company officials enacted regulations requiring plots for pigs that could provide salted provi-sions essential for the twice yearly refurbishing of the fleet in Table Bay. Batavia, conceived and constructed on a grand scale, was submerged beneath its own pollution, a combination of the lack of sanitary arrangements and the greed of upriver plantation owners who stripped away the natural vegetation for sugar farms, leading to massive sedimentation and the clogging of canals which had been intended to rival the Netherlands in the East. Batavia's colonial population died in numbers unprecedented in other colonial settlements and had to retreat to the hills. Mauritstadt was destroyed through the brevity of the Dutch occupation of Brazil. Within a few years, the Portuguese were back, and made a determined effort to eradicate the Dutch idea of a colonial capital. Today, traces of the Dutch presence are confined to a small number of buildings and some obscure statues. On Manhattan Island, the Indian community may have been outgunned by the Dutch, but steadfastly refused to walk where intended. Eventually, the colonial sense of order was eroded and the Indian path that violated the principles of the orthogonal grid was allowed to become a street in its own right – Broadway.

There is, then, an inherent instability in this discourse of possession and control, whether at the global or the local scale. And what could be more local than the individual body itself. Francis Barker has teased apart the combination of assertion and anxiety that is characteristic of colonial discourse in his analysis of Rembrandt's painting, *The Anatomy Lesson of Dr Nicolaas Tulp* (Figure 3.5).

Every year, the Guild of Surgeons gathered in Amsterdam for the public dissection of an executed criminal (in this case, the unfortunate Aris Kindt). On the one hand, there could be no more confident assertion of the patriarchal order. But Barker shows how Rembrandt succeeded in capturing an underlying current of unease and anxiety: the inaccurate representation of the tendons of the executed criminal's left hand, the averted gaze of most of the

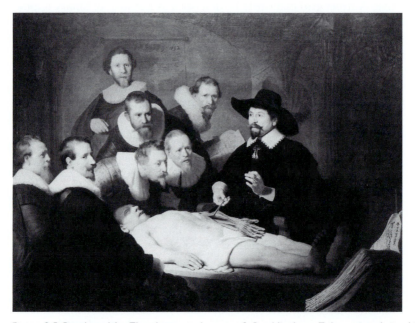

Figure 3.5 Rembrandt's *The Anatomy Lesson of Dr Nicolaas Tulp*, painted in 1632 (Mauritshuis, The Hague).

men in attendance on Dr Tulp, who prefer to look at the anatomical atlas at the subject's feet, rather than at the opened corpse itself. This is the intrusion of 'desire, disease, the mess of the body and its passions': 'neither wholly present, nor wholly absent, the body is confined, ignored, exscribed from discourse, and yet remains at the edge of visibility, troubling the space from which it has been banished' (Barker 1984: 6–7, 63). The public dissection was followed by a commemorative banquet:

> To execute, to dismember, to eat. It is difficult to imagine how much more thorough than this an act of corporal punishment could be ... The scene of dissection is thus the exercise of a jurisdiction over the body of Aris Kindt, an act of penal and sovereign domination which is exemplary and substantive, symbolic and material, at one and the same time.
>
> (Barker 1984: 73–4)

Chapter 4

Substantial identities

The previous chapters have shown how the colonial world was both a world system of order and a set of intensely local systems of meaning. How, then, was material culture employed in the daily 'microphysics of power' of these different domains?

This question leads us to a third theme (along with phenomenology and structuralism) in recent explanatory approaches of the archaeology of the modern world. Termed 'critical materialism', this approach builds on structuralism, seeking to avoid the trap of ahistorical reasoning that waits in the concepts of mental templates and world-views. This approach is best represented in Mark Leone's interpretations of the material world of the early Chesapeake and Matthew Johnson's *Archaeology of Capitalism* (1996), a reinterpretation of early modern history and material culture in Britain, and one of the few studies to draw global inferences from intensely local detail. Through work by Leone, Johnson and others, the 'Georgian order' of structuralism appears in a new light. Now, rather than being the expression of mind, material culture and the interwoven verbal evidence that are the rich transcripts at the heart of historical archaeology appear as manifestations of a new, capitalist, class.

What were the ways in which these material expressions of power were expressed? Most obvious were the often exotic practices that prompted regulation through sumptuary laws. Sumptuary laws ranged from limits on the number of footmen (and their appropriate livery) according to the standing of their employers, through regulations that sought to control which women were allowed to carry parasols, to laws that limited the consumption of marzipan in the Venetian court. Sumptuary laws were matched by practices and customs that included the use of clothing to mark servitude (at the Cape, slaves were not allowed to wear shoes) and the conspicuous frugality practised by leading Dutch burghers who regarded the colonies as devoid of taste and who wore nothing but black to indicate their superiority.

Some interpreters have mocked sumptuary laws, seeing in them examples of the irrationality of early modern cultural life. This was certainly the view of many contemporary commentators. Others have shown how these uses of material culture are rich indicators of the plays of power. Simon Schama (1988), in his now-classic study of the sixteenth- and seventeenth-century Netherlands, has shown just how much these cultural displays meant. Arjun Appadurai (1986) has demonstrated the centrality of sumptuary laws in early modern economies. Both of these studies fall within the rubric of a historical archaeology that explores the integration of material culture into day-by-day histories at a detailed local level.

This consideration of generalized practices leads to some specific examples of individual agency that show how ordinary day-by-day objects structured interactions. A fragmentary record of a few months in the life of a Cape free-burgher shows how everyday objects such as wineglasses and smoking pipes were used to express forms of social interaction at the opening of the eighteenth century. Moving on in time, the surviving work of a craftsman in the employment of the Dutch East India Company at the Cape shows how workmanship (today celebrated as high art) used complex sets of references to express ideas in material form. Gardens had a particular role in these material expressions of power. This was because the layout of paths and parterres were an obvious use of artifice to contain and control the disorderliness of nature. And gardens take the argument back again to houses, and a place beneath the stark face of Table Mountain where excavation in both the soil and the archives reveals the sumptuary affectations of a minor Dutch East India Company official who aspired to be more than he was.

Louis XIV and the theatre that was his Versailles and France is a suitable avatar for identity given substance in materiality. Versailles was the envy of Europe – 'the first image of the modern nation state at continental scale' (Scully 1991: 16), the inscription of the king himself on the landscape.

> The king is everywhere over France; his eyes are made to shine with light looking out to vast differences. His hair is water and fire, like the fountains that tell his story in transparent silver screens. Most of all, in the flat parterres, drawn tight as wire and clothed in his livery, the king himself achieves the Neoplatonic dream: he is the individual at the center. The diagonals of his body's action project out across the circles and the squares and his will becomes more than regional, shaping the land of France in celestial *étoiles* and so, like the medieval kings before him, linking the kingdom to a cosmic order.
>
> (Scully 1991: 16)

The King's contemporaries and later admirers were bowled over. Prince Maurits petitioned to have a record of his exploits in Brazil displayed at the Sun King's court. William Byrd stocked his new Library at Westover with treatises on garden design. Governors at both Cape and the Chesapeake aspired to courtly mansions and formal gardens that, likewise, blended their authority with the cosmic order.

Were such accoutrements of everyday life significant in contestations of power and identity? Many who jealously guarded their authority thought so. Dutch colonial administrations, in common with others before them, promulgated sumptuary laws in an often-futile attempt to enforce a tight connection between status and its material signifiers. Men of position in the Netherlands marked their position by conspicuous displays of frugality, and were appalled by the excesses of the east. Here is one outraged description, written by Nicolaus de Graaff in the mid-seventeenth century:

> what astounds one ... is the extreme splendor and hauteur which the women in Batavia – Dutch, Mestiza and Half-Caste too – display, especially on going to and from church ... for on such occasions each is decked out more expensively than at any other time ... Thus they sit by the hundred in church making a show like lacquered dolls. The least of them looks more like a Princess than a burgher's wife or daughter, so that Heaven itself is filled with loathing, especially as they go and come from church, when even the most inferior has her slave follow behind to carry a parasol or sunshade above her against the fierce heat. Many of these have great hanging silken flaps embroidered with golden dragons and ornamental foliage.
>
> (quoted in Taylor 1983: 41)

Such excesses worried successive governors-general of the East Indies, challenging their own perquisites of power. The first Batavian sumptuary laws were introduced in the mid-seventeenth century, but the most extensive code – the 'Measures for Curbing Pomp and Circumstance' – was issued by Jacob Mossel in December 1754. Numerous clauses sought to regulate the use of carriages, livery, parasols, men's clothing (including buttons, silk shirts and shoe buckles), women's dress and the number of slaves permitted in a retinue (Taylor 1983). Local discretion in the application of Mossel's regulations was allowed in the 'outer offices of the Indies', and in July 1755 the Council at the Cape issued regulations that emphasized and modified some aspects of the Batavian code. Members of the Council were allowed carriages, but without coats of arms, gilding or liveried drivers, all of which were reserved for the Governor. Only Council members were allowed to have their clothes embroidered and lace-edged trappings, and the wives and daughters of those below the rank of undermerchant could not use large sun umbrellas or have their clothes seamed with silk.

At the other end of the social scale were slaves and servants, also marked by their appearance (Figure 4.1). Regulations at the Cape dictated that clothes worn by slaves must be 'entirely plain and without cuffs or collars of another

Figure 4.1 Master and slave at the Cape. Clothing played a major role in indicating status (Cape Archives, L1379).

colour' (VOC 1754–86). Changes in clothing signified change of status. Thunberg, a Scandinavian visitor to the Cape, found slaves easy to pick out:

> The male slaves wear their own hair, upon which they set a great value, wrapped up in a twisted handkerchief like a turban, and the females wreath up their hair and fix it on their heads with a large pin. Trowsers constitute the other part of their dress; and as a token of their servile condition, they always go barefoot, and without a hat.
>
> (Thunberg 1986: 26)

Freedom, appropriately, was also publicly marked: 'as soon as a slave is enfranchised, he wears shoes, stockings and a hat, as a mark of his freedom' (Thunberg 1986: 35). But servants were not to be allowed to appear like their betters. In 1765, the Political Council at the Cape passed regulations limiting the dress of free black women in the colony, prohibiting coloured silk clothing, hoop skirts, fine lace, adorned bonnets or earrings, and prescribing chintz and striped cotton, and black silk in church (Shell 1994).

Both contemporary commentaries and graphic sources attest the importance of material things in marking out who people were, or whom they thought they should be. Otto Mentzel, offering his readers a characteristically stereotypical vignette, describes a couple setting up house on the frontier:

the young man takes with him his rifle, powder and shot, tobacco, axe, hatchet, saw, drill, chisel and similar tools, while the young wife takes along tea, coffee, sugar candy, soap and some porcelain or other dishes, plates, tea cups and a hundred other trifles . . .

(Mentzel 1944: 113)

Equally stylized, but nonetheless instructive, is the way in which Mentzel punctuates his account of the stages in the transformation of his patron, Rudolf Siegfried Allemann, through changes of clothes. Fleeing Prussia, Allemann marks the beginning of his new history by selling his uniform and horse to pay his way, donning new clothes when he eventually reaches the Cape and is garrisoned at the Castle. Finding favour as one of the Governor's huntsman, Allemann takes the appropriate livery: 'His old uniform was bought by the sergeant of his company, and with the money that he obtained for this and for his bed, he procured a green coat. A musket, together with powder and shot, was given to him, so there he was, transformed into a huntsman' (Mentzel 1919: 38). But this way of life was too difficult, and Allemann returns again to the Castle, changing his uniform back to that of a soldier. Rising to the rank of Sergeant, he is awarded a new coat – 'blue with double bands of broad gold braid on the pockets and cuffs' (Mentzel 1919: 58) – while promotion again, to Ensign, brings 'red cloth, trimmed with silver lace, and the hat is embroidered with silver point d'Espagne' (Mentzel 1919: 68).

Other indicators come from the popular art of the seventeenth-century low countries. There are frequent depictions of men with clay tobacco pipes and stoneware flagons, suggesting that they were part of male identity. Arent Diepraem's *A Peasant Seated Smoking* uses a grey and blue Rhenish stoneware jug in the foreground of the picture as a focal point (Figure 4.2), while a similar association, seen from behind, is in a detail of Jan Steen's *Skittle Players outside an Inn*; here, a man sits on the grass, legs slightly apart, holding a pipe and with a stoneware jug on the upturned barrel in front of him. Adriaen van Ostade's *A Peasant Holding a Jug and a Pipe* is, like Diepraem's picture, a character study and again the man is portrayed with a jug and pipe. Other pictures show smoking and drinking as a less solitary activity. For example, in Hendrick Sorgh's *A Woman Playing Cards with Two Boors* one man holds a jug and the other a pipe, while Adriaen van Ostade shows everyone smoking and drinking in *The Interior of an Inn with Nine Peasants and a Hurdy-gurdy Player*. Gabriel Metsu's *A Man and a Woman Seated by a Virginal* is a more sophisticated setting, but there is again the same association between the man and the stoneware jar at his feet (all these examples are in the collections of the National Gallery, London; Maclaren 1960). Although it is not surprising that flagons and pipes should be prominent in genre paintings, with their 'low life' penchant for scenes in inns, brothels and public feasting, this

Figure 4.2 Arent Diepraem, *A Peasant Seated Smoking*, painted in about 1650 (National Gallery, London).

does not detract from the message that stoneware jugs and clay tobacco pipes were part of the paraphernalia of male identity.

The use of parasols, shoes and hats, stone jugs and tobacco pipes to mark out identity is what Daniel Miller has described as 'objectification': 'the inevitable process by which all expression, conscious or unconscious, social or individual, takes specific form' (Miller 1987: 81). One approach to theorizing such objectification has been what Orser and Fagan (1995: 194) have termed 'critical materialism'. These interpretations – as diverse as Mark Leone's (1988) reading of the street plan of Maryland's early capital of Annapolis and Paul

Shackel's (1993) perception of a regime of personal order in the archaeology of toothbrushes – build on structuralism, and combine the recognition of general patterns in material culture with a Marxist model of historical change (Hall 1992a).

Leone's interpretation of Annapolis illustrates this critical materialism at work. Leone takes the broadest view of that which constitutes archaeological evidence: street plans, architecture, garden layout and domestic artefacts are all woven into an elegant and comprehensive reading (Leone 1988). He starts by mapping out the changing distribution of wealth. These data show a dramatic economic realignment between 1690 and 1730, during which period the wealth held by the poorest group in the sample fell from 28 to 3 per cent of the total, and the richest group, while comprising only 18 per cent of the population, came to own over 78 per cent of the total wealth of the town. This trend continued after 1730, albeit at a slower pace, and by 1775, the top stratum of Annapolis society owned 85 per cent of measurable wealth. Leone argues that economic change of this scope had to cause changes in the way that people thought and lived, and these changes were accommodated in the 'culture' of capitalism.

This leads Leone to three propositions about the role material culture played in accommodating the expansion of the capitalist order in Annapolis. First, he argues that, between 1710 and 1730, clocks, scientific instruments and musical instruments were introduced, not as the playthings of an already-established elite, but to represent wealth as legitimate. Instrumentation enabled the ordered, baroque plan of Annapolis to be realized. Leone suggests

> that the order initiated was thought to be natural and thought to have been discovered by one's own instrument-aided hand, in the heavens or some other part of the natural world. The order – whether or not it was in sight, sound, or time – was ideological, not cognitive, and contained a misrepresentation of the material relations ordinary humans were in.
>
> (Leone 1988: 243)

Secondly, Leone interprets the increasing popularity of individual place settings among poorer people in Annapolis after 1730 as evidence for an 'internalized work discipline'. Leone sees the strong emphasis on individualism over corporate identity as an ideological device that enabled capitalists to control wage labour and direct their workers towards high-production goals: 'the ideology represented by the place setting celebrates the self as an autonomous individual', leading to circumstances in which 'unequal wealth could be continually generated and held without violent resistance in a capitalist setting' (Leone 1988: 247). Thirdly, Leone argues that, in the uncertain years immediately prior to the Revolution, the wealthiest citizens of Annapolis created houses and gardens to demonstrate their power over the natural world and, therefore, their right to power in the political and economic worlds: 'landscape architecture and architecture itself were used to create the dual illusion that their builders or owners could reproduce the laws of nature and, in so doing, could convince others that the owners had or deserved the power that they were actually soon to seek in leading the Revolution. The gardens and homes were statements of wishes rather than statements of fact' (Leone 1988: 240–1). In gardens such as these, the lesser citizenry of Annapolis could marvel at the breathtaking parterres, the vistas across the terraces and the noble house standing above, and could believe that their superiors had been granted at least a small portion of divine power.

A second, related, example of this approach is Paul Shackel's tracking of the development of 'modern behaviour', using Braudel's 'scales of history'. Shackel sees histories as individual, social or long term. 'Each scale builds on and is dependent on the other scales, revealing social and material change as historical developments rather than as evolutionary and predetermined patterns' (Shackel 1993: xiii). Objectification in 'individual time' can be understood through the study of appropriate collections of artefacts, in Shackel's context, ceramics and toothbrushes that reveal how ideas of personal discipline were disseminated through society. Objectification in 'social time' can be revealed through collective data (e.g. the study of probate inventory data from Annapolis). 'Long-term history' is revealed in sources that are distributed and employed at the global scale.

> A comprehensive analysis of the meanings and uses of goods should consider material culture in the context of long-term history. Long-term history can be discussed in terms of centuries or even millennia. It reveals trends and broad changes and filters out the idiosyncrasies of individuals and short-term events.
>
> (Shackel 1993: 129)

One writer who has extended this critical materialist approach across both local and global scales is Matthew Johnson. Johnson interprets the emergent ideology of capitalism in Britain and the eastern seaboard of North America through the objectification of power in landscapes, domestic architecture and everyday material culture. He sees the enclosing of the British landscape, in which privately owned fields replaced commonly held lands, as primarily a deployment of space, a creation of boundaries, and a cultural redefinition of the land. It is part of the process of taming nature and expresses a redeployment of power. The consequence was 'the emergence of categories of thought that we consider modern':

> The material presence of that landscape, and the material culture that went with it, thus changed its nature: from being a carrier of meaning in an embedded way, to one which might be drained of meaning, or that

might be more freely reassigned meaning, and in which symbolic meaning
and practical usage might actually be opposed.

(Johnson 1996: 77–8)

Johnson shows that there were parallels between the enclosure of the
landscape and transformations in domestic space. The late medieval peasant
house centred around a central hall open to the roof. This changed, with the
hall losing its central importance, the construction of additional rooms at
either end of the house, which became centres of activity in their own right,
and the addition of upstairs rooms. 'If open fields mapped complex social
relations on the ground, the enclosed landscape masked such relations . . . So
it was with traditional houses. As the open hall declined in importance, the
layout of houses became rationalized, divided according to function. Layout
became less a matter of marking social relations within a body of space to be
negotiated at a face-to-face level. It became more a matter of segregating, of
providing separate rooms for master and servant, or between the world of
work and the 'domestic' world' (Johnson 1996: 82). The end of this process
was the eighteenth-century Georgian house, characteristic of both Britain
and the eastern seaboard of North America.

Changing perceptions of space were also associated with more distanced
modes of describing, in texts on agriculture, in maps and in other documents,
which departed from the 'embeddedness' of earlier practice. Similarly, com-
modification 'involved the placing of goods in secular rather than spiritual
domains, giving freer rein to the acquisition and accumulation of goods; it
thus 'de-spiritualized' the material world' (Johnson 1996: 200).

Together, then, this critical materialist school has offered several analytical
tools. Mark Leone has shown how the naturalization of orders of authority
occurs through the deployment of material culture and the relationship of
individual domestic life to these shifting orders of authority. Paul Shackel
and Matthew Johnson have revealed 'scales of history' – the mutual interdependence of the global and the local, and some of the ways in which
general shifts in the world were played out in mundane daily life, whether
toothbrushes, house layouts or the ways in which possessions were listed and
recorded. Approaches such as these contribute to understanding the objectification of identity within the discourses of colonialism, reflecting the ways in
which Foucauldian concepts of power have been formed from a common,
broad, stream of Marxist thought.

The information that we have about two lives in the eighteenth-century
Cape shows how substantial identities were formed in different registers. The
colonial edifices of town and country required builders and craftsmen who
could interpret the wishes of their masters in bricks, mortar and timber.
Many were skilled slaves. Others were servants on loan from the Dutch East
India Company, while a few were freeburghers making a tenuous living by
their trade. The best known today is Anton Anreith, who entered Company

service in 1777 at the age of 22 and as an ordinary soldier, and worked as part of a large gang of house carpenters and masons on Cape Town's new hospital for the next 9 years before being promoted to the unusual position of 'Master Sculptor' in 1786 (de Bosdari 1954). Anreith has been celebrated as the founder of an indigenous South African fine-art tradition, distinct from an anonymous 'vernacular', although this is more due to the fortuitous survival of a segment of the documentary record rather than a quality specific to Anreith's life and work. It mattered little to him; he lived and died in abject poverty.

In late 1782 or early 1783, Anreith was commissioned to build a pulpit for the new Lutheran Church – a focal point of authority equivalent to a gable. His wooden sculpture was of two life-size Hercules figures, each with a lion's pelt slung over his shoulder, carrying the weight of the structure above (Figure 4.3). Two mastiffs behind were a rather amateurish representation of

Figure 4.3 The pulpit in the Lutheran Church, Cape Town. Designed and built by Anton Anreith in 1782–3, and photographed by Arthur Elliott in the early twentieth century (Cape Archives).

Cerberus (each should properly have three heads), while the lion recumbent between men and dog was also part of the Hercules myth. The pulpit box above had the winged heads of four smiling cherubs, and a fifth cherub was depicted full length (de Bosdari 1954). This work was clearly well regarded, for 6 years later Anreith was similarly commissioned by the elders of the Dutch Reformed Church. Here, two lions supported the weight of the pulpit. There was particular emphasis on the beast's heads and jaws, the woodwork of which was originally painted with white teeth and red mouths (de Bosdari 1954). In the words of an eighteenth-century British visitor: 'these lions gape and grin in a most formidable manner, and exhibit their teeth in the true Dutch taste; but the whole is not badly executed' (Semple 1968: 16).

In his work, Anreith was clearly relying on a broad sculptural lexicon. For example, the use of Hercules figures to support superstructures was a frequent European device used to support a balcony or other projection on the façade of a house, and the lion figured widely in European mythology and iconographic representation, conveying terror, worldly power, magnanimity and bravery, and the impossibility of forgetting an injury. This use of common ideas was an example of Shackel's 'social time' – the circulation of ideas about material form, linked to a shared mythology. It was also an example of the naturalization of authority recognized by Leone – the founding of patriarchal control in a mythology claimed to be timeless.

But, equally, such a lexicon offered many different possibilities for more individual expression. Hercules's twelve labours demonstrated strength, amorous exploits and the consumption of food and drink. They also included the liberation of the triple-headed Cerberus from the underworld and the slaying of the Nemean lion – oblique references, perhaps, to the final success of the Cape's Lutherans in being allowed to build their own church against the opposition of the 'Dutch Lion'. The Lutheran Church's muscular pulpit was a celebration of masculine strength. But Hercules was betrayed by his wife Deianeira, who killed him with the blood of the Centaur, which she believed would secure his love, but which was instead a powerful poison. In this aspect, Anreith's work objectified the far more individual scale of politics and power at the Cape – saying in sculpture that which would have been treason in words – and then again naturalizing the local plays of power by grounding them in global streams of ideas and mythology.

Adam Tas, who arrived at the Cape 80 years before Anreith, was no sculptor. The record of him that has survived was also intended to be private – like his contemporary, William Byrd, his diary was written as a personal journal. But because of this, and because of its very mundanity, the fragments of his record are particularly useful in revealing the way in which identity was constructed.

Tas was born in Amsterdam in 1668 and, through an aunt, had a connection with a wealthy and influential merchant at the Cape, where he settled in 1697. In 1703 he married the widow Elizabeth van Brakel, thus coming to own a comfortable farm on the outskirts of Stellenbosch. But his bucolic calm was short lived. Embroiled in a dispute with the Governor and a faction of wealthy Company officials benefiting from the perquisites of office, he found himself accused of high crimes and, for a while, incarcerated in the Castle (Fouché 1970). During the Cape government's investigation of the issue, Tas was discovered to have kept a diary. This was mostly an undramatic account of his everyday life. But the Governor's party saw in it evidence for idleness, confiscated its pages and had them copied into court testimony, ensuring their survival in the colonial archive.

First, Tas's diary reveals a socially segmented world. This is shown in the way in which Tas differentiated between the people he encountered in his everyday life. Tas used a largely invariable system of naming that reveals his sense of social hierarchy. Equals and betters are designated with titles. Kin are given a kinship designation, without differentiating between relatives by descent and relatives through marriage: Sister Tas, Uncle Husing, Brother van Brakel, Sister Barbara. Other equals or betters (almost always men – women are identified as their husband's wives) are invariably 'Mijnheer': Mr Starrenburg, Mr Bek, Mr Appel, Mr van Heiden, Mr van der Bijl. The form of reference was the same whether the individual was a bitter enemy (such as the Magistrate Starrenburg – one of the Governor's functionaries) or a close friend (such as Van Heiden or Van der Bijl, with whom Tas spent many hours eating, drinking and plotting). In contrast, inferiors are never 'Mijnheer'. Such people are usually recalled by their first name only, and identified further by a descriptive designation ('the cripple Vulcan', 'Louis the Hottentot') or by their craft ('Hans the smith', 'Jacobus the shoemaker', 'Dirk the sexton', 'our manservant Jacob'). Yet further down Tas's social scale, and beneath the small farmers and craftsmen, was the underclass of slaves and labourers. Tas declined to recognize such people as individuals at all, even though their labour was vital to him. His diary underlines the difference by resorting to collectives: 'our slaves', 'our boys', 'our labourers', 'our servants'. These were the people who ploughed, carted manure, sowed the fields, pruned the vines, carted wood, cut straw and weeded the corn. The diary entry for 10 July 1705 gives an impression of the farm on a winter's day; three slaves and two 'Hottentots' were working on the farm and six more fishing on the False Bay coast. None of them, however, warrants an individual identity in Tas's hierarchical nomenclature.

There was little possibility of spatial differentiation in Tas's early eighteenth-century world. Slaves, craftsmen and estate owners such as Tas – with aspirations to grandeur that assailed the Governor's standing – lived around and on top of one another. Consequently, terms of address would have been crucial in maintaining, and challenging, social hierarchy. Tas's diary reveals that the non-verbal language of material culture worked alongside words, contributing to the daily recreation of the social order.

Tas recorded some 170 social encounters in the diary fragments that have survived, noting that, in just over half of these interactions, he drank or smoked as he exchanged gossip or carried out his business. On 5 August 1705, for instance, the magistrate rode through Tas's farm in the company of his pre-decessor and they 'alighted from the coach for a while to light a pipe of tobacco, and then boarded the coach again to set forth in company ...' (Fouché 1970: 101). A month or so earlier, on 7 July 1705, Tas had been more relaxed at van der Heijden's farm, where 'we talked, drank and smoked mightily, not forgetting the eating'. The next morning Tas recorded that 'on rising I discovered that my head ached a good deal' (Fouché 1970: 73). On the first day of the diary fragment – 13 June 1705 – Tas had spent time with Hans the smith:

> after Hans, the smith, and his wife had spent a little time with us, the lady had drunk a dish of tea, etc., and we two together had partaken of a glass or two of wine and smoked sundry pipes of tobacco, they sauntered home.
> (Fouché 1970: 37)

These social encounters in which material culture mediated can be broken down further into individual elements, each of which implies the use of a different category of artefact. The least frequent activity was tea or coffee drinking, which took place in about one in ten encounters. Tas recorded a con-signment of tea (amongst other goods) being sent him from Cape Town early in June and, when in Cape Town later in the month, a significant proportion of his debts was for tea (Fouché 1970: 47). On 6 August 1705, Tas received a pair of shoes and three pounds of coffee beans from Cape Town (Fouché 1970: 103). Tea drinking was invariably tied to Asian porcelain (Jorg 1982) and Adam Tas probably owned such teaware. But the ritual was neither gender nor status specific, for Tas records both men and women drinking tea. He offered tea to men as socially diverse as Hans Jacob the Stellenbosch smith and Abraham Poulle, the Secretary to the Council in Cape Town. Eating a meal in company was a more frequent form of socialization – about one-fifth of the encounters recorded in the diary fragment. But the most frequent mediators in social encounters were smoking and drinking; about one-third each of the total encounters recorded in the diary fragment.

Wine was of course plentiful, as Tas had his own vineyard, and he recorded receiving gin from Cape Town on account from Johannes Phiffer. As with tableware, Tas does not mention acquiring drinking utensils, but this is not surprising, as such commodities would not have been bought with sufficient frequency to occur in a short journal fragment such as this one. However, he clearly had glassware – there are several references to drinking 'a glass of wine'. Smoking pipes were more fragile, and were easily discarded. On 4 July 1705, Jacob brought a consignment of goods 'from the mother country' back to the farm, including a gross of long clay pipes, which Tas had got for his friend van der Heijden (Fouché 1970: 69). The diary shows that drinking wine and spirits, and smoking tobacco, invariably involved men meeting with men. What is more, such exchanges seem to have covered a broader social range than did eating. Although Tas does not record smoking with his slaves, he did light up a pipe with the smith from Stellenbosch (who was clearly of lower social standing) with his friends and peers, and with the magistrate (the agent of his enemy, the Governor). Smoking and drinking were gendered activities, repetitively constituting masculinity.

Tas's diary shows clearly how the 'conditions of materialization' were worked though on a day-by-day basis in the domain of Shackel's 'individual time'. And, in using the imported commodities of a global system of distribution – coffee, tobacco, glassware and ceramics, Tas was constructing a local identity focused on his own bodily positioning in a small social world by using the material culture of this same global system; the same process that connected the household regimes of particular localities in early modern England with the broad flow of ideas that united contemporary cultural systems across the full span of the Atlantic.

Adam Tas's domestic life gained unintended public notice when the Governor had his farm searched and his papers confiscated as part of his attempts to suppress opposition to his policies. And Willem Adriaan van der Stel was only too aware how material things could be used to promote position in the world. His father – Governor before him – had built a fine mansion at Constantia, and the ostensible reason for Willem Adriaan's recall to the Netherlands a few years later would be his own excesses in the construction of his elaborate estate at Vergelegen (Markell *et al.* 1995). Van der Stel's contemporary, Governor Spotswood of Virginia, shared many of his ambitions of grandeur in the tradition of Versailles and, consequently, his vulnerability to his political enemies.

Alexander Spotswood, it will be recalled, arrived in Williamsburg in 1710. As with his predecessor, he aspired to build a capital worthy of the direct representative of the King, and centred these ambitions on the construction of a new garden for the recently constructed Governor's Palace. However, the garden project was as valuable as a vehicle for political opposition as it was for the assertion of control, and the seeds of dissent blossomed, eventually smothering the Governor and forcing his resignation. The gentry's complaint was not that Spotswood had built a mansion and garden, but that the scale of his monument suggested absolutist rule rather than the oligarchic control that the elite had come to expect by the early eighteenth century. From 1718, the Governor and the House of Burgesses bickered continually about the extent of the Palace garden, and in 1721 Spotswood relinquished the governorship in disgust.

Initially, the General Assembly of the Colony had specifically indicated the need for the Palace to have an appropriately sized and enclosed garden. The

'Act for finishing a House for the Governor of this Colony and Dominion', passed in 1710, specified:

> that a Court-Yard, of dimensions proportionable to the said house, be laid out, levelled and encompassed with a brick wall four feet high, with the ballustrades of wood thereupon, on the said land, and that a Garden of a length of two hundred fifty-four foot and the breadth of one hundred forty-four foot from out to out, adjoining to the said house, to be laid out and levelled and enclosed with a brick wall, four feet high, with ballus-trades of wood upon the said wall, and that handsome gates be made to the said court-yard and garden.
>
> (quoted by Martin 1991: 44)

Archaeological work has shown that these specifications were met in the construction. Peter Martin (1991) has suggested that the combination of low brick walls and balustrades prevented the enclosure of the Palace gardens from being visually complete, allowing vistas of parkland and landscape beyond, to the north. Thus the view from the north face of the Palace would have moved from nature-as-art in the foreground (a flower garden laid out in parterres with diamond-shaped centres), across nature-modified in the middle distance (parklands stocked with deer) to the untamed landscape beyond. At the front of the Palace, facing the street, was a small forecourt garden with oval flower beds and gravel walks, and flanked by two, symmetrically placed wings of the house – a detail confirmed in a contemporary image of the house. This south garden connected the Palace, with its formal public rooms, to the gridded streets of Williamsburg. Thus an axis through Williamsburg's Palace and gardens served to integrate town, house, garden and landscape into a single system of representation.

Trouble with the Burgesses probably began when Spotswood decided to transform the ravine west of the house into elaborate terraces overlooking a formal canal and fish pond, creating a theatrical effect in Italian Renaissance style. By 1718 his opponents were claiming that his obsession with the Palace garden was draining away the finances of the colony while Spotswood responded that he was spending large amounts of his own money to the public benefit. In frustration, Spotswood turned his attention to the development of his private plantation of Germanna, far away on the Rappahannock River. The author of an anonymous tract against Virginia's governor claimed of Germanna in 1721 that 'he is building a very fine House there & has encouraged artificers of all sorts to people his new town which I hear is regularly laid out in streets and squares and a pretty many houses are already built' (Martin 1991: 43). In the following year Spotswood was removed from office.

Virginia's gentry – although quick to condemn Spotswood for his perceived excesses, were no strangers to grandeur. In Rhys Isaac's words, from early in the eighteenth century the main residences that stood at the centres of the sprawling domains of Virginia gentlemen were being fashioned as declarations of the owners' status, not only by sheer scale but also by means of elaborately contrived formal relationships.

(Isaac 1982: 35–6)

One such estate was the Byrd seat of Westover. William Byrd's father had augmented his fortune through exporting tobacco, trade with the Indians, and by importing slaves, indentured servants and cask after cask of rum. He built the first house at Westover in 1688. No evidence for this structure survives, but it was probably timber frame, with planks cut at the Byrd sawmill upriver at Falling Creek. Returning to Virginia to take up his patrimony, William Byrd II had grand plans, but financial difficulties prevented him from finishing his building programme before his death in 1744. The construction of the great house was completed by William Byrd III between 1751 and 1755 (Wenger 1980, and personal communication, November 1989).

Thus three generations of the Byrd dynasty gave effect to the passion for building that was a mark of the contemporary gentry (Figure 4.4). It is probable that William Byrd II's first building project, in inheriting his father's estate in 1704, was the construction of the library, completed in 1712. This was a dependency of the main house, balancing the washhouse on the other side (later rebuilt as a kitchen), and presenting a symmetrical façade to ships approaching from the James River. Later, he built a clairvoyée in front of the landward façade, balanced by the symmetrically placed privies, or 'Necessary Houses', at each end. Attention was also given to the mansion's precinct. By 1712 a new formal garden had been completed, and Byrd continued his interest in gardening in the years that followed. Among other volumes, his library contained a wide selection of gardening books, including volumes such as Quintinye's 'Compleat Gardiner', Hugh's 'Flower Garden and Vineyard' and Mortimer's 'Art of Husbandry' (Wenger 1980).

In the design of their estates, both Governor and gentry played out a political dialogue. Aspirations for greater power could be dangerous if expressed merely in words; a Governor's ambitions could be seen as usurping the authority of the Crown, while members of the Burgess who openly defied the King's representative would be sailing close to the perils of treason. But houses and gardens provided material metaphors, rendered powerful because their meanings were clear, but deniable, and were substantial in their transformation of the visual landscape. Nicholson and Spotswood – and Byrd and numerous other Chesapeake gentry – used their building projects to extend verbal representations. In these actions, they laid claim to long-established practice, whether in the grandeur of Louis XIV political allegories at Versailles, or in the more modest claims of lesser gentry throughout the colonial world.

Figure 4.4 William Byrd II's Westover mansion, as it is today (photograph: author).

Similar plays of power were characteristic of town life in the Chesapeake. Anne Yentsch has shown how the Calvert family used both the position of their house site – 58 State Circle, Annapolis – within the landscape and the urban plan of town, as well as the architectural design of the building, to mark their power and status in the community:

> its placement gave its dwelling visual representation among buildings of rank in Annapolis. Men back then would have looked at it and known there was no way it danced fifth flowerpot. Through contiguity, the

house and its land assumed greater symbolic importance than if it had been located elsewhere ... The ascending location – the spirit of the place symbolically defined – was an essential element in its persona.

(Yentsch 1994: 97)

By the late 1720s, the Calvert household comprised some sixty individuals. Buildings were spread over two town lots and set in formal terraced gardens. Interest in horticulture contributed to the definition of status:

> wealthy men – curious about nature, plant-lovers, avid horticulturalists – built orangeries in the Chesapeake to assert prestige and compete with their peers. Orangeries, with their exotic contents, socially accrued the luminescent qualities that made a man a 'brighter light'. Orangeries spoke to the issue of power within society ... Owning an orangery gave a family symbolic control over the plant kingdom.

(Yentsch 1994: 113)

Power also resided in the vista: 'the Calvert house, located on a high terrace on the hillside above a formal, ornamental garden ... furnished its owners with a panoramic view of the town and Chesapeake Bay, and provided townfolk in turn with an evocative status-telling imagery' (Yentsch 1994: 127).

Contemporaries of the Byrds and Calverts on the other side of the Atlantic also worried about their place in the world, and the ambiguities of nature. From the earliest years of Dutch settlement at the Cape, travellers had commented on the abundance of nature at the southernmost tip of Africa, and the quality of the gardens that expressed and contained this abundance – an appreciation often accentuated by months of deprivation on board ship (Figure 4.5). Here is one example, an account by Georg Meister who visited the Cape in 1677. The Company's garden, Meister wrote, was enclosed, 'protected around with thick quickset hedges, beside which a wall a rood high and a moat half a rood wide were under construction while I was there, on the side of the so-called Devil's Peak, which will in time be continued all around'. Inside its walls the garden was 'rich in fruits and flowers', with 'many fine double laurel hedges a good pike's-length high and 2 to 3 ells [old Dutch measurement] thick, which are diligently kept to their shape year in, year out with shears or other sharp cutting-irons on long handles.' The hedges enclosed regular planting beds,

> divided and bounded, in part with rosemary which is cut at the due season like our current-bushes, in part with hyssop and sage, which I thought an oddity in this so large and long garden. Besides these the most excellent and never-sufficiently-praised tree- and ground fruits are to be seen there, brought from the Indies ...

(Raven Hart 1971: 198–9)

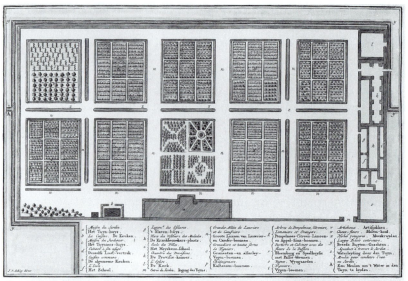

Figure 4.5 Plan of the Company's garden at the Cape of Good Hope (from Pieter Kolbe's *Present State of the Cape of Good Hope*).

Meister had once been a gardener at the Court of the Duke of Saxony and knew his trade – his account focuses succinctly on three essential qualities in a garden. First, it is enclosed and distinct from the landscape beyond; 'thick quickset hedges', a wall and a ditch, with the 'so-called Devil's Peak' unambiguously outside. Secondly, it was designed geometrically and kept in strict control; regular beds and walkways, laurel hedges 'diligently kept to their shape'. Thirdly, it was a showpiece for the exotic; the tree and ground fruits from the Indies.

These themes were echoed in other early accounts. For Johann Wilhelm Vogel, who came to the Cape 2 years later, the Company's garden was 'a brief epitome of all the finest plants, flower herbs, and fruit-trees to be found in Europe, Asia, Africa and America', all enclosed within neat beds hedged with rosemary (Raven Hart 1971: 212). Father Guy Tachard drew out the comparison between the 'avenues . . . as far as the eye can see, of citron, pomegranate and orange trees, growing in the ground and protected from the wind by thick and high hedges . . .', and the untamed landscape beyond, 'a land that seems the most sterile and horrible in the world' (Raven Hart 1971: 276–7). François Valentyn made the same comparison, turning from Table Mountain, 'barren and rocky', 'everything that is horrid and frightening' to the 'very fine and delightful arbours roofed with foliage, where one can long sit hidden from everyone' and where 'Nature and Art seem to have brought together in unity all that can give pleasure' (Valentyn 1971: 107).

Art and pleasure – nature reconstituted within the contained space of the garden's walls; Valentyn and Tachard's comparisons are themes that echo through representations of the garden, pointing to its role as the essential corollary of landscape (Pugh 1988). In comparison with the openness of the untamed landscape, gardens were known and limited – representations of human power to contain and transform wild nature, symbols of the essence of colonial settlement and transformation.

Gardens such as these were, of course, not intended just for contemplation – they were also meant to be used. In this regard gardens continued the symmetry and geometry of house plans into parterres and paths and linked conceptually the orthogonal grids of streets with the corridors and reception rooms of house interiors. Earlier visitors to the Cape consistently made the connection between buildings and nature-as-art in the garden, noting the unusual absence of structures. Meister thought this was a pity, a missed opportunity to model Cape Town's garden on 'the famous Versailles'; 'the loveliest and most healthful water from the cloud-threatening and most renowned Table Mountain could with very low costs be led for about 3 to 400 paces and then watermains and fountains could be made as high as the highest towers'. To such 'ornamental water devices' could be added 'pleasure-pavillions' and 'grottos' (Raven Hart 1971: 198–9).

Governor Simon van der Stel, Willem Adriaan's father, made it one of his priorities to correct this deficiency. By 1682 he had had a new 'pleasure house' built in the garden, which he used for entertaining visitors of rank (Theal 1964). This was designed specifically to provide vistas of both the garden and the wilderness of the Mountain. 'The ground floor contains an open vestibule that looks towards the fort and the garden, with two rooms on either side. Above there is a chamber open on all sides, between two terraces paved with bricks and surrounded by balustrades, one of which faces North and the other South' (Tachard writing in 1685 and quoted in Raven Hart 1971: 276–7). Pleasant as this pavilion sounds, it did not satisfy the Commander, for the following year, when Tachard returned to the Cape, he noted that it had been demolished 'in order to be rebuilt more magnificently' (Raven Hart 1971: 306). The second 'pleasure house' had been completed by 1691, when William Dampier noted the 'stately Garden walled in with a high Stone-wall', and its 'large House' (Raven Hart 1971: 381–2). Three years later still Christoffel Langhansz observed (probably in reference to Meister's earlier account) that the Governor was having 'various grottos and fountains' built as additional ornamentation (Raven Hart 1971: 403–4).

Given this focus of interest, it was hardly surprising that the Cape's notables were intensely interested in the designs of their houses, and their positioning within the landscape. Martin Melck's history is particularly striking in this respect. Like Anton Anreith, Melck arrived at the Cape as an artisan in Company service. But unlike the sculptor, who spent his life working for the glorification of the powers of others, Melck became a very wealthy man. Using his knowledge of brick making and agriculture, he found employment on the farm Elsenburg, outside Stellenbosch. In 1752 he married his master's widow, Anna Margaretha Hop, ensuring his fortune (Pama 1981). A little over 20 years later, Admiral Jan Splinter Stavorinus paid a visit. By now, Melck had constructed a massive estate on the foundations of his wife's first husband's modest house, described by the Admiral as a 'whole village', set to advantage 'upon the gentle declivity of a high ridge'. The manor house 'more resembled a gentlemen's villa than the mansion of a farmer' (Stavorinus 1969: 65).

Elsenburg had probably stood since 1698; the land was originally allocated to Samuel Elsevier, *Secunde* under Governor Willem Adriaan van der Stel (Fransen and Cook 1980). There is little direct information on the early design of the house, although the inventory made in 1747 when Anna Margaretha Hop inherited the property hints at the plan (Archaeology Contracts Office 1993). This room-by-room probate list gives the contents of a front room, or *voorhuis* (some furniture, and a good deal of porcelain) and of a room off to the right. Behind was a 'large back room' (*groot agterkamer*) containing porcelain and glasswork, pictures and a mirror, several tables and stools, and a bed. There was also a *binnen camer*, or 'inner room', with more beds, a kitchen and a pantry. Anna Margaretha and her first husband had clearly been affluent by contemporary standards, and lived in a practical, irregular sort of house that had probably had additional rooms, such as the *groot agterkamer*, added as necessity demanded and prosperity permitted. Like Adam Tas, they had created an identity marked out in a clutter of possessions.

Melck lived in the old house for almost a decade after his marriage but then, in 1761, completely demolished the dwelling to make way for a new mansion; archaeological excavations have shown the detritus of the earlier phase of the estate's history to be sealed beneath building rubble and cut by the new foundations (Archaeology Contracts Office 1993). Melck's new house had a U-shaped plan with a symmetrical front façade, a front room with equal-sized rooms to the left and the right, and two side wings, one containing the kitchen. The visitor's gaze was captured by a richly ornamented front door and a moulded, Baroque-style front gable directly above. Four large barns, a smithy, carpenters' and cartwrights' workshops, houses for slaves and kraals for cattle, sheep and horses completed the precinct, or *werf* (Stavorinus 1969: 65). All were carefully aligned to complement the regularity of the manor-house's façade.

Like William Byrd II, Martin Melck had a power of personality that echoes through the historical record. Illiterate, he ran his affairs from memory: 'he had the whole in his head of what was necessary for the due management of his extensive concerns ...' (Stavorinus 1969: 65). Nonchalance about the extent of his wealth has the hallmark of conspicuous consumption, and he professed to Stavorinus that he did not know the exact number of his slaves, and did not mind the ravages of disease among his livestock:

> a small proof of the numerousness of his herds, was his informing me, in a careless manner, as if it were a circumstance of no consideration, that he had lost one hundred and twenty head of cattle, a few days before.
>
> (Stavorinus 1969: 63)

Further, and undoubtedly to the consternation of the Company's administration in the Castle, Melck was a Lutheran, and would donate the building in Cape Town that was eventually converted into the Lutheran church that Anreith was commissioned to adorn. Melck was also a Prussian nationalist, and surprised Stavorinus with 'his steady love for his king, of whom he always spoke with the deepest respect and affection' (Stavorinus 1969: 61). This patriotism was expressed graphically by a life-sized ivory and ebony Prussian eagle above the *voorhuis* fireplace, crowned by Melck's monogram (Figure 4.6; Fransen 1987).

Just as Byrd's Westover was one of a set of great houses in Virginia, so Melck's reconstruction of Elsenburg as a symmetrical structure was one instance of a general pattern, definitive of a local tradition of eighteenth-century colonial architecture. A further example of a house where such a building project has been verified by archeological excavation – and can be correlated with documentary sources – is the house at Paradise, on the side of Table Mountain.

The first documentary record for the Paradise area was an entry in the Company's log in October 1657, when it was recorded that the Commander went to inspect the forest close to his own estate of Bosheuvel (Thom 1954: 164–5). Van Riebeeck granted the rights to cut wood to a man called Cornelis (or Cornelissen) who built a house in the forest which he subsequently fortified with a palisade to fend off the Khoikhoi who, not unreasonably, believed the land to be theirs. But Cornelis took to drink, let his house fall into disrepair, and was sent back to Batavia because of his 'debauchery'. Some years later, and certainly by 1710, the Company took direct control of the forest and built an outpost at Paradise (Hall *et al.* 1993).

The Paradise buildings were sited to take advantage of a flatter promontory of land on an otherwise steep slope, backed by the rocky mountain face and looking out over the valley of the Liesbeek River (Figure 4.7). The first direct evidence for architecture is the remains of a rectangular, stone-foundation house with three rooms, each different in size and floor finish. Irregularities in the wall footings suggest the positions of door openings leading between the rooms and to the area outside the building. As with Elsenburg, this phase ended dramatically. Sometime after 1734, the building was completely razed, and levelled evenly down to the level of floors and stone-wall footings. Fill, incorporating building rubble and artefacts from

Figure 4.6 Martin Melck's Prussian eagle for the main fireplace, Elsenburg.

the demolished house, was roughly flattened across the site, red brick debris was tamped down to a level surface and yellow clay was laid to support and seal new floors. Landscaping of the hillside behind extended the building platform. A new, stone-walled dwelling was raised, utilizing the earlier foundations to reinforce the downhill front walls (Hall *et al.* 1993).

The new house at Paradise consisted of four rooms, three symmetrically laid out in the front of the building and one to the rear. The tail area of this

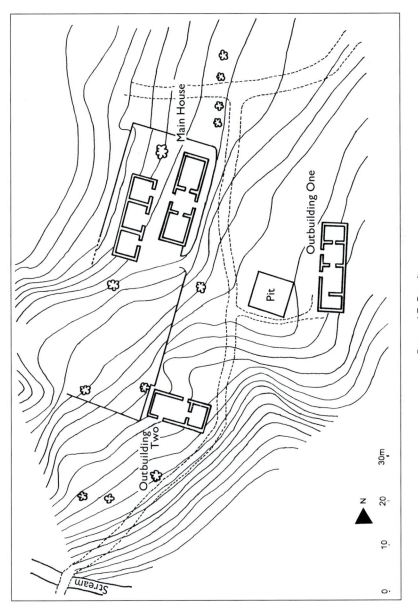

Main House

Outbuilding One

Pit

Outbuilding Two

Stream

N

0   10   20   30m

Figure 4.7 Paradise.

T-plan building (probably the kitchen) may only have been partitioned off at this stage, as the back-wall footings of the front-middle room abut the main walls rather than being keyed into the stonework, suggesting that the wall was built later. Over the years that followed, alterations were made to this second building. The walls of the back wing were stripped down to the tops of their foundation platforms and the ground filled back to the level of the front rooms. The building site was extended backwards again with a further cut into the hillside and a retaining wall was put up to protect the back of the house. Two new rooms were built in this back area, separated from the front wing of the house. The southernmost of this pair of new back rooms was cobbled and had a wide brick threshold laid in a stone-lined trench. The cobbled-floor surface had carefully laid drainage channels which led into a similarly cobbled inner yard between the two wings. The northern of the new back rooms had a floor partially surfaced with mortar and broken window glass, probably as protection against rodents. A brick footing is all that remains of a hearth. At a still later stage, an additional room was added to the south end of the back wing, again with a hearth. These alterations preserved the symmetrical design of the overall structure (Hall *et al.* 1993).

Who built this new house, matching Melck's project at Elsenburg with an equally comprehensive rebuilding at Paradise? The Company must have been involved in some way, since it held the title to the property. But the principal instigator was probably one Salomon Bosch who arrived at the Cape in Company service in 1747, was appointed Master Woodcutter for the forest in 1751, and lived at Paradise until he died in 1768. Bosch had ample reason to extend his house once it had been reconstructed. First married to Elisabeth de Nys, with whom he had seven children, Bosch was married again in 1765, to Gesina Maartens, to whom two sons were born before their father's death (Hall *et al.* 1993). Surrounded by his numerous children, and looking out from his symmetrically fronted house over the forests and farmlands of the upper Liesbeek River valley, Salomon Bosch would have rivalled William Byrd II as a model of patriarchy.

The record of Bosch's possessions at his death brings alive the bare foundations and floors of Paradise's archaeology, animating the sherds of glass and ceramics – the rusting fragments of metal – in the low middens around the site (Cairns 1980). We learn that, in the three front rooms of the house, there were nine tables of various shapes and sizes, twenty-four chairs, three cabinets, two four-poster beds with hangings, a kist (chest), a desk and a birdcage. On the walls were fifteen pictures, four mirrors and a cuckoo clock. The kitchen, at the back of the house, was fully equipped with a wide range of pots and implements, and there was a horse, with saddle and bridle and a supply of barley, in the stable. Something of Bosch's personality and appearance also hovers behind the document; the horde of gold and silverware locked away in the room to the right of the house's entrance; personal posses-

Figure 4.8 William Hogarth's *Marriage à la Mode* (National Gallery, London).

sions such as a silver pocket watch and pocket clip, a silver tobacco box, twenty steel buttons set in silver, a pair of silver trouser buckles, a gold neck clasp and one pair of gold double shirt buttons, two canes with silver knobs, two daggers and a sword with silver fittings.

Despite his rustic calling, Salomon Bosch had clearly cut a fine figure when out and about in the streets of Cape Town. Paradise was not Versailles and Bosch was not the Sun King. But there was common ground in the way that claims and counter-claims to power and authority were mapped out in personal possessions, household goods, the design of house and garden and remodelled landscapes.

Critical materialism helps to show the way in which public transcripts were put together through acts of individual agency that deployed material culture. Whether Adam Tas or the nameless subjects of genre paintings, everyday utensils expressed identity through their very mundanity. Material culture was everywhere implicated in the day-by-day 'microphysics' of power.

This relationship was captured with characteristic satire by William Hogarth (Figure 4.8). Here we see a transaction being finalized. On the one side of the table is the aristocrat, well-bred but penniless. His asset is the title that he will pass to his son once he is dead. On the other side of the table is the newly made merchant. His daughter and her dowry will secure social elevation. The historical archaeology of Hogarth's painting lies in the background. Before the ink can dry, the architect will have given fresh instructions to the builders at work outside the window. The merchant's money will allow the mansion make-over that is essential if this aristocratic family is to remain 'in society'. Hogarth's wit may be a parody of custom rather than law, but it is sumptuary action in play, and an incisive demonstration of the importance of material culture in the artist's eighteenth century world.

Chapter 5

Hidden voices

Hogarth's painting of the aristocratic but decrepit father negotiating the dowry of his daughter-in-law in bricks and mortar (Figure 4.8) illustrates the relationship between power and performance well. As the previous chapter showed, material culture gives form to the expression of identity, whether at the scale of cities, streets and houses, or in the everyday objects of an Adam Tas, marking out both gender and social status in sets of domestic utensils.

This chapter moves beyond the insights that come from this use of critical materialism and looks for the impress of 'hidden voices'. These are the people who did not even leave Deetz's 'small things forgotten' in the archaeological record. They are Spivak's subalterns – the women, slaves and servants who were the engines of colonial society but who can only be seen partially – or not at all – in the material culture and documents that are the historical record.

This approach recognizes that the limitation of critical materialism is its focus on the public transcripts of domination. This emphasis, whether in Mark Leone's work on domestic settings in the early years of merchant capitalism in Maryland, or Matthew Johnson's study of the transition to capitalism in Britain, leaves those who were in positions of subjugation as the inevitable victims of manipulation. Other approaches (and the principal influence on this book has come from writing by Scott, Spivak and Bhabha) have shown how the subaltern inevitably answers back. In the face of everyday acts of opposition, or in anticipation of resistance, the behaviour of those in positions of power is affected. As a consequence, the impression that the 'hidden transcript' makes on the public manifestations of power can be read as an indication of the form of these hidden voices of the past. The process is rather like deducing the impact of a fist that remains on a sandbag. The drama of the blow is over and the sound of the impact has faded. But the impression of the clenched fist remains for all to see.

The route into this argument will be a consideration of the way in which houses, churches and other public spaces worked to frame and form the relationships between people. Houses and gardens were rather like stages in an experimental theatre. The performances that were set in them were intended for both audience and actors, and the settings were constantly shifted and developed in reaction to the volatility of the plot.

Many of the participants in this theatre of colonialism had been dispossessed by the relentlessness of European settlement. At the Cape, this included the Khoikhoi, the herders who had lived in this part of southern Africa for some 2,000 years before the Dutch had arrived. For the first 50 years, the Khoikhoi were engaged in a series of one-sided wars with the garrison at Table Bay. Following this, their communities were largely decimated by smallpox, and survivors were trapped in the colonial system as indentured labourers or were incorporated in colonial society as wives or concubines. But despite this history of dispossession and violence, the Khoikhoi had a crucial formative influence on the Cape's colonial culture through miscegenation and cultural diffusion, contributing to the rich creole culture that twentieth-century apartheid idealists were to work so hard to eradicate.

The impression of the subaltern is well illustrated in the life of Krotoa, who left ripples of impact far wider than the scarce mark of her explicit presence in the historical record. A 'woman between', Krotoa was a Khoikhoi notable who moved between the world of the Dutch at the Castle and her own community, camped some way off and attempting to read the rapidly changing historical circumstances in which they were living. As this chapter will show, Krotoa's performance with material culture vividly illustrates this aspect of the power dynamics of early colonial settlement.

The wider reaction of Dutch colonial settlers to the Khoikhoi well illustrates how the impress of transcripts of resistance created what Bhabha has called the 'third space'. Contemporary descriptions of the Khoikhoi take an ethnographic approach, describing customs such as those associated with marriage and death. Here, the nervous repetitions and carnivalesque inversions of the ethnographer show the complex way in which, at first, European customs, assumed superior, are read into the colonial subject, and then the manner in which this is contradicted by the assertion of difference, and finally the complex and revealing confusion in these descriptions that reveals the effect of day-by-day forms of resistance.

Of course, the Khoikhoi were not the only subjugated group in colonial society. As we have already seen, colonialism was predicated on patriarchy and the set of assumptions of male superiority. As a result, women had particularly complex positions in colonial society. This chapter develops understanding of this complexity further, again in a closely detailed case study. Through a reading of genealogies, probate records and other documentary sources, the apparently self-sure male world appears more complex, and to some extent a masquerade that hid complex sets of dependencies. This documentary evidence shows that the symmetrical Cape houses that stood proudly in the landscape marked connections between men that depended almost entirely on family connections through women. Although the owner of such a house may have stood proudly beneath an ornate gable, thumbs in his belt and long clay tobacco pipe to hand, women held a degree of economic and social power that has gone largely unrecognized. Again, this shows the complex way in which words and objects worked in tandem in forming colonial discourse.

The consequence of reading architecture in this way, and of appreciating the ability of the Khoikhoi to destabilize the confidence of the colonizer merely by their presence, is to sketch a 'landscape of power'. Rather than a static dominant ideology that was imposed on a compliant population, we see a dynamic vista made up of words of all sorts and objects at all scales. This is Carter's (1988) 'travelling epistemology' at work – the mapping of colonial discourse at the point of its formation, creating a rich historical record that connects the present with many decades of previous history.

Yvonne Brink has explored the concept of performance by interpreting the eighteenth-century Cape manor house as a stage, framing what she terms the 'inscribed text' of the façade and plan, and the 'oral discourse' of the face-to-face encounters between people within the structure of the building (Brink 1992: 135). Such interactions started with the first sight of the buildings. The vista was controlled by a number of different architectural devices, but in one way or another attention was directed to the symmetrical façade of the manor house itself. Often, this first sight was stressed by the barrier of the low perimeter wall of the *werf*, or enclosure, separating the wilderness of the countryside from the order within this local boundary of civilization: 'arrested in his progress, the visitor was made to gaze upon the full vista of the symmetrical, gabled façade at the end of a tree-lined carriageway' (Brink 1992: 148). The next barrier to the visitor's progress was the centrally placed front door, sometimes embellished to emphasize the position and standing of the house's occupant. This threshold gave access to an internal hierarchy of spaces, initiated by the *voorhuis*, which lay directly beyond the front door.

Such performances – declarations of relative status – continued the performances of the streets – the funerals, executions and carnivals that ritualized social relations. Cape Town's Lutherans, taking advantage of Martin Melck's generosity, seemed to understand this when they commissioned Anreith to design the façade of their new church (Figure 5.1). Anreith gave the building a pediment, running the full width of the building, which was split in the centre and had a tall obelisk rising from the gap. Drapery garlands hung down both sides of the façade. Life-size statues, said to represent Africa and Europe, stood at each end of the cornice, and the Lutheran symbol of the swan was placed above the entrance (de Bosdari 1954). The effect was of a theatre curtain opening on a performance. Robert Semple, an English visitor to the Cape a few years later, was unimpressed, and mistook the species of bird: '[The church] is without a steeple, but is adorned externally with three or four chubby figures which seem to have

Figure 5.1 Anne Barnard's drawing of the façade of the Lutheran Church, Cape Town, 1797
(South African Library, Cape Town, SAL INIL7058).

perched themselves rather clumsily upon the roof. An ostrich is carved out
over the door . . .' (Semple 1968: 16).

Although the Lutheran Church may indeed not have been consistent with
the broad trends in ecclesiastical architecture, both its exterior and interior
elements were consonant with the emphasis on a patriarchal authority, both
secular and divinely directed. William Byrd would have shuddered at
Anreith's taste, but spent most of his life playing the same game in his architectural contests with the likes of Governor Spotswood and the other Virginia
gentry. Salomon Bosch and Martin Melck would probably have heartily
approved if they had lived long enough to see the new façade. Buildings were
for expressing status and commonality with gentlemen of like standing, for
contesting the standing of those higher up the ladder, and for defending
position against usurpers from below.

Performances that objectified everyday contestations of power were
important in other spheres of the colonial world. Dutch settlement at the
Cape – as with colonial settlement in almost all other parts of the world –
resulted in the dispossession of the indigenous population. The subsequent
consolidation of occupation depended on a combination of the eradication of
resistance and the incorporation of local communities into the new colonial
order. This set up plays of domination and resistance that can also be
approached through the lens of performance. The life and death of Krotoa
illustrates this well.

The Goringhaicona, a Khoikhoi tribe that visited the Cape regularly in its seasonal grazing rounds, had long had intermittent contacts with visiting European trading vessels in the bay. Their chief, Autshumato, had acted as an informal agent of trade at Table Bay, having been taken some 20 years earlier to the Javanese port of Bantam by the British, where he had learned some English. Krotoa was kin to Autshumato, and a young girl when the Dutch first settled in 1652 (Malherbe 1990). Over the next decade, Krotoa played an increasingly complex role as a 'woman between', serving the Dutch in Van Riebeeck's household (as a maid to Van Riebeeck's wife, Maria de la Quellerie), and as a well-connected Khoikhoi notable.

Krotoa's work was partly with words, using her increasing knowledge of Dutch and Portuguese to interpret between the garrison, desperate for trade, and the chiefs, ever wary of Dutch intentions and good faith. But she also used a rich panoply of material representations, as did the Dutch. The garrison fired muskets, offered baubles and trinkets, tobacco and liquor, and kept Krotoa on hand to interpret. One attempt to represent simultaneously their own superiority over the Khoikhoi and the Khoikhoi to themselves seems to have gone wrong. A delegation from the Chainouqua were shown into the fort:

> later on ... [they] were led to a large looking-glass in the Commander's room, they were obviously very much alarmed, first thinking that they were looking at people in another room and then, when they recognized themselves and other people reflected, they imagined that they were seeing spirits.
>
> (Thom 1958: 261)

For their part, the Khoikhoi dazzled the Dutch with promises of livestock too numerous to count, and with the riches of a mythical ruler in the interior, 'Chobona', who accorded closely with European preconceptions of Monomotapa and Prester John (Malherbe 1990: 15).

Krotoa's particular command of symbolic representation was shown by her use of the codes of appearance. To the Dutch, she was 'Eva' – a servant and convert to Christianity. To the Goringhaicona she was a relative of their chief. As Krotoa moved between the colonial world of the fort and the settlements of her Khoikhoi relatives she changed her clothes, as well as her name. This was by no means lost on the Dutch, as the Journal recorded:

> towards evening they thanked us politely and gratefully in good Dutch words for the presents they had received. They then left. When Eva reached the matted hut of Doman, also known as Anthonij, outside the fort, she at once dressed herself in hides again and sent her clothes home. She intended to put them on again when she returned to the Commander's wife, promising, however, that she would in the meantime

not forget the Lord God, Whom she had come to know in the
Commander's house . . .

(Thom 1954: 343)

Once on the other side of the frontier, Krotoa was a woman of position in
Khoikhoi society, related through marriage or by descent to at least three
chiefs – a lady's maid no longer (Malherbe 1990). Her standing was made
abundantly clear: 'Like her sister and brother-in-law [the chief and his wife]
she was, according to native custom, mounted on an ox as if she were a lady
of quality instead of travelling on foot with the rest' (Thom 1954: 373).

Understanding the dialectics of the relationships of power across the grids of
status and gender is crucial in the interpretation of localities, the conditions
of their materialization, and the rituals played out within them – whether
these localities were the interior of the household, the precinct of a settlement,
or garden and landscape. Adam Tas, Martin Melck and Krotoa all played
out complex histories that defined and contested their positions in the world.
These sorts of dimension have been well captured in James Duncan's
nuanced interpretation of landscape in the Sri Lankan Kingdom of Kandy.
Duncan sees landscape as a signifying system, and part of 'culture' in the
sense defined by Raymond Williams. Within this cultural sphere are 'discursive fields' – a range of competing positions constituted by narratives related
to social practice: 'The landscape . . . is one of the central elements in a
cultural system, for as an ordered assemblage of objects, a text, it acts as a signifying system through which a social system is communicated, reproduced,
experienced, and explored' (Duncan 1990: 17). The king ruled over his
people in the same way as the Buddhist King of the Gods, Sakra, ruled over
the gods in heaven . . . a narrative of the cities of the kings during Lanka's
'golden age'. Both were encoded together within a given element in the
urban landscape. The King's reading of the landscape entailed moving
backwards and forwards between sacred texts and landscape in order to
legitimate claims to political power. This reading was acted out in civic
rituals, such as royal funerals and inaugurations and the reception of foreign
ambassadors. In contrast, the nobility of Kandy used the same landscape to
enhance a different reading of sacred texts, claiming dereliction and
sacrilege, and their own rights to power. And then again, there were the
peasants' interpretation, reflected in rituals and traditions of injustice and
false claims to divine status – James Scott's 'hidden transcripts' of resistance.

One of the limitations of the 'critical materialist' school in historical archaeology has been a failure to move beyond the delimitation of dominant transcripts, leaving such subtle contestations – in which the material world
played a central role – largely uncharted. Leone and Shackel's work in the
Chesapeake, while representing a significant advance from the ahistoricism
of structuralism, has been mired by the concept of a blanketing 'dominant

ideology' – a pervasive false consciousness that prevented the dominated from seeing their entrapment, and from resisting (Hall 1992a).

Similarly, the world that Matthew Johnson maps out is the persuasive view offered by those with power. For example, in considering the role of inventories and architecture in imposing the new order of capitalism, Johnson writes:

> so the inventory, as part of the structure of probate records in general, is patriarchal: women are rendered silent, made into objects. At the same time this is what the architecture of the sixteenth century house does. The central hall is both public space and an arena for the playing out of unequal social relationships. Women, servants, children are rendered 'silent' by the architecture.
>
> (Johnson 1996: 113)

But were women and servants really rendered silent? Other contemporary documents demonstrate otherwise. Johnson himself points out that the sixteenth century was a time when men perceived a major threat from women to the patriarchal order, with a rise in prosecutions against scolds and witches. The error is to elide the historian's narrative with the representation of their contemporary world made by those holding power. In other words, to take the self-proclaimed dominant transcripts of the past at face value – as was intended by those who expressed them – is to do as those in the past intended, rendering invisible the subaltern voices.

This point can be amplified by a detailed example from the same material domain that interests Johnson in the archaeology of early modern England. The Cape has long been known for its eighteenth-century colonial architecture, commonly named 'Cape Dutch' – an inappropriate label, since the stylistic connections with the Netherlands are indirect and many of the free-burghers who were to build at the Cape came originally from other areas in Europe such as France, Germany and Scandanavia (Obholzer *et al.* 1985). When men like Martin Melck and Salomon Bosch built such mansions, they were clearly asserting their own dominance, in much the same way that Johnson describes for sixteenth-century England. But was this all? A closer look suggests not. There is evidence that the connections that linked men and their houses across the eighteenth-century landscape were manipulated by women, who were far from being passive objects.

Academic interest in the Cape's manor houses has been almost exclusively in stylistic connections and influences, rather than in a history within the context of colonial settlement in this part of southern Africa. However, the work of Yvonne Brink is a notable exception. Through a close study of probate records, she has shown that the development of the symmetrically centred front room, the *voorhuis*, was synonymous with the development of the Cape manor house as an architectural form. Earlier buildings in the colony had a *voorhuis*, but in these cases the room was probably not centrally placed. The probate records imply a systematic change beginning in the 1730s, with the *voorhuis* regularly placed in the centre of the front wing of the house, and with equal-sized rooms providing a balanced symmetry to left and right. Behind such a *voorhuis* was a hierarchy of additional rooms, which could include a *gaanderij*, or dining room, and an *agterkamer* beyond (Brink 1992). Further emphasis was added to the building by ornamentation, and in particular by high gables at the centre of the front façade, directly above the front door, and optionally to the ends of the wings as well. The most elaborate of the ornamented manor houses had six gables on an H-shaped ground plan: at the centre of the front and back façades and on each of the four wing ends. Such gables added three-dimensional volume to the pavilion of the dwelling standing in its *werf*.

The earliest suggestion of such a gabled façade is in Stade's 1710 panorama of Stellenbosch (reproduced in Smuts 1979: 84–5). This picture shows at least one building with a gable above its front façade; it is, however, unadorned and it is not possible to establish the ground plan associated with it. In Cape Town, no domestic buildings put up before 1756 still stand today in unmodified form. The Governor's pleasure house in the Gardens had a fully fledged centre gable, covered by later building work, that may date back to 1751, while Rach's drawings of Cape Town made in 1762 show several gables; it is likely that some of these buildings had been standing for some time (Figure 5.2; Fransen 1987). All this evidence, frustratingly partial as it is, is consistent with Brink's argument that the Cape manor house, with symmetrical floor plan and ornamented centre gable, was initially developed in the 1730s and had become a fully established building tradition within two decades.

Several different typologies have been offered for these curvilinear gables

Figure 5.2 Gabled buildings bordering the Parade Ground, in front of the Castle, Johannes Rach, 1762 (Cape Archives, M163).

(e.g. Baker 1900; de Bosdari 1953; Pearse 1959). In recent years, Fransen and Cook's three-part summary has generally been accepted as standard. The earliest form was a frame of simple, convex lobes, dated to before the mid-1750s. This was followed by the concavo-convex, or 'holbol' gable, beginning in the mid-1750s and continuing to be popular until the beginning of the last decade of the century. This type was characterized by curved, in- and out-swinging outlines, and included various subtypes which became more and more elaborate as the century progressed. Finally, from the 1780s onwards, neoclassical styles began to become popular, characterized by distinctive arrangements of pilasters and pediments (Fransen and Cook 1980). Such frames could contain a variety of different decorative forms, although many of the earlier 'holbol' gables seem to have had little surface decoration beyond the date of construction. However, from about 1770 plaster surface features began to become more common as curvilinear outlines themselves became more complex. Dates were elaborated and the initials of the owner and occupier of the house – and sometimes those of his wife as well – were used in cartouches or as part of florid, applied plaster work. Other decoration included free-flowing plants, pineapples, the 'tree of life' and the stylized 'all-seeing eye' (Fransen 1987).

Clearly, such decoration developed as part of an aesthetic tradition, and styles were copied and elaborated as part of the 'proper' ornamentation of a Cape house of quality. But, at the same time, there is also clear reference to a more general iconographic code, and to assertions of position within the world. The 'all-seeing eye', although not a particularly common attribute of gable plaster work, invokes the notion of controlling patriarchy; the gabled house standing high in the landscape and reminding those who see it of the sur-veillance of the head of the household. Classical motifs invoke the memory of Greek and Roman imperial authority – 'Augustus' dominion', 'conquering Alexander' and the 'cornerstone at Earth's extremest end' (Gray 1989). Such military authority was made explicit in the relief on the portico parapet over the entrance to the Governor's apartments in the Castle, constructed between 1785 and 1790. The moulded images include a crowned shield with the Lion of the Netherlands, military trophies and helmeted putti (Fransen 1987). Originally, urns stood on the two extremities of the parapet (de Bosdari 1954). The doors below have lions' heads set in their centre panels, holding the door knockers and making sure that the parapet's message is not lost on the visitor about to cross the threshold to the seat of Company authority.

There are few buildings or building complexes surviving intact today in which a full suite of gable, outbuilding and interior decoration comes together to present the comprehensive effect of such patriarchal signification. One example, though, is the farm of Meerlust, on the Eerste River down-stream from Stellenbosch (Figure 5.3). Originally granted to Henning Hussing, a colonial notable, Meerlust was considerably enlarged in 1776 by Johannes Albertus Myburgh, who added extra wings to create a variant of

Figure 5.3 Meerlust (photograph: author).

the symmetrical H-plan. Myburgh signalled his connections with his forebears and contemporaries by incorporating Hussing's pentagonal-motif front door in the new structure (it became Myburgh's back entrance) and by copying Melck's Elsenburg architrave to add dignity and emphasis to the doorway in the new front façade. 'Holbol' front and side gables added volume and emphasis to the pavilion's presentation and the front gable incorporated moulded plaster work; wheatsheaf-like motifs that have survived generations of overpainting. Other buildings were adorned with applied plaster work – outbuildings with cartouches to designate their functions, a decorated poultry yard, scrolls supporting an outside stairway and an elaborate slave bell. The gable motif was continued into the woodwork of the house, picked up on still-surviving interior doors and built-in wall cupboards, symmetrically placed in the *voorhuis* (Fransen and Cook 1980; Obholzer *et al.* 1985). Meerlust's gabled sign system extends, as well, beyond the immediate *werf* and beyond the life of its principal architect. The farm's graveyard has a gable fronting its main vault, ensuring that Myburgh's patriarchal standing survived his own mortality. Others had the same idea: Paarl's churchyard has a number of gabled vaults, miniature dwellings for their occupants, with façades reflecting the building fashions of different periods.

Who were the elite who built the Cape's manor houses, decorated their gables and went to such pains to differentiate themselves from the run-of-the-mill, *mestizo* society of the colony? Gable designs combined familiar baroque elements with local innovation to create a new aesthetic which has frustrated a smooth connection with the broad streams of traditional art history. Brink has argued that this was just the point. The genre of gable building which began at the Cape in the 1730s was the product of a class of peasants-made-good, who were taking old European approaches to gentry architecture and twisting them into a new aesthetic strand:

> the Cape Dutch gable conjures up a vast architectural intertext which includes the aesthetic. Gables beautify the Cape Dutch dwellings and in appropriating beauty for their houses, the free burghers also appropriated it for themselves, contradicting established intertexts, almost clichés, in European art and literature where peasants are depicted as ragged, dirty, dull and ugly. Symmetrifying and gabling the basic peasant house showed how the ragged could put on grand new clothes . . .
>
> (Brink 1992: 165–6)

One advantage of taking houses as instances of the use of material culture in extending the language of words is that buildings can be related to the documentary record through deeds of transfer and owners identified. Sequences of such documents constitute the 'biography' of a house through the years following its construction. Together, such biographies allow the men who claimed these houses as the expression of their position in the world to be placed in their contemporary context.

There are forty-one surviving (or recently standing) eighteenth-century gabled manor houses with traceable histories of ownership in the Cape. These are listed, with the names of the title-holders to the property deeds in the years that the gables were put up, in Table 5.1.

The two earliest surviving, dated examples are Joostenburg and Klipheuvel, both with gables erected in 1756. The busiest building years seem to have been 1767 and 1792, each with four new gables that still stand today. The last two gables in the group (those at Rhone and Zeekoegat) were put up in 1795, when the Dutch East India Company lost the Cape to the British. All these houses could be encompassed within a single patriarchal era. Thomas Arnoldus Theron, who had his initials cast in plaster on his gable at Languedoc in 1757 when he was 41 years old, was still on his farm in 1783. Jacob Marais, who built a gable at Plaisir de Merle in 1764, lived until 1787, when the property passed to his son Pieter Marais; the combined lifespans of father and son exceeded the span of baroque gable building in the Dutch Cape.

Taken together, this set of gabled buildings shows a tight pattern of distribution (Figure 5.4). Almost all of them are in the fertile catchments of the Liesbeek, Eerste, Berg and Upper Breede Rivers – the established winelands of the Cape countryside. These locations suggest specific farming activities – an inference that is supported by the documentary sources. The census

Table 5.1 Title-holders of gabled buildings

Date	Estate name	Family	Title-holder
1756	Joostenburg	Grové	Gerrit van der Byl
1756	Klipheuvel	Louw	Paul Hartog
1757	Languedoc	Louw	Thomas Arnoldus Theron
1759	Kromme Rhee	Grové	Dirk de Vos
1761	Elsenburg	Van der Merwe	Martin Melck
1763	Zwaanswyk	Grové	Nicolaas Russouw
1764	Plaisir de Merle	De Villiers	Jacob Marais
1767	Spier	Van der Merwe	Albertus Johannes Myburgh
1767	Olyvenhout	De Villiers	Hermanus Bosman
1767	Buffelskraal	De Villiers/Retief	Jacob Hugo
1767	Karnemelksvlei	Van der Merwe	Schalk Willem Burger
1768	Lemoenbult	De Villiers/Retief	Jacob Hugo
1769	Landskroon	De Villiers/Van der Merwe	Pieter van der Merwe
1771	Kromme Rivier	Groenwald	Jacob Groenwald
1771	Loevestein	Van der Merwe	Hendrik Oostwald Eksteen
1771	Libertas	Groenwald/Louw	Johann Bernard Hoffman
1773	Vergenoegd	Grové	Johannes Nicolaas Colyn
1774	Nooitgedacht	Van der Merwe	Hendrik Cloete
1776	Meerlust	Van der Merwe	Johannes Albertus Myburgh
1777	L'Arc d'Orleans	Retief	Pierre le Riche
1778	Groenhof	Groenewald	Hendrik Albertyn
1779	Morgenster	Van der Merwe	Philip Hendrik Morkel
1780	Blaauwklip	Van der Merwe/Retief/Louw	Dirk Wouter Hoffman
1781	Hazendal	Van der Merwe/Van Breda	Joost Rynhard van As
1781	Klaasvoogdsrivier	De Villiers/Van der Merwe	Hendrik van der Merwe
1782	Rheezicht	Van Breda	Alexander van Breda
1789	Vredenburg	De Villiers/Retief	Jacob Roux
1789	Ida's Valley	Groenewald	Samule Johannes Cats
1790	Boesmansvlei	Van der Merwe/Retief	Daniel Hugo
1790	Zevenrivieren	Van Breda	Johannes Jacobus Haman
1790	Doornrivier	Van der Merwe	Willem Hendrik van der Merwe
1791	Burgundy	De Villiers	Jacob Marais
1792	Kleinbosch	Retief	Guillaume du Toit
1792	Uiterwyk	De Villiers	Johannes Krige
1792	Hartebeestkraal	Eighth family	Arend van Wielligh
1792	Groot Constantia	Van der Merwe	Hendrik Cloete
1793	Dwars-in-die-Weg	De Villiers/Grové/Retief	Isaac Stephanus de Villiers
1793	Groenfontein	Retief/Louw	Adriaan Louw
1794	Rotterdam	De Villiers	Anthony Faure
1795	Rhone	Eighth family	Gerrit Victor
1795	Zeekoegat	Retief	Hillegert Muller

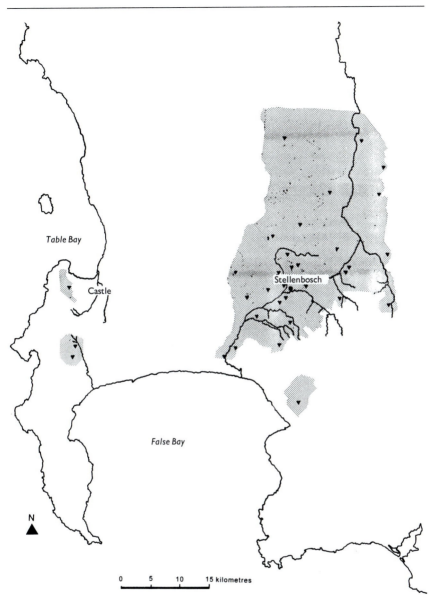

Figure 5.4 Eighteenth-century gabled buildings (▼) at the Cape were located in areas with soils suitable for wine production.

returns reveal the same profile over and over again; variable numbers of sheep and cattle, wheat and barley, and extensive vineyards. The census returns also record the ownership of gangs of slaves and, often, *kneghts* (servants) on loan from the Company. In contrast, eighteenth-century gabled buildings are rarely associated with poorer farmers or with pastoralists pushing the frontier on beyond the Hottentots' Holland mountains (Hall 1994a).

There is an equivalently tight patterning in the kinship of the people (all men) who held the titles of the forty-one manor houses when the gables were built. All can be connected to a maximum of eight families, seven of which can be specifically identified from the genealogical records, and the eighth implied from fragmentary sources. Just over half these freeburghers were connected with the De Villiers family, which traces its descent to three brothers who arrived together at the Cape in the late seventeenth century. A second major group is attached to the Van der Merwe family, originating with Willem Schalk van Der Merwe, who arrived at the Cape from the Netherlands in 1661. Five other families – Groenewald, Grové, Retief, Van Breda and Louw – link together almost all the remaining manor houses. The only gabled buildings that cannot be associated with one of these seven families can be connected with one another, suggesting an eighth family which is only partially documented. Both Salomon Bosch and Martin Melck were members of this group of families by virtue of marriage. By the end of the eighteenth century there were some 2,000 family names in use in the Cape (Pama 1981); title-holders to gabled manor houses were clearly a very small subset of the colonial population at large.

So far, this is a familiar story of patriarchy. At first pass, these buildings seem individually male – Cape equivalents of the Byrd dynasty, signifying themselves in brick and plaster. However, a closer look at the documentary evidence reveals a more complex play of power and influence.

Some of the forty-one surviving gabled manor houses listed were connected through their owners. Two men held the titles to more than one building (Jacob Hugo of Buffelskraal and Lemoenbult, with gables dated a year apart, and the houses adjacent, and Hendrik Cloete of Nooitgedacht, which he inherited, and Groot Constantia, which he purchased more than a decade later). There are two fathers and sons in the list (Jacob Marais of Plaisir de Merle and his son, also Jacob Marais, of Burgundy, and Johann Bernard Hoffman of Libertas and his son Dirk Wouter Hoffman of Blaauwklip), and two uncles and nephews (Johannes Albertus Myburgh of Meerlust and his nephew, Albertus Johannes Myburgh of Spier, and Jacob Hugo of Buffelskraal and Daniel Hugo of Boesmansvlei). There is one pair of brothers (Hendrik van der Merwe of Klaasvoogdsrivier and Willem Hendrik van der Merwe of Doornrivier), and one pair of distant cousins, sharing the same name (Isaac Stephanus de Villiers of Dwars-in-die-Weg and his second cousin once removed, Pieter de Villiers of Landskroon). But, nevertheless, there are still thirty-three different family names associated with forty-one houses (Hall 1994a).

Another way of looking at this sociological landscape is through building histories, traced through title deeds. Often, these histories show frequent changes in title-holders' family names. In addition, transfers often specify a purchase price, even when the change of ownership is part of the settlement of a deceased estate. This suggests, again at first glance, the operation of a free market, with few associations between particular families, and with few estates staying in the ownership of individual families through time. But the closer examination of individual estate biographies shows that the situation was far more complex. For, although the history of each property, and the biographies of the people who were born, lived and died there, was unique, there were discernible trends and, in particular, a few distinct patterns of descent.

Only one estate in the group of forty-one, Plaisir de Merle, had a history of ownership that approximated to primogeniture. A few other farms – Olyvenhout, Vergenoegd, Morgenster and Hazendal – had histories with strong male lines. However, in each case women played crucial roles in the farm's history: a daughter providing the link between grandfather and grandson, a granddaughter re-establishing the male line, a connection through cousins, marriage between cousins with a great-grandfather in common. In other cases there is a recurrent pattern, in which a male title-holder transferred ownership of the estate to the husband of either his daughter or of his niece. Such 'male histories' were, however, in the minority; more often, male title-holders played only a nominal role in histories which had women as their central players. For example, Joostenburg, one of the earliest still-surviving farms to be given a gable, had been purchased by Anna van der Byl in 1734 while she was married to Burchard Heinrich Brand; the property was never in her husband's name. Anna did not remarry after her husband died in 1738 and continued to farm her land for a further 14 years; the 1741 census recorded 'Widow Brand', 4 children, 13 slaves, 30 horses, 30 cattle, 500 sheep, 10,000 vines, wheat and barley. On her death, Joostenburg was purchased from her estate by her brother, Gerrit van der Byl. Gerrit van der Byl himself died 15 years later, in 1767, and the farm was inherited by his widow, Elizabeth Grové. She in turn transferred it to Dirk de Vos, the son of a further sibling of Anna van der Byl and Gerrit van der Byl, Maria Sophia van der Byl (who had been married to Wouter de Vos). Gerrit van der Byl and Elizabeth Grové's twelve children were bypassed in this transfer history, in which Anna van der Byl continued to play a role long after her death (Hall 1994a).

Read in this way, many of the estate biographies map out a 'shadow lineage' of women, standing behind the formality of male legal ownership. For example, Kromme Rivier was purchased by Pieter Venter in 1732, and he clearly made this his family estate; the Opgaaf Roll of 1741 records 6 sons, 2 daughters, 12 slaves, 20 horses, 30 cattle, 200 sheep, wheat and 16,000 vines. By 1761 he had died, but his widow, Hester Nel, was still living on the farm. Although she was to live until 1785, in 1763 she transferred ownership of the estate to Jacob Groenewald, her niece Martha Susanna Conterman's husband. This transfer bypassed three of Pieter Venter and Hester Nel's married sons, and their six sons and eight daughters born by 1763. By 1773,

Martha Susanna Conterman and Jacob Groenewald were, in their turn, established at Kromme Rivier, with the Opgaaf Roll recording 2 children, 9 slaves, 20 horses, 30 cattle, 200 sheep and 40,000 vines.

Estate biographies such as this show that women gained access to property through their widowhood, and that they could exercise discretion in choosing how to apply their power over property ownership. The history of a further farm amplifies this dimension of gender relations. Zwaanswyk was farmed in the early decades of the eighteenth century by Frederik Russouw, married to Christina Diemer. By 1735, Christina Diemer had been widowed, but was head of a substantial establishment of 10 children, 3 overseers, 66 slaves, 37 horses, 260 cattle, 1,200 sheep, wheatfields and 30,000 vines. Her first child had been born 19 years earlier and her youngest son, Nicolaas, had been baptized in 1732. Successive entries in the Opgaaf Roll show that Christina Diemer continued to farm Zwaanswyk; there is no evidence that she remarried. In 1741 the establishment was much the same size, but there was only one overseer. Ten years later, only three daughters remained at home and there were no overseers; there were still, however, 68 slaves, a herd of 360 cattle, 1,250 sheep and 30,000 vines. The absence of a man is underlined by the note in the census return that there were no weapons on the farm. Ten years later again (in 1762) the Opgaaf Roll recorded 57 slaves, cattle, sheep and vineyards that had been increased to 40,000 vines. By this time, none of Christina Diemer's ten children was living with her. In 1765, after Christina Diemer had farmed at Zwaanswyk for 30 years, the property was transferred to her youngest child, Nicolaas Russouw, probably in anticipation of his marriage the following year (Hall 1994a).

Patriarchal control of the Cape countryside was, then, more complex than it at first seems. There may often have been a 'sale' of a house – a transaction between men – in the sense that a son-in-law would 'purchase' a farm from, for instance, his wife's widowed mother, or goods would be auctioned to allow the patrimony to be divided and distributed. But the constraints of tradition and consanguinity were such that there was rarely a movement of economic capital in any free market. The juristic basis for this system was the Roman-Dutch principles of inheritance and, although it was possible to modify such inheritance through a will, this was rarely done. The effect of the application of this legal practice, coupled with the tradition of cousin marriage, was constantly to fragment estates between widows and children, and between the children of successive marriages, and then to reconsolidate capital in new conjugal estates (Hall 1994a).

Such a system had clear benefits for male 'insiders'. Cousin marriage (in various forms) kept the accumulating capital of the Cape gentry circulating among a tight group of families. Some men, not born into this elite, were able to gain access through marriage, although this happened comparatively rarely for, although about a third of the male title-holders associated with gabled buildings were married to women from the eight families (rather than being lineal descendants themselves), only two had got to the Cape as Dutch East India Company soldiers and then bettered themselves.

Such male benefits, though, could only be obtained through giving women considerable power. The network of women that established the connections between members of the Cape's slave-owning elite had particular qualities. It is notable that, despite the prevalence of miscegenation in establishing new freeburgher households at the end of the seventeenth century and in the early eighteenth century, the women who made the connections between the gabled houses were mostly of European descent. Those 'women of the house' in 1780 – when the Cape's manor-house architecture was at its apogee – whose descent can be traced had, for the most part, lineages with 'founding mothers' born in Europe (five in France, four in the Netherlands and one in Germany). Only two were emancipated slaves or the daughters of slaves (Hall 1994a). This is consistent with contemporary opinion about the importance of racial purity for upper-class women. Stavorinus (1969) commented on the scarcity at the Cape of women born in Europe, easily distinguishing them from the *mestizo* population. Anne Barnard, who arrived at the Cape in the entourage of its first British administration of 1795, was ever quick to spot social niceties. She described the predicament of Elisabeth van den Berg, 17 years old and in the news for defying her father and insisting on marrying Captain Hamilton Ross of the Scottish Brigade. But it was genetics, rather than filial disobedience, that resulted in Elisabeth's ostracism: 'the dutch ladys will not visit her I dare say, she has a dash of the Blew, her mothers mother having been a slave . . .' (Robinson 1973: 174).

The power that women could have within the ranks of the Cape farming elite is epitomized in the life of Sibella Pasman. Baptized in 1693, she was first married, in 1714, to Jan Albert Loubser. In the same year her mother, Sophia Schalk van der Merwe, bought the farm Nooitgedacht, transferring the property into her son-in-law's name 4 years later. In 1722, after her first husband had died, Sibella married Jacobus Cloete. This was a family with which she already had connections; her uncle Hendrik Schalk van der Merwe had married Catharina Cloete 5 years earlier, and her aunt Petronella Schalk van der Merwe had married Johannes Cloete, Jacobus Cloete's cousin.

Sibella was widowed for the second time in 1757. During this last quarter of her life, she clearly had great influence, exercised through patronage. Sibella had inherited Nooitgedacht (and thus her mother's investment) and she transferred the estate to her son Hendrik Cloete in 1761; by now Hendrik was in his late thirties, had been married for 8 years, and already had four children. In 1771, she drew up a new will, amending it 6 years later, when she was about 85 years old. She directed her town house into the female line of descent; it was to go to her daughter's (Sophia Cloete) husband, Petrus Michel Eksteen, provided he would pay the estate 10,000 guilders for the property. Sophia was to have all her mother's clothes, and Hendrik Cloete was given an assortment of furniture and utensils. Twelve named slaves were left to specified children and grandchildren and four more were passed to the children on condition that they never be sold.

Although she had transferred title of the farm to her son 15 years earlier, Sibella Pasman clearly still exercised considerable influence over Nooitgedacht's affairs. Her will makes it clear that she lived in the main house (she refers to her bedroom), and also particularly favours one of many grandchildren, Rudolf Johannes Loubser, who was to receive three beds, cushions, chests and the horsecart outside the smithy. Rudolf Johannes was also left Nooitgedacht's entire cattle herd. The interpersonal politics that lay behind these bequests remain unknown, but it is clear that Sibella Pasman had power, and that she used it. Lest she be forgotten, she directed that her daughter Sophia Cloete should have her gold chain, and that Rudolf Johannes Loubser should get 'one pair single gold shirt buttons to wear in memory of me'.

Sibella Pasman's son Hendrik Cloete built the gable at Nooitgedacht in 1774, almost 20 years before he started work transforming Groot Constantia, and presumably with his mother's consent. Eight more of Sibella Pasman's male relatives had held titles to houses when gables were built, or were to hold such titles. Three female relatives were married to men who were, or would be, title-holders to estates when gables were built. In sum, Sibella Pasman had direct family connections with more than a quarter of the dated eighteenth-century gabled buildings that survive today (Hall 1994a).

Manor-house architecture serves as a metaphor for estate biographies such as these. In front were façades of male ownership – holders of title deeds, the men who asserted ownership of the landscape. But behind such façades were complex patterns of connections that depended critically on women; the ties that bound estates together across the countryside; the 'shadow lineages' which seem to have organized changes in ownership through time.

One man well practised in the performance of power was Governor Willem Adriaan van der Stel. Called to account by his superiors in the Netherlands, he represented his house at Vergelegen as a modest country villa (albeit with impossible architectural proportions – Markell *et al.* 1995; Bogaert 1711). In the background, beyond the boundary of the orderly vineyards, he had drawn huge marauding lions, descending on the edifice of civilization from the mountains behind. In the foreground, on the margins of the tamed landscape, were a group of Khoikhoi, standing in contemplation of the Governor's achievements (Figure 5.5). Van der Stel's defence was not successful, and Adam Tas's time in the Castle's dungeons was rewarded by his return to his farm. But the juxtaposition of colonial villa, wild landscape and the Khoikhoi well represents the complex ways in which such different elements were intertwined in the statements that made up the discourse of colonialism, and how these relationships were played out.

Figure 5.5 Willem Adriaan van der Stel commissioned this engraving of Vergelegen in support of his claim to have built a modest country estate and a bastion of civilization in the face of wild nature (published by N. Bogaert in *Historiche Reizen Doort d'Oosterssche Deelen van Asia*, Amsterdam, 1711).

The mountains behind Vergelegen – the backcloth for anyone looking north from the shore of Table Bay – had been traversed, described and mapped in a series of expeditions that began shortly after initial Dutch settlement. Pieter van Meerhoff, who arrived at the Cape in 1659 after the gruelling voyage from the Netherlands as a common Company servant, was a particularly energetic participant in such expeditions. Over the next 5 years he was a member of six parties that left Table Bay in search of the fabled wealth of Vigiti Magna, the Monomotapa and the other mythologies squeezed inside the newly surveyed African coastlines. These adventures gained him notice, 'a reputation as a man who was both persevering and brave' (Malherbe 1990: 45). Van Meerhoff's third expedition, which left the fort at the end of January 1661, was the first in which his voice is directly heard, for he was responsible for keeping the expedition journal, later transcribed into the official Company log (Thom 1958: 343–56).

The 1661 expedition comprised thirteen Company soldiers (van Meerhoff was second-in-command), two Khoikhoi interpreters and five pack oxen. Following convention, van Meerhoff kept the record in terms of general directions between prominent topographical features. Some of these were known from previous journeys – the Tiger Mountains, the Berg and Oliphants Rivers – and others were not sufficiently significant to be named: 'a beautiful river', 'a small, well-watered valley'. But others were new and deserved formal recognition: 'Riebeeck's Kasteel', the 'Little Berg River' and, with a twitch of vanity, 'Kasteel Meerhoff', 'a most prominent feature visible from 17 or 18 miles away'. Remembered superstitions had their influence; the 'Blocxbergh' was probably named after Prussian mountains notorious as a place of devil worship (Mossop 1927).

Van Meerhoff's cartography was a contribution to the dominant transcript of colonial possession – a system of names that attempted to domesticate the wild continent. But his was not a sole, uncontested, account. The expedition's journal was a single interpretation, to be locked away in Cape Town's fort as part of the Dutch East India Company's burgeoning bureaucracy, and there were other recollections, incorporating different sets of names. For van Meerhoff's Khoikhoi interpreters, Heijbingha and Donckeman, the landscape would already have been named and known, allowing them to lead the thirteen Europeans on a sure route to the Oliphants River in the north. This landscape was not the carte blanche of Dutch fantasy, waiting for the inscription of 'holy Christendom's' story (in the words of the Castle's founding poet). The mountains and valleys on Cape Town's horizon were peopled with a history – Soaqua hunters, other groups of Khoikhoi and the Namaqua.

We do not have a record of the Heijbingha and Donckeman expedition in their own words. But something of their experience is embossed on van Meerhoff's record – the trace of a subaltern voice that directs events without being formally recognized in the dominant transcript. This comes over in the crisis of an encounter with a group of Namaqua men. It seems reasonable to surmise that for Heijbingha and Donckeman, van Meerhoff's 'perseverance' and 'bravery' was the foolhardiness of a man who did not know the Namaqua's warrior reputation. But for van Meerhoff, his interpreters' reticence was cowardice:

> towards the evening a fire was lit W.S.W. of us on a mountain. I, Pieter van Meerhoff, took our two Hottentots with me and made off in that direction. When we were halfway to the mountain, Donckeman began calling out, 'Meester Pieter – Namaqua!' I looked up and counted 23 of them standing on rocks and looking at us. I climbed a little higher, but my accompanying Hottentots were so frightened that they took off their shoes and were about to scuttle back, crying out 'Namaqua boeba kros Moscoqua! [roughly, 'look! Namaquas with karosses and shields']. I raised my telescope to see if this was true and saw that the Namaquas were armed with dry hides and had a skin hanging over the left arm, bows and arrows slung over their shoulders and an assegai in each hand. I spoke encouraging words to my Hottentots and told them not to be afraid, for the Namaquas would do us no harm, promising them some reward if they would go with me. I told them that if they would not do

this I would report them to my lord [Van Riebeeck] when I reached the Cape. At this they could hardly utter a word, such was their fear, so finally they did go with me.

(Thom 1958: 350)

Here, we see two landscapes and the dialectic between them. One was the pre-colonial topography of named mountains, rivers and plains with established grazing rights and rules of obeisance and sovereignty. The other was the newly colonial, with its renamed places, mapped-out boundaries and vengeful violence, symbolized by the four-bastioned fort squatting on the shore of Table Bay. J. M. Coetzee's novel *Dusklands* captures this complexity of meaning with the latitude afforded to fiction: an imagined expedition to the Namaqua a century after van Meerhoff's encounter. On the one hand is the stark deposition submitted by the traveller to the Governor: a sequence of named places and new designations, and a summary of possibilities for trade. Set against this is an internal narration; the traveller's own suppositions of savagery, brutalization of those around him and eventual 'blurring of bound-aries'; his 'exploration of the Hottentots, trying to find a place for them in my history'; his mass execution of the occupants of a Namaqua village:

Through their deaths I, who after they had expelled me had wandered the desert like a pallid symbol, again asserted my reality. No more than any other man do I enjoy killing; but I have taken it upon myself to be the one to pull the trigger, performing this sacrifice for myself and my coun-trymen, who exist, and committing upon the dark folk the murders we have all wished. All are guilty, without exception. I include the Hottentots. Who knows for what unimaginable crimes of the spirit they died, through me? God's judgement is just, irreprehensible, and incom-prehensible. His mercy pays no heed to merit. I am a tool in the hands of history.

(Coetzee 1982: 106)

The complexity and uncertainty of the dominant transcript of this landscape – and the influence of the subaltern voices ever present beneath its surface – can be revealed further through Kolbe's historical ethnography. Kolbe's work has been widely used as an objective account – one of the few records of Khoikhoi society before the ravages of the smallpox epidemic of 1713 and the subsequent assimilation of the Khoikhoi in the urban underclass, and in the indentured labour force of the colonial countryside. However, in a different reading, his *Present State of the Cape of Good Hope* seems more a rich source of ambivalence that demonstrates how colonial anxiety about the maintenance of control fuelled the 'third space'.

Kolbe's technique is rhetorical. He starts by setting up the Khoikhoi as equal to 'all the other Nations upon Earth'. Their 'Munificence and

Hospitality' are excessive, and they show 'a noble Simplicity and Largeness of Heart' in excess of all known people except Europeans. Furthermore, they have been maligned in claims that they 'cohabit promiscuously with their Women' and enjoy public orgies 'in the Presence of any one, without Fear or Shame'. To the contrary: a Khoikhoi wife

> lies not every Night, nor any whole Night, with her Husband. They have always separate Beds. No Kissing, no soft, leering languishing Looks do you see. Night and Day, for any Thing that appears, they are so cold and indifferent to one another, that you would think there was no such Thing as Love or conjugal Relation between 'em . . .

This admirable restraint and separation extends into the spheres of daily work. Apart from the joint task of looking after the cattle, 'they neither of 'em meddle in the Province of the other' (Kolbe 1968, I: 160–5).

Testing the credulity of the eighteenth-century reader further, Kolbe idealizes the Khoikhoi wife. She shares some of the vices common to women the world over; 'the same Emulation to excell in Dress and Equipage, which we see among the Women of Europe, is found among the Hottentot Women . . .' And, 'like Multitudes of the Sex in Europe', they are 'seiz'd with the Vanity of Painting their Faces' (Kolbe 1968, I: 191, 199). But nevertheless, the Khoikhoi woman is the perfect wife, 'doom'd to all the Toil of getting and dressing Provisions for him, her self, and Children, when they have any, and to all the Care and Drudgery within Doors . . .'. Rather than complaining, she smiles from beneath her daily burden, ever at her husband's service – 'he issues his Command, and she silently obeys' (Kolbe 1968, I: 160–2).

But while Kolbe is setting up this patriarchal and pastoral ideal, he is also undermining it with contradictory ethnographic snippets. As well as being as industrious and house-proud as any *huisvrouw* (housewife), the Khoikhoi are also presented as bone idle – 'without doubt, both in Body and Mind, the laziest People under the Sun' (Kolbe 1968, I: 46) They are paragons of bodily decorum, defecating with extreme modesty ('in the Case of Easing the Body, there is not a more shamefac'd People upon Earth . . .') and putting their conquerors to shame in the matter of flatulence:

> . . . they will not let a F- - - in the Presence either of Europeans or of One another. And when the Europeans take that Freedom among themselves, if a Hottentot be by, he is much displeas'd at it; and makes no Scruple to tell 'em, They ought to be asham'd.
>
> (Kolbe 1968, I: 162–3)

But the Khoikhoi also fulfill all the requirements of the *wilde*, eating the uneatable and living in filth and degradation. 'In the Matter of Diet' they are, quite simply, 'the filthiest People in the World' (Kolbe 1968, I: 47).

Thus, despite his ethnographic inclination, the Khoikhoi are for Kolbe as they are in other seventeenth- and eighteenth-century descriptions of the Cape – stereotypes of the wild man and wild woman. The creation of such stereotypes was central to the discourse of colonialism – an attempt to fix the essential differences between the colonizer and the colonized. But, at the same time, the search for stereotypes introduces a paradox. For the stereotype must be both a representation that is so self-evident that it can be taken for granted and need not be repeated, but also an image that is constantly restated in order to emphasize its effect. The result is a phenomenon that particularly characterizes what Coetzee (1988) has called 'white writing' – the constant repetition of a small set of unoriginal anecdotes and attributes of the Khoikhoi; the stories must be told over and over again, and are repeatedly both gratifying and terrifying.

Such a paradox, along with the ambivalence characteristic of the 'third space', further opens up weaknesses in patriarchy's edifice, for the subject in the tales of a colonial storyteller like Kolbe can mimic the storyteller himself. The nervous, constant repetition of descriptions which are self-evident and should not need repeating begins to transform the civilized standard itself into a parody. This becomes evident by bringing together contradictions scattered around in different parts of Kolbe's text. If, for example, Khoikhoi women are 'the filthiest people in the world' and are often 'seized with the vanity of painting their faces', what does it mean to assert that similar behaviour is to 'be found among the women of Europe?'

This ambiguity becomes acute when Kolbe comes to deal with ceremonies close to the heart of the male patriarchal world – public parades and connections between men. His solution is to make the parody overt, abandoning completely his rhetorical technique of setting the Khoikhoi up as superior or equal to 'all the other nations upon earth'. Here, for example, is his description of a funeral:

> When the Corpse is brought out, the Circles before the Door of the Hut rise and follow it to the Grave, but in no manner of Order, saving that the Men and Women generally march in separate Bodies. And all the Way both Men and Women make such a wretched Howling of Bo, Bo, Bo, wring their Hands in such a Manner, make such Grimaces, and put themselves into such ridiculous Postures, that the Europeans at the Cape ever repair to a Hottentot funeral when they have a Mind to have their Bellies full of Laughing. And indeed I could never see a Hottentot Funeral without laughing very heartily.
>
> (Kolbe 1968, I: 314)

A second example, in which relations between men are described, Kolbe diminishes male prowess by concocting an 'Order of the Piss' with the hope that he can give his reader 'a little Entertainment.' After returning to his kraal, the successful hunter is led to the centre of a circle of men, where an elder 'pisses upon him from Head to Foot; pronouncing over him certain Terms, which I could never get the Meaning of ... The more Piss, the more Honour ...' (Kolbe 1968, I: 249–50). And Kolbe himself is aware of both the mimicry and the inversion:

> Strange! The different Notions different Nations entertain of the same Thing! The Force, the Witchcraft of Custom! To be piss'd upon in Europe is a Token of the highest Contempt: to be piss'd on in the Hottentot Countries is a Token of the highest Honour. Pissing is the Glory of all the Hottentot Ceremonies.
>
> (Kolbe 1968, I: 316)

The contradiction expressed in Kolbe's text is true to the contradiction in the colonial society at large. At one and the same time, the colonizer wants the colonial subject to be both the same, and different. The consequence is the 'traumatic impact of the return of the oppressed' (Bhabha 1994: 72) – the origin of both fear and desire, and an inevitable weakness in patriarchy itself.

Rather, then, than a simple matter of a dominant ideology at work, imposing a patriarchal order on compliant subjects, the discourse of colonialism seems more like a Chinese box, with complex layers of relations defined in the intersections of race, gender and status. Male assertion of the dominant transcript – the house in the landscape – is undermined by the shadow lineage of women and their influence. This dialectic is in turn mapped on to the grid of race, since women's status is graded by their pedigrees. In turn, attempts to assert the patriarchal order through parody – mapping the dominant transcript against the inverse image of the colonial subject – result in self-subversion, accentuating the insecurity of colonial control.

Implicated at all levels of this complex puzzle is the objectification of complex interrelations in material culture, whether the house façades of the colonial countryside, or the coding of possessions and clothing – the 'mobile, conflictual fusion of power, fear and desire in the construction of subjectivity' about which Peter Stallybrass and Allon White have written:

> A recurrent pattern emerges: the 'top' attempts to reject and eliminate the 'bottom' for reasons of prestige and status, only to discover, not only that it is in some way frequently dependent upon the low-Other ... but also that the top includes the low symbolically, as a primary eroticized consti-tuent of its own fantasy life. The result is a psychological dependence upon precisely those Others which are being rigorously opposed and excluded at the social level.
>
> (Stallybrass and White 1986: 5)

Not only, then, do the texts and artefacts of one particular segment of society form part of a semiotically rich recreation of existence, but they also contain the consciousness of statements by those to whom they stand in opposition (Hall 1992a).

How does this complexity relate to individual experience – to the global order mapped on the body of the individual, in the spirit of the Guild of Surgeons' ritual dismemberment of Aris Kindt? One incident in the account of the Cape by Anders Sparrman, a consummate naturalist caught out by his nature, reveals the way in which patriarchal domination and its ambiguities was played out in the mundane violence of everyday life.

Sparrman, an Uppsala graduate who arrived at the Cape in 1772 to work as a tutor and botanist, was a new sort of ethnograher – students of Linnaeus, concerned with ordering and classifying the world, following a 'messianic strategy', 'turning up everywhere collecting plants and insects, measuring, annotating, preserving, making drawings, and trying desperately to get it all home intact' (Pratt 1992: 25). This was Science as a global system of knowledge, 'the cumulative, observational enterprise of documenting geography, flora and fauna.' All human presence was marginal, the narrator self-effacing and presented as innocent and vulnerable; a 'surveillance of possibilities', rather than an assertion of dominance (Pratt 1992: 61).

But, despite such rigorous preparation, the instincts of patriarchal dominance could prevail. Visiting a farm near Riviersonderend, Sparrman and his companions encountered two young Khoikhoi women. Sparrman was immediately the ethnographer, observing that they were 'well besmeared, and, in their fashion, very smartly dressed', and offering them 'a fine piece of roll-tobacco, of which they cut off a little, filled their pipes with it, and smoked in a very elegant style'. But the farmer suggested that brandy might promote some entertainment, and Sparrman obliged: 'we therefore brought a couple of glasses of it for each of them, and they stuck pretty close to it, applying to it with great assiduity while they were smoking their pipes'. Sparrman now became the moralist, noting that, although they became 'a little lively', they 'took their leave of us in a very discreet manner, and I was very much pleased to see so much modesty and decency in girls belonging to so uncivilized a nation' (Sparrman 1975: 208–9). There is something of William Byrd's ethnographic description of the 'family of mulattoes' in Sparrman's account up to this point. But, just as the detached ethnographer dissolves into the randy Shoebrush in Byrd's 'Secret History', so Sparrman's desires got the better of him. As the women left the farm, Sparrman interpreted their behaviour as flirtatious:

> when they got out of doors, these mad-caps had the boldness to defy us to run after them and catch them. We soon gave over the chase, but as often as we turned back they came after us, and defied us again. At length the elder of them while she was running, not only fell down, but even seemed

to wait for us in that position. So unexpected a circumstance gave us no
small concern, as it made us begin to suspect the girl's virtue.

Sparrman and his friends, though, were mistaken, for one of the women 'drew
a large knife, and threatened to plunge it into our hearts, if we dared to
approach any nearer' (Sparrman 1975: 208–9).

Particularly striking in this account – typical of innumerable encounters in
the unfolding path of colonial expansion – is that Sparrman could not see the
incident as a misreading of sexual signals; had he done so, he would hardly
have included the account in his natural history of the region. Indeed, he
went on to ascribe such behaviour to diet and lack of exercise that 'deaden
and benumb both the physical and moral sensations'. This is colonialism at
work at the level of individual action, enabled by a view of the world in
which the moral superiority of the colonizer is unassailable, but undermined
by an ambivalence that requires this superiority to be acted out in everyday
acts of possession and domination.

Krotoa's later life at the Cape was the inverse of Sparrman's confident assertions. Baptized as Eva and largely rejected by the Khoikhoi, she was married
to Pieter Van Meerhoff in 1664, in a ceremony in the fort over which
Zacharias Wagenaer presided (Malherbe 1990). The marriage, however,
was neither long-lived nor peaceful. Van Meerhoff was soon killed on a
beach in Madagascar, where he was leading an expedition to capture more
slaves for the Cape. Destitute, and reviled as a drunkard and prostitute by
the same town burghers who had witnessed her marriage a decade earlier,
Krotoa died in the winter of 1674. Nevertheless, she was a Christian and so,
with a touch of very material irony, she became the first person to be buried
in Wagenaer's new Castle. The Company's journalist at the Cape used the
opportunity of her death to offer a philosophy. Noting that she had been
'transformed from a female Hottentot almost into a Netherland woman', the
diarist observed that her subsequent debauchery proved that 'nature,
however closely and firmly muzzled by imprinted principles, nevertheless at
its own time triumphing over all precepts, again rushes back to its inborn
qualities' (quoted by Malherbe 1990: 51).

A more fitting epitaph is an extract from Karen Press' evocative narrative
poem.

> no word came for me from Oedasoa, ever
> and so I stayed among those people
> became a dutch wife, learned
> to speak in long dutch sentences,
> became a widow, standing like a wild buck
> in the yard of the foreigners
> they would not take me in, hottentot woman
> nor would they let me run away, they broke my legs

mine are the crippled footprints
worn into the rocks along the harbour wall
the beginning was an exploding sun
I ran dancing into the fire
the end unravelled like an old root,
dry with sorrow, lasting forever.

(Press 1990: 66)

This chapter has sought out the 'hidden voices' of colonial domination and has revealed some of them. We know something of the life of Krotoa through the words of the Dutch East India Company's journal. The attention to detail, the degree of incredulity about Krotoa's behaviour, and the homilies about Christian behaviour and character indicate the fascination of the diarist with this performance. Taken in the context of the anxiety of the Dutch East India Company garrison to secure reliable supplies of meat for provisioning the fleet, van Riebeeck's dependency on Krotoa as a go-between with the

Figure 5.6 A Man and Woman at the Cape of Good Hope, first published in London in 1677 (African Studies Library, University of Cape Town).

Khoikhoi gave her for a while an extraordinary degree of authority. Heijbingha and Donckeman's expedition into the interior was one of many similar colonial adventures through which the landscape of power was mapped out. Their presence indicates many different transcripts that underlay the dominant voice of the written journal account. The nameless Khoikhoi girls in Sparmann's account of his visit to a Cape farm lead the celebrated naturalist into an ellipse in his narration – a momentary slip that reveals the chasm that lay beneath his seemingly confident voice.

These muffled voices are Homi Bhabha's 'third space' at work. With this in mind we can go back to one of the best known and most frequently reproduced early colonial images of the Khoikhoi (Figure 5.6). It has long been recognized that this depiction, emphasizing nakedness and savagery, and their effects on a people who were content to feed off the intestines of their animals, is a racial stereotype. But is there not perhaps a deeper significance to this image – the same anxiety about the tenuous hold on civility that led Kolbe to seesaw between portraying the Khoikhoi as noble savages with the graces of simple living and barbarous semi-humans who deserved nothing but ridicule? When this depiction is read alongside Rabelais' carnival-like representation of contemporary European society, with its accounts of gargantuan excesses that involved a massive consumption of viscera, something of the anxieties that Dutch settlers felt on encountering the Khoikhoi can be appreciated. Just as the Indian subjects passing the Bible around beneath the tree at Delhi induced nervousness and the repetitive insistence on the superiority of European civilization in the words of the missionary, did not the depiction of the Khoikhoi represent the nervousness among colonizers of the potential for failure in the outrageous enterprise of conquering the world?

Chapter 6

Bodily uncertainties

The argument that has been developed in this book has moved from the global networks of the early modern world to more specific manifestations of the colonial order, and then on again to the most localized uses of material culture in individual dress and behaviour. At the global level, we have seen how the rich trade in commodities that conferred social status through their exotic nature was matched by the circulation of ideas – the rumours, myths and fantasies about the outer reaches of the known world that plied backwards and forwards through colonial settlements. At the regional level, houses and gardens enabled the stamp of colonial authority to be made visible and real. Individuals indicated their own claims and aspirations through uses of material culture that ranged from gold braid and buttons to smoking pipes and tableware. These complex and varied constructions of words and objects created rich strands of discourse that connect us with the past through the many remaining traces on the landscape, as well as archives of documents and material-culture assemblages.

An undoubting authority led the directors of the early chartered trading companies to plan with confidence networks of trade that spread outwards from Europe to the edge of the known world. This confidence, at first so sure and unchallenged, can now be seen as a mask that disguised a far less certain view of the world. Van Meerhoff confronted suddenly by a band of armed Namaqua warriors, William Byrd at the margins of Virginia's self-image of civility, Kolbe trying to make sense of Khoikhoi customs or Sparrman faced with a knife, wielded by a girl whom he had assumed to be compliant – all seem far less confident than the public image of colonialism portrayed. Rather than a neat cognitive system in which cultural expression and actions were predetermined by a mental template, or a regime of order in which false consciousness prevailed, this historical archaeology of colonialism reveals an inherently unstable system, constantly under challenge.

These trajectories from global to local and confidence to anxiety have brought us closer to the particularity of the body. In some respects, ambiguity of the body in this colonial world is matched by the rather strange quality of many archaeological and historical approaches to corporeality.

Conventional approaches to material-culture assemblages from archaeological sites serve to disarticulate them from the context in which they were created. Ceramic sherds, metal objects, food remains and other categories of artefacts are separated from one another, sent off to different specialists and are reported under different sub-headings in the site report. In a similar fashion, the archive dismembers the records of past lives. Probate records are filed separately from diaries and personal correspondence. Maps might well be found in a different place to wills. Specialist historians concentrate on the interpretation of one or the other category, and historical archaeologists focus on subsets of documents and material culture. The result is a curious displacement of the evidence that constitutes a central purpose of historical archaeology – the understanding and interpretation of individual agency within the world at all its scales.

In this chapter I try to reverse this centrifugal momentum by pulling some of the categories of evidence back together again. I start by looking at the way in which the presence of an individual can be revealed through the intersection of the verbal and material elements of discourse. Here, my approach is to build on the key idea of ambiguity that has been developed in previous chapters. My argument is that the discordance between an assemblage of material culture (in this case the excavated collection from a well) and a collection of documentary sources (in this example a probate record) can show revealing elements of individual agency. The projection of the 'heroic individual' portrayed in the selected evidence of the probate record is undermined by the material evidence of other presences, and particularly by the presence of slaves, probably the most persistent form of ambiguity. A second example uses the same approach to interpret an ethnographic account of early Cape Town. Here, inconsistencies that at first sight seem inconsequential can be seen to reveal the ways in which the daily behaviour of individuals was structured around the anxieties of colonial society.

Understanding anxieties of the body in this way allows us to look again at some of the details of early colonial architecture, and to find in them new evidence. Now, traditions of decoration such as the symbols of fecundity and plenty that have long been celebrated as the definitive element in Cape colonial architecture can be seen in a different light. Given that these buildings were a façade of male superiority (their notional masters owed everything to their wives and mothers) the ebullient gable decorations of the colonial countryside now seem to represent some very persistent concerns. This, in turn, takes us back to the Chesapeake and William Byrd's extraordinary contribution to historical analysis. By following him in his expedition to mark the boundary between Virginia and Carolina, and then going back with him to his James River mansion of Westover, we are able to read both the public transcript of patriarchal control and the private record of anxiety and uncertainty. In consequence, the colonial order emerges as a fragile edifice.

Sparrman's inability to connect two parts of his persona – the enlightenment objectivity of the Linnaean scholar and the instinctive *droit de seigneur* over the female native subject – is an example of the sort of fissure that makes the study of travel writing so rewarding in understanding colonialism. Van Meerhoff's journal of the expedition into the Cape's interior fails to reconcile the trope of naming and mapping with the latent violence in encounters with the Namaqua and in Dutch–Khoikhoi relations. Later, the Governor's mendacious wish that van Meerhoff and Krotoa's marriage will symbolize the civilization of the Khoikhoi under the benign rule of the Dutch East India Company unravels as the husband is killed while out slaving and the wife is vilified as a drunkard and a prostitute by the colonial settlement that claimed her as Eva, the first woman. Kolbe, seeking to tap the ready European market for exotic ethnographies, tries both to naturalize the patriarchal order of his own society by finding in it a universal human quality, and to take advantage of the market in horror stories about Khoikhoi society. Other textual sources are eloquent in their silences, similarly revealing hidden transcripts. Thus, while the Cape's wine and wheat farmers stood confidently in front of their baroque-adorned mansions, seeming to embody the patriarchal order, the deeds and transfer documents fail to advertise a far more complex pattern of connections that made women like Sibella Pasman and Christina Diemer powerful influences in the colony.

This same approach can be used in interpreting the material elements of the discourse of colonialism. Just as textual sources reveal, in themselves, ambiguities, contradictions and absences, so the ways in which the networks of social relations across the grids of race, gender and class were objectified reveal the active agency of hidden transcripts.

The result is a carnivalesque parody that undermines patriarchy at the same time as asserting it. And at the centre of all carnival are the ambiguities of the body – the corporeal focus of acts of domination and resistance and anxieties of representation and vulnerability. These bodily uncertainties are explored further in this chapter. They can be introduced through an example from the late eighteenth- and early nineteenth-century Cape that shows how the person emerges through even the most unpromising assemblage of material culture.

From 1791 until his death in 1829, one Philip Anhuyzer owned and ran a retail store in Ziekedwars Street, a slightly disreputable part of Cape Town. Like Melck, Bosch and many others, Anhuyzer had first come to the Cape in the service of the Company (first as a soldier, and then as a cook at the Hospital – Hoge 1946). His house stood long enough to be photographed in about 1880 (Figure 6.1) – a building with a symmetrical façade, an ornamental fanlight over the door, a cornice and a pediment with a swan in bas-relief (Hall *et al.* 1990b). Anhuyzer's neighbours were bakers. The house next door was owned and occupied by Everhard Cruywagen, who baked bread there

Figure 6.1 Philip Anhuyzer's house and store in Ziekedwars Street, photographed in about 1880 (Cape Archives E2622).

from 1802 until he died in 1815; after this his widow ran the shop until 1824, when William Cairncross took over the business.

Today, nothing is left of either premises. But, in common with many other contemporary houses, the Cruywagen and Cairncross's bakery had its own well, relieving the household from reliance on the town's few public pumps. This well was uncovered during renovation and reinforcement of the modern building on the site. It had been carefully built with sides and base of dressed stone and a total depth of almost 6 meters. There was a clear stratigraphy, with four distinct levels. The lowermost strata – layers 4 and 3 – accumulated at the same time that Philip Anhuyzer was living in the house next door. They contained rich assemblages of domestic utensils: fine display porcelain from Asia, refined earthenware from the Staffordshire potteries, glassware, some common earthenware, domestic utensils, barrel staves, knives and nails. There were also personal possessions: a decorative brass box hinge, brass thimbles, hairpins and buckles, part of a leather belt and remains of shoes, stem fragments and bowls of clay tobacco pipes (Hall *et al.* 1990b).

There are no surviving probate records for the bakery. However, Anhuyzer's property was inventoried on his death in 1829. These listed household possessions can also be read as an assemblage, allowing them to be compared with the material record of the well.

Comparison of the furnishings listed in Anhuyzer's probate inventory with furnishings from the next-door well show little coincidence. Chairs, tables and pictures were the most common items of furniture in Anhuyzer's house: layer 3 from the well contained a single chair leg and a picture frame. This lack of correlation is not surprising, as wardrobes, cupboards and writing desks would hardly have fitted into the well, and the Cruywagens and Cairncross would have got rid of unwanted furniture elsewhere. Tableware shows a closer correspondence. Glassware – decanters, wineglasses and tumblers – is similarly represented in the two assemblages, while the ubiquitous 'crockeryware' in the inventory undoubtedly encompasses the variety of porcelain and earthenware known in far greater detail from the archaeological assemblage. The main distinction is the absence of eating utensils from the well. This can be explained by the inventory. Anhuyzer's knives, forks and spoons were made of silver and kept – presumably for safety – in an upstairs room. Valued possessions such as these would be far less likely to end up in a well than would broken plates and glasses (Hall et al. 1990b).

Household utensils – those items in everyday use – show the greatest degree of correlation. About one-fifth of the items listed in Anhuyzer's inventory were also found in layer 3 of the well. In contrast, the two sources of information diverge when it comes to provisions. Either the probate appraisers listed only those provisions of obvious value – linen, lumber and cotton – or else food and other supplies had been removed from the household in the 4 days between Anhuyzer's death and the inspection of his house. As is common in most archaeological assemblages, layer 3 in the well contained the remains of food preparation and consumption, and in addition a variety of containers for everyday needs such as ink, salt, blacking, wine, coconut oil and medicine. Finally, the category of personal possessions shows a similar divergence. The probate inventory lists no clothing, but the well contained shoes, belts, buttons and badges. Anhuyzer's appraisers concentrated on personal possessions of value, such as guns, a silver watch and a sword. The well reflects a more prosaic image: a hairpin, buttons, a brooch and two thimbles (Hall et al. 1990b).

By setting Anhuyzer's inventory against the layer-3 assemblage (the more contemporary of the two archaeological units), the differing taphonomic 'filters' of the two sources become apparent. Thus large items of furniture will not be represented in a well assemblage, for obvious reasons. Appraisers particularly noted valuable items, such as silverware, while the more expensive a possession was, the less likely that it would be lost or discarded in the well. However, there is more than just a comprehensive list of household goods to be gained by reading these two texts together, for by focusing on the contradictions between the sources, the undercurrents that characterized life in early Cape Town begin to be revealed.

The list of personal possessions from layer 3 of the well reveals men (military badge, cane, shoes) but also women (hairpin, brooch, small bells, shoes, thimbles, cotton reels, a doll and a doll's tea service). The probate record, on the other hand, is an overwhelmingly masculine document. The image that emerges from the list of personal possessions is of Philip Anhuyzer himself: perhaps suffering from gout (the crutches), sword and pistol beside him while reading his bible and occasionally peering at his silver watch through his spectacles. The underclass – the slaves and servants who constituted the majority in Anhuyzer's household – are excluded from the image that is developed in the probate record. In both this and in the street directories, Anhuyzer, his house and his possessions are almost as one. But the assemblage from layer 3 of the well hints at other presences: the common soldiers who left behind buttons and a uniform badge, and the servants and slaves.

This archaeological evidence is coincident with other historical evidence. In 1840, following an outbreak of smallpox in Cape Town, the city was inspected by special wardmasters. Ward 10 (which included these two households) was found not to be as bad as some other areas. However, 'the habitations were generally too thickly occupied . . . in one case . . . we found a house of very modest size occupied by upwards of 50 inmates'. The average occupancy was more than fifteen per household. This life of the streets, backyards, kitchens and cellars – and the poverty which Shirley Judges (1977) has shown was so prevalent in Cape Town in the early nineteenth century – is precisely the life that was obscured in documents such as Philip Anhuyzer's probate record and the published directories (Figure 6.2).

Anhuyzer's wife was also excluded from the image of his household presented in the documentary sources. This is particularly interesting, because Anhuyzer had married a former slave, Cecilia van der Kaap. The presence of slavery was overwhelming in the eighteenth-century Cape. In the early years of the colony, slaves had been brought mostly from India and Indonesia, while in the late eighteenth century the African mainland and Madagascar became the most important sources. By the end of the eighteenth century, some 63,000 slaves had been imported. With the exception of the Company's Slave Lodge, most slaves were held in small numbers, and by the second half of the century, more than half of the householders in the town were slave owners (Shell 1994). This profile throws the denial of the character of Anhuyzer's household into sharp relief. The appraisal that was made on his death – probably by neighbours, following the standardized requirements of local officials – presents a back-street patriarch as other men thought that one of their own should be seen. The parallel source of material possessions picks out and emphasizes the omissions.

In addition to the material things of everyday life, the well in Ziekedwars Street contained food refuse. Meals in the baker's household were dominated by mutton, with some beef and occasional pork. But there were also fish bones – small quantites of Cape cob, stumpnose, silverfish and geelbek, and far larger amounts of snoek, a pike-like sea fish characteristic of Cape cuisine and, in the eighteenth and nineteenth centuries, particularly associated with slave and underclass culture (e.g. in January 1876 an article in the *Cape Argus*

Figure 6.2 Coffee Lane, Cape Town (behind Ziekedwars Street), photographed in the late nineteenth century (Cape Archives E7979).

reported that the staple food in Cape Town's poorer districts was 'snoek heads ... the only variation in the family diet being crawfish and rice', Bradlow 1977; Hall *et al.* 1990b).

As in so many cases, food is a rich and rewarding domain, and contemporary descriptions of meals, whether celebratory or ordinary, reveal still further cracks in the edifices of patriarchal order. Otto Mentzel's description of the wedding feast at the Cape is a case in point.

Not surprisingly, where descent and marriage provided the crucial ordering framework in colonial society, a marriage was an event of considerable importance. Appropriately, then, the catering was lavish: 'It is almost incredible what an infinite variety of foods find their way on to the table at a fashionable wedding. I have myself, seen at least 50 different dishes on the table, including the vegetable dishes. The table is so crowded that the smaller dishes have to rest on the rims of the larger ones. I have seen enormous porcelain salad dishes, a yard in diameter, the like of which is a rare sight in Europe'. Such wedding feasts, Mentzel noted, included 'boiled and fried fish' prepared in a number of different ways (Mentzel 1925: 104).

This, though, introduced a source of ambivalence, for fish was food routinely allocated to slaves. Consequently, Mentzel becomes inconsistent on the subject of fish. At one point, he recognizes only the existence of the small quantities of game fish caught by line in the Indian Ocean, on the opposite side of the peninsula from Cape Town: red roman, galjoen, silverfish and red steenbras (repeating much of the inventory from the Ziekedwars Street well).

> The commonest kind of fish caught here is the so-called Rooy-manns. They retain their blood red appearance even after they are boiled, and are about two feet long and proportionately heavy . . . Besides the above-named red fish and another kind known as galleon-fish there are few other fish available.
>
> (Mentzel 1921: 81–2)

But elsewhere, Mentzel emphasizes the shoal fish, netted on the Atlantic seaboard: the 'vast quantities of fish' that are caught from small boats with dragnets at night and which are used as food for slaves (Mentzel 1925: 88–9). Now, away from describing the wedding feast, Mentzel is again the detached ethnographer, allowing slaves' food back into his account.

A matching area of ambiguity is to be found in explicit references to slaves. Mentzel pities the arduous workload of slaves and their frequent bad treatment at the hands of their masters, yet elsewhere he provides, without comment, a detailed account of flogging, the rubbing of salt water into wounds, riveting in chains, breaking on the wheel, crucifixion and breaking on the rack (Mentzel 1925). In contrast again, the reader is presented with an apology for slavery:

> Generally speaking the servants themselves know what their daily task is, and it may be said that even the slaves are quite happy in their bondage. This may be clearly perceived in fine weather and on moonlit evenings. For although the slave has worked fairly hard and suffered from heat during the day, yet he is happy and sings, and plays on his raveking (ramkie) and even dances. But on winter evenings they sit round the fire with a pipe of tobacco and tell each other stories of their fatherland . . .
>
> (Mentzel 1944: 109)

But elsewhere again, Mentzel reveals his disgust at contact with slaves, their habit of chewing betel leaves (*Piper betle*) and shell lime, and the offensive smell of hair oiled with coconut oil, 'clammy and offensive to European nostrils' (Mentzel 1925: 131).

Why these contradictions? The ambiguities of slavery went to the heart of colonial settlement at the Cape, as in many other parts of the early colonial world, because of a shortage of women as marriage partners. The tables at wedding feasts such as those that Mentzel took part in were loaded with more than vast dishes laden with food. At issue was the continuation of colonial life within its complex milieu of race, status and gender. And behind this were the anxieties of the body.

Early garrisons such as that at Table Bay were usually overwhelmingly male. But subsequent expansion required viable domestic units. A first solution was to send women from Europe. In Valentyn's words, 'there were no women there of their race, for which reason it was thought good to send thither some girls from the Orphanage at Amsterdam and elsewhere ...' (Valentyn 1973: 161). But this scheme was unsuccessful – it seems that relatives too often prevented the girls' export (Mentzel 1921: 53) – and the only alternative was to turn to slaves. This, though, brought together a plethora of contradictory issues: doctrines of racial superiority and inferiority, the public transcript of moral behaviour, and the standing of European women within the colony. Mentzel, as usual, excelled himself in his confusion. In some parts of his account he follows Kolbe, who saw the 'Negro-Women at the Cape' as 'very lascivious Creatures' (Kolbe 1968: 340). But elsewhere, he applauds the sexual freedom of the colony, reporting that boys, during their 'impressionable years', often got entangled with 'a handsome slave-girl belonging to the household':

> These affairs are not regarded as very serious. The girl is sternly rebuked for her wantonness, and threatened with dire punishments if she dares to disclose who was responsible for her condition; nay, she is bribed to put the blame on some other man. True enough, these tactics are of no avail; her fellow slaves know what really happened, and the story leaks out. Nothing matters, however; it is nobody's business to take the matter further. It would be extremely difficult to prove it; besides, the offence is venial in the public estimation. It does not hurt the boy's prospects; his escapade is a source of amusement, and he is dubbed a young fellow who has shown the stuff he is made of.
>
> (Mentzel 1925: 109–10)

These same confusions marked official Company policy. On the one hand, the administration took a moral line. In 1681, visiting commissioner Ryklof van Goens had complained that white men and slave women danced naked together in the slave lodge. Four years later, Commissioner van Rheede commented on the number of children living in the slave barracks in the Heerengracht who had European fathers: fifty-eight at the time of his inspection. Heavy punishments were dictated for such dalliance. But, nevertheless, the slave lodge was run virtually as a licensed brothel:

> From 1655 through 1714 the Lodge housed the largest number of un-
> attached women in the male-dominated Cape. If a Cape Town bachelor
> (free or slave) or a visiting seaman were sexually lonely, the Lodge was
> the place to visit.
>
> (Shell 1994: 71)

And, despite his moral rectitude, van Rheede set up a system which effectively
turned the transformation of mixed-descent women from the slave barracks
into a commercial arrangement. At the age of 22, such women could obtain
manumission if they could speak passable Dutch, had embraced reformed
Christianity and could pay the Company a fee of 100 guilders – the reimburse-
ment of the cost of their upkeep. If the prospective husband could not afford
the price, the Company would accept an antenuptial contract, marking its
claim against the estate of the husband should he die (Heese 1984; Shell
1994). The rub, of course, was the fee. Few slave women aged 22 were likely
to have such money, encouraging them to accept sponsorship in return for
marriage.

Another option was for a European man first to establish a family with a
houvrouw (concubine), or kept woman, and then to legitimate his line through
marriage and baptism. Heese has shown how this form of concubinage
increased in popularity through the eighteenth century. Children from such
marriages were fully absorbed within freeburgher society, and the daughters
of such parents became 'European' marriage partners. Mixed marriages
became a feature of life at the Cape from the earliest years of the settlement.
The first to be recorded was in 1656, between Jan Woutersz van Middelburg
and Catharina Anthonis van Bengale. Van Middelburg was appointed super-
intendent of Robben Island, where the couple's first child was born, thus
anticipating the marriage between van Meerhoff and Krotoa by several
years. Between 1652 and 1795, just over 1,000 former slave and indigenous
women married freeburghers of European descent (this out about 65,000
imported slaves, and about the same number of slave births, over the same
period; Heese 1984; Shell 1994).

This was consistent with practice in other Dutch colonies. The Dutch East
India Company generally did little to promote female migration, and often
actively discouraged it. Extramarital relationships were proscribed (largely
unsuccessfully), but lawful unions between low-ranking employees and slave
women were usually encouraged on condition that the women were manumitted and baptized with new, Christian, names. The Company also
purchased women in Asian slave markets and transported them to Batavia
for sale as brides, occasionally recovering costs through monthly deductions
from soldiers' salaries (Taylor 1983). Stoler has shown how practices such as
concubinage and marriage to manumitted slaves (or the daughters of slaves)
permitted the cheap growth of a colony by reducing the costs of maintaining
Europeans and by combining domestic and sexual services (Stoler 1991).

Such miscegenation had the advantage of producing generations of Cape-born women whose servile and lascivious origins could be deracinated to effect a transformation to *huisvrouw*. But the contradictions that such practices set up fed into, and amplified, the wider contradictions and ambiguities of slavery as an institution. Sparrman, for instance, had very different perspectives on the household seen from afar – the ideal of domestic industry – and circumstances that could be experienced closer to hand. Looking down from Table Mountain in September 1772, the countryside seemed a paragon of tranquillity and order:

> Several neat compact farms scattered up and down, the houses belonging to which were white with black roofs, at the same time that the grounds were laid out in a regular and judicious manner with verdant orchards and vineyards, lay distinctly open to the eye in all their respective ground-plots, forming a most natural as well as beautiful picture.
>
> (Sparrman 1975: 71–2)

But back at sea level, and seeking the shelter in 'an elegant house, the property of a private gentleman' not far from the town, Sparrman's impressions were very different:

> After I had stood out the attacks of a number of dogs, there came out a heap of slaves, from sixteen to twenty. These fellows were so malicious as not to answer me, though certainly some of them understood me extremely well, and though, after having promised them some money, I asked them the way in tolerable good Dutch; on the contrary, they conferred with each other in broken Portuguese or Malay, in such a manner, as to make me suspect, that they had no better will towards me, than they have to others of a different nation to themselves, who are accustomed to sell them here, after having partly by robbery and open violence, and partly in the way of bargain or purchase, got them from their native country, and thus eventually brought them to the grievous evils they then sustained. Had the master of the house been at this time at home, of which however I much doubt, it would have made very little dif-ference to me, as even in that case I could not have spoken with him; for every body in this country is obliged to bolt the door of his chamber at night, and keep loaded firearms by him, for fear of the revengeful disposition of his slaves. This being the case, it was still easier for them to murder me, and afterwards conceal the deed by burying my body, or drag it into a thicket to be devoured by wild beasts; I therefore took again to the road, in search of a better fate.
>
> (Sparrman 1975: 73–4)

Many householders and estate owners would have shared Sparrman's fears.

Figure 6.3 Flat roofs were adopted in preference to thatch to reduce the risk of damage from fire (*Long Street*, painted by W. H. F. Langschmidt in about 1850: William Fehr Collection, Castle, CD115).

People who owned property and slaves lived in perpetual fear of attack – a paranoia considerably in excess of the recorded incidents of resistance and rebellion, as Robert Ross has shown. In the hot summer months of 1735 and 1736, for example, three town fires were popularly attributed to a band of slave runaways that had achieved an exaggerated notoriety over the previous decade. Fears were accentuated by the heroic status given runaways by other slaves, and the general knowledge that fugitives regularly came down from the mountain under cover of night to join their fellows in illicit gatherings. Consequently, anxiety had already reached fever pitch when a further fire broke out in the autumn, leading to what Ross has termed a 'general crisis of authority' (Ross 1983).

Such eddies of panic had a direct effect on Cape Town's architecture. Mentzel recalled the widespread fear of orgies of 'robbing, pilfering and murdering' that would attend the general confusion of a fire jumping from thatch to thatch across the town houses (Mentzel 1921: 134). In reaction, many rich officials and freeburghers began to build in the 'Italian style', with a flat roof built of klinker bricks set in lime plaster, and waterproofed with oil, resulting in turn in the distinctive rectangular façade (Figure 6.3). The first of these buildings was recorded in 1717 (Fransen and Cook 1980), but the design only became widespread after 1736, when Mentzel could remember it as still a 'new type of house' (Mentzel 1921: 135).

Contemporary accounts show how this paranoid dominant transcript was imposed on the body of the slave – more a sacrifice than a simple punishment. The appropriate response to arson – an attempt to 'break' the town – was the breaking of the bodies of the alleged perpetrators, and the slaves executed in 1736 were destroyed in ways considered apposite to the crime: 'five were impaled; four were broken on the wheel; that is to say each arm and each leg was twice beaten in two with an iron club, and then they were bound living on the wheel; four were hanged, and two women were slowly strangled while the hangman's assistant waved a burning bundle of reeds about their faces and before their eyes'. 'In warm weather', Otto Mentzel further observed, 'it is usual for slaves impaled and broken on the wheel to live between two or three days and nights, but on this occasion it was cold and they were all dead by midnight' (Mentzel 1919: 102).

The Cape's colonial economy and society depended completely on the labour of slaves, and the reproduction of colonial households relied substantially on the deracination of slave women. But slavery depended on an impossibility – the suppression of slaves' humanity, their 'social death' (Patterson 1982). And the conversion of lascivious natives into respectable housewives depended on moral and practical contortions that set up cascades of contradictions. For slaves, open rebellion was a high-risk form of resistance that would, at the Cape, have been comparatively easy to suppress. But the everyday acts of defiance – the hidden transcript – were daily reminders of the instability of slave society and the constant possibility of violence. For many women, marriage to a freeman meant escape from bondage; such opportunities could be taken by exploiting the contradictions in colonial society.

Mentzel, wishing to claim accuracy for his memoir and advertise the virtues of the Cape, needed to describe slavery and make a claim for its benefits. But its ambiguities led him, at the very same time, to want to wish it away, to deny its presence in paradise. Thus shoal fish, the staple food for slaves, could not be acknowledged at the wedding feast, a primary rite in the continuities of colonial society. Ever present in these complex transcripts is the objectification of social transactions in material culture – 'small things' that were not so much 'forgotten' (in the celebrated title of James Deetz's book) as constantly remembered, but not put into words without paroxysms of contradiction and ambiguity.

Women, then, whether wealthy estate owners commanding considerable resources and influence, or newly emancipated slaves baptized into the church and dressed in Dutch respectability, set up a complex nexus within the discourse of colonialism. Such ambivalence can be tracked in aspects of architecture, in gardens, and in concepts of the landscape beyond, again

Figure 6.4 The façade of Willem Berg's tavern in Dorp Street (early twentieth-century photograph of a now-lost drawing: Capt Archives E2365).

contradicting the easy view of patriarchal domination. For example, in about 1777, Willem Berg had an ornate gable put up over the front door of his canteen in Dorp Street, a few blocks from the Lutheran Church (Fransen 1987). Exuberantly curved mouldings enclosed figures of soldiers and of mermaids (Figure 6.4). The unknown artist who executed Berg's façade could have drawn on a wide stream of Biblical and pagan iconography in coming up with a design for which the tavern's owner was prepared to pay. But such iconography was, in itself, frequently ambiguous, and the image of the mermaid carried specific connotations of magical powers, misfortune and the danger of shipwreck. Folktales retold stories of men who married mermaids after stealing some possession of their brides, only to lose their wives once the theft had been discovered. For Willem Berg's inebriated clientele, the sign above his door must have evoked a complex cocktail of titillation and desire, wariness and misogyny.

On a more ornate scale was Anreith's pediment for Groot Constantia's wine cellar, commissioned in 1790 or 1791 (Figure 6.5). The scene symbolizes winemaking. Ganymede descends on Zeus's eagle and pours wine from a beaker. On either side of him is a leopard, the emblem of Bacchus, and a confusion of frolicking putti. Above, a lion mask presides, indicating strength and virtue (de Bosdari 1954). As with his pulpits, Anreith was clearly calling on the

Figure 6.5 Anreith's pediment for the Groot Constantia wine cellar, built in 1790–91.

lexicon of baroque imagery in his design. The lion mask and skin probably refer to Hercules as well as to generalized qualities; in the engraving of 'decorum' in Hertel's eighteenth-century edition of Ripa's *Iconologia*, the personification of this virtue wears a lion skin and mask over his shoulder (Maser 1971, engraving 123). But the mythological basis for the imagery carries deep-seated ambiguities. Ganymede was carried off by Zeus, disguised as an eagle, to serve as cupbearer to the gods, and Ganymede's father received the gift of the vine in compensation for his loss; there is a strong subtext of Zeus's homosexual passion for the boy. Bacchus, or Dionysus, was the god of both wine and ecstasy. He was associated with women's festival rites carried out in his honour. While under Dionysus's inspiration, women were believed to possess occult powers over nature, and Athenian men were punished by impotence for dishonouring the female cult.

An early nineteenth-century visitor was shocked:

> some beautifully executed, but most indecent, statues – a naked goddess riding upon an eagle in a manner calculated to give offence to one's chaster feelings, and pouring out nectar for the gods; the while she is surrounded by a crowd of bacchantes in like nudity and lascivious posture.
>
> (quoted by de Bosdari 1954: 98)

De Bosdari, writing with the superiority of aesthetic judgement, laughs at a lack of taste and naivety. But this visitor, although mistaken in the central figure's gender, was perhaps closer to some of the popular associations that such imagery carried; the way in which the architectural ornamentation of the Cape manor house, of associated buildings, and of other public spaces in the colony had an underside to their classical form – a constant reminder of the presence of the threatening power of women.

Similar ambiguity is suggested by sculptures adorning other buildings. In 1771 Bernadin de St.-Pierre (later to gain acclaim as a novelist) visited the Groot Constantia manor house, reporting that above the front door was 'a bad painting of a Lady Constantia, a strapping young woman, fairly ugly, leaning on a column' (quoted by de Bosdari 1954: 100). Like Plenty, Constancy was a standard eighteenth-century iconological image, symbolizing firmness and stability, and often shown as a young woman in classical robes, embracing a column (Maser 1971, engraving 139). At the end of the century the estate's new owner Hendrik Cloete – Sibella Pasman's son – commissioned a statue of the goddess of Plenty for the front façade. Also probably made by Anreith (Fransen 1987), the goddess holds an overflowing cornucopia high in one hand, repeating the standard contemporary iconography for abundance (Maser 1971, engraving 34).

Symmetrical, ornate manor houses were associated with the 'classical' elite women who enabled the connections between men, and held considerable power themselves. Such women also stood for fecundity – both in the importance of their own reproductive powers, giving birth to the children who would allow the extension of connections of conjugality and consanguinity, and also as metaphors for the fecundity of vineyards and wheat fields which would further build the capital value of elite estates. This is evident in the ornamentation of gables. Images are of fertility – wheat sheaves, grapes, vines, sometimes the entwined initials of husband and wife. But, as with the garden, a consistent theme that runs through such ornamentation is ambiguity and sexual danger – disaster (mermaid), homophobia (Ganymede), sexual excess (grapes and vines), poison and betrayal (Hercules).

Ambivalence extended outwards from the construction of the household to embrace the colonial landscape. Thus the garden was a place for plants to thrive and orchards to bear fruit, demonstrating the success of men's labours. But it was also dependent on female qualities of fecundity. Kolbe, in a passage that matches his uncertainties about the qualities of women, revelled in the female qualities of what he celebrated as one of 'the noblest and most beautiful Curiosities in all Afric':

> Nature has Little or Nothing to set her off there besides her own Charms and the Hand of the Gardener: And she is more charming than I have seen her in any other Part of the World. Thousands of various

Flowers strike your Eye at once, vying with each other for superiour Beauty.

(Kolbe 1968: 346–7)

For Valentyn as well, the Cape's Garden was evidently female:

I saw here also astonishingly large nurseries of melons, whole rooms full, and incomparably lovely large water-melons in abundance, so that all the gardens and fine plantations which I have seen in our own country and elsewhere are unworthy of comparison with this noble Garden, since all that is useful and rare which all the famous gardens of the world produce is here closely assembled, as if in the womb of this African Mother-Garden.

(Valentyn 1971: 105)

Apart from this promise of fecundity, Valentyn's prose is laden with the implication of sexual pleasure and desire. Thus his Garden gives 'exceptional relief' to 'the worn-out and scurvy-smitten seaman' who, however, can never be 'sated' because he 'continually experiences a new desire to be in it again' (Valentyn 1971: 107).

Here, Valentyn seems to be projecting his own body on to the desired 'body' of the garden in the same way that William Byrd associated the rape of 'dark angels' and 'fresh-colored wenches' with the subjugation and mapping out of the Virginia landscape. Not surprisingly, such a projection brought this Dutch Reformed Church predikant his share of anxieties – ambiguity about the consequences of indulgence. Valentyn comments particularly on the Cape's vineyards:

One of the noblest fruits here is the grape, which here is unusually lovely, sweet and varied ... it is a pleasure to stroll through the vineyards, both at the Table Bay (where there are various owned by the Servants of the Hon. Company and especially by the freemen) ...

(Valentyn 1971: 115)

But steeped as he must have been in the iconographies and parables of his time, Valentyn would have also made the then-standard association of grapes with sexual pleasure and excess. For example, Ripa's *Iconologia* made the connection clear (Figure 6.6). All three personifications of explicitly sexual vices are associated with grapes and the vine. Adultery is a richly dressed, fat young man, wine bottle at his feet and grapes hanging over his head. Lewdness is portrayed as a beautiful woman, scantily dressed, reclining on a rumpled bed and fondling a blindfolded Cupid with bunches of grapes at her feet. Debauchery is envisaged as a naked, goat-footed satyr crowned with a wreath of vine leaves and drinking from a wine bottle (Maser 1971, engravings

Figure 6.6 An image of lewdness from Ripa's *Iconologia*, 1758–60. Grapes evoked associations with excess and sexual pleasure.

46, 70 and 132). Valentyn must have been aware of these connections – he probably made extensive use of them in his sermons.

Given this context, the continuation of Valentyn's description of the Cape's vineyards implies a weight of anxiety equal to the pendulous, promising weight of the bunches of full, ripe fruit: '... so many thousand unusually lovely, large and fully ripe bunches hang on very low plants, that one does not know which to choose ...' And the consequences of indulgence, although generally acceptable, are closely associated with the grotesqueries of the body:

> ... they usually agree with people very well, as I found in my own case, daily eating several pounds or more (if I may admit it) in the mornings, afternoons and evenings without their ever disagreeing with me, although they also served me uncommonly well very gently to open my

bowels, as if obstructed and hardened by the stale provisions, and then cleanse them, especially if the skins are also eaten.

(Valentyn 1971: 115)

Valentyn's consciousness of this other dimension of the Cape's landscape extends deep into its history. Here, the predikant introduces an archaeological allusion, announcing that he 'will now dredge up from the ground the things which have occurred here . . .' (Valentyn 1973: 127). These include the story of 'Manuel de Sousa de Sepulveda's pityful end', probably as widely known in Europe as Ripa's *Iconologia*, and originally published in Lisbon as an account by sailors who survived the shipwreck on the Cape coast in 1552 (Axelson 1973). Valentyn recounts how the party ran out of food, was attacked by wild animals and betrayed by natives. 'Eleonora' (Dona Leonor) was ravished, weakened, and could not carry on, digging a grave for herself in the sand and lying in it for 3 days before dying. After completing the burial, her husband

went back alone to the forest, refusing to take anyone with him, and since then no word nor sign of him was perceived, from which it was decided that he was eaten by some wild beast, unless from sorrow he helped himself to his end in some other manner.

(Valentyn 1973: 145)

In the original account, Dona Leonor was robbed of her clothes, buried herself up to her waist in the sand and covered her upper body as best she could with her long hair (Axelson 1973).

Thus Valentyn 'dredges from the ground' the story of the destruction of an epitome of the 'civilized woman' at the hand of untamed nature, and the subsequent destruction of the civilized man as a consequence of his wife's actions. Elsewhere, Valentyn captures this dangerous quality of the landscape by telling of the curiously selective behaviour of lions: 'There are examples where they have dragged out Dutchmen from among a whole troop of Hottentots, and torn them to pieces before their eyes' (Valentyn 1973: 115). Mentzel makes a similar point with an inverse of Valentyn's lion story, which serves to put women in nature along with baboons:

In order to hunt them [baboons] one should dress up as a woman for they do not seem very frightened of women. But when they see men approaching, they immediately cry a-hu! and retreat to the mountains and rocks where they cannot easily be reached.

(Mentzel 1944: 220)

Such mountains are threatening and inaccessible. Mentzel tells his readers that, to the east, the colony is bounded by 'immense and well-nigh impassable mountains' while to the north lies the 'impregnable chain', the 'Mountains of the Moon', believed by 'credulous country folk' to be 'peopled by dragon-winged four-footed serpents' (Mentzel 1921: 71).

Valentyn, Mentzel and others at the Cape were aware of two different land-scapes of power. The one was assertive and dominating – the unquestioned authority of the male order. The other was subterranean and uncertain – a place that was threatened by the power of women and the latent violence of slavery and all potential of resistance to control. Turning now to Virginia, the same 'third space' is evident, but in the multiple texts of one man, whose complex presentations of his world, and its objectification in material culture, make the trace he has left in history invaluable in seeking to under-stand the discourse of colonialism.

William Byrd's *History of the Dividing Line betwixt Virginia and North Carolina Run in the Year of our Lord 1728* was a public transcript of the boundary commis-sion's work. In this account, the differences among members of the expedition-ary party are minor. Overall, the men stand together, looking outwards at a wilderness that must be tamed. The North Carolinans are presented as part of this wilderness, in the same way that the Namaquas were set alongside mountains and rivers in Pieter van Meerhoff's account of his journey into the interior of the Cape a generation earlier:

Both cattle and hogs ramble into the neighboring marshes and swamps, where they maintain themselves the whole winter long and are not fetched home till the spring. Thus these indolent wretches during one half of the year lose the advantage of the milk of their cattle, as well as their dung, and many of the poor creatures perish in the mire, into the bargain, by this ill management. Some who pique themselves more upon industry than their neighbors will now and then, in compliment to their cattle, cut down a tree whose limbs are loaded with the moss afore-mentioned. The trouble would be too great to climb the tree in order to gather this provender, but the shortest way (which in this country is always counted the best) is to fell it, just like the lazy Indians, who do the same by such trees as bear fruit and so make one harvest for all. By this bad husbandry milk is so scarce in the winter season that were a big-bellied woman to long for it she would tax her longing. And, in truth, I believe this is often the case, and at the same time a very good reason why so many people in this province are marked with a custard complex-ion. The only business here is raising of hogs, which is managed with the least trouble and affords the diet they are most fond of. The truth of it is, the inhabitants of North Carolina devour so much swine's flesh that it fills them full of gross humors.

(Wright 1966: 184–5)

Byrd's gentlemen-commissioners stand with their backs protected by the edifices of colonial settlement, assessing 'human substance' that can never be more than 'an imperfect state of oneself' (Todorov 1984: 42). In the *History of the Dividing Line*, the North Carolinans have almost ceased to be human; in order to take their place on the edge of Byrd's landscape, furthest from the focal point of his Westover mansion, they have been cast almost as semi-human forms. One suspects that, through eating so much swine's flesh, the North Carolinan's are about to turn into pigs. In this confident public transcript of the expedition, the landscape is carefully plotted and measured, captured on maps and within beacons; 'care was taken to erect a post in every road that our line ran through, with Virginia carved on the north side of it and Carolina on the south, that the bounds might everywhere appear' (Wright 1966: 211). Nature was no obstacle as the surveyors pushed on through mire and across mountain; even the Great Dismal Swamp did not prove an impassable hindrance. And just as swamps and rivers were tamed with the surveyor's staff, so the North Carolinans were tamed with the Chaplain's touch; 'we christened two of our landlord's children, which might have remained infidels all their lives had not we carried Christianity home to his own door' (Wright 1966: 211).

In contrast, *The Secret History of the Line* presents a different set of images – the underside of the confident public document. Here, the bad habits of the North Carolinans receive only cursory mention and the main tension – as Arner, Bain and others have noted – is between Steddy/Byrd and Firebrand/ Fitzwilliam, both of whom are Virginian gentlemen. Steddy and Firebrand battle out their differences throughout the pages of the *Secret History*, reaching a denouement in a brawl between Firebrand and Steddy's ally, Meanwell:

> Soon after, when I said that our governor expected that we should carry the line to the mountains, he [Firebrand] made answer that the Governor had expressed himself otherwise to him and told him that thirty or forty miles would be sufficient to go beyond the Roanoke River. Honest Meanwell, hearing this and, I suppose, not giving entire credit to it, immediately lugged out a pencil, saying in a comical tone that since he was for minutes, egad, he would take a minute of that. The other took fire at this and without any preface or ceremony seized a limb of our table, big enough to knock down an ox, and lifted it up at Meanwell while he was scratching out his minutes. I, happening to see him brandish this dangerous weapon, darted toward him in a moment to stop his hand, by which the blow was prevented; but while I hindered one mischief, I had like to have done another, for the swiftness of my motion overset the table and Shoebrush fell under it, to the great hazard of his gouty limbs. So soon as Meanwell came to know the favor that Firebrand intended him, he saluted him with the title he had a good right to, namely, a son of a w - - - e, telling him if they had been alone he

durst as well be damned as lift that club at him. To this the other replied that he might remember, if he please, that he had now lifted a club at him.

(Wright 1966: 106–7)

In the *History of the Dividing Line* the starting date for the expedition is set by the careful deliberations of responsible men of substance; 'all the persons being thus agreed upon, they settled the time of meeting to be at Currituck, March 5, 1728' (Wright 1966: 171). But in the *Secret History* this rationality is consciously inverted, and the starting date is determined by astrology; 'the fifth of March was thought a proper time, because then Mercury and the moon were to be in conjunction' (Wright 1966: 43). The *Secret History* is presented as a vortex, revolving madly around one stable point – Steddy (Byrd) himself. The *History of the Dividing Line*, in contrast, is presented as a dialectic, in which the expedition as a whole takes on the chaos of nature in mapping out a landscape.

Byrd was simultaneously aware of the potential for profit and advancement – the public stance of the confident patriarch and boundary commissioner – and conscious of the potential for corruption. North Carolina could clearly be tamed:

I question not but there are thirty thousand acres at least, lying all together, as fertile as the lands were said to be about Babylon . . . Besides grazing and tillage, which would abundantly compensate their labor, they might plant vineyards upon the hills, in which situation the richest wines are always produced. They might also propagate white mulberry trees, which thrive exceedingly in this climate, in order to the feeding of silkworms and making raw silk. They might too produce hemp, flax, and cotton in what quantity they pleased, not only for their own use but likewise for sale. Then they might raise very plentifully orchards both of peaches and apples, which contribute as much as any fruit to the luxury of life . . . In short, everything will grow plentifully here to supply either the wants or wantonness of man.

(Wright 1966: 290)

But 'wantonness' was a considered allusion – North Carolina's very fertility was a source of danger. In the *History of the Dividing Line*, North Carolina is the Cockaigne of medieval mythology, where the 'slothfulness of the people' stems from 'the great felicity of the climate, the easiness of raising provisions' (Wright 1966: 204). As a result the North Carolinans are 'just like the Indians', surrendering their manliness to their women: 'they make their wives rise out of their beds early in the morning, at the same time that they lie and snore till the sun has risen one-third of his course and dispersed all the unwholesome damps' (Wright 1966: 204). Indeed, the very landscape is an untamed woman, to be brought under man's control.

This combination of public transcript and private anxiety is evident in other aspects of the record of Byrd's life. His assertive confidence in the public transcript of the boundary commission was matched by his plans for Westover's reconstruction as a symmetrical mansion fronting the James River – verbal and material elements in the public transcript of domination reinforced one another. But at the same time, Byrd revealed an anxiety about his position that is manifested in the overdetermination of his building projects – the obsessively defined architectural form that was considered appropriate for a gentleman, and the coterminous expression of domination and anxiety in the interior of his privy:

> entering the privy from a dramatically high set of steps, one passes between two rows of seats. Those to the left flank a fireplace, and they are small and low, presumably for children. On the opposite wall a brick apse has been constructed inside the square walls, forming the backdrop for a semicircular seat that faces the fireplace. The seat is pierced by three holes – those at the sides are of medium size and that at the center is slightly larger.
>
> (Chappell 1984)

One could well attribute this wish to assert rank and hierarchy in the most private domain to a personal idiosyncrasy. On the other hand, the symmetry of the interior of the privy matches the symmetry of the manor house and its offices, taking the anxiety for repetition to the extreme.

This private, material, world of the privy is matched by the private, verbal, world of Byrd's diary, written in code and clearly meant for his eyes only – a further source for understanding the ambiguities that he felt about his position. Byrd's anxiety about his own sexuality and about sexual access to women are concerns that are ineluctably linked with his role as patriarch. For, rather than there being a distinction in his consciousness between his own body and his position in the world, he constantly merges the two, dissolving metaphor into a continuity that makes his own bodily health and the health of his flocks and herds, bondsmen and bondswomen seem one and the same.

This is well illustrated by the pattern of his life in January and June 1710; a winter when his wife was sick and an outbreak of 'distemper' was threatening the health of his slaves, and a summer when he became ill himself. Byrd spent much of his time in the cold first week of January in the company of other men or in reviewing the situation on his plantation: playing billiards, walking on his estate, visiting a neighbour, settling his accounts and going to church. In between he ministered to his wife, largely through diversion (playing cards and sex, even though she was 'very sick'), and to his slaves by administering emetics. Byrd's language is custodial and paternal, patrolling his territory and asserting with his body: 'I gave my wife a flourish', 'I took a walk about the plantation', 'I gave a vomit to six of my people', 'I beat Jenny severely', 'I went and took a long walk about the plantation and looked over my people', 'I gave a vomit to several more of my people', 'I gave a vomit to my negro children ...' (Wright and Tinling 1941: 125–7; extracted from diary entries made between 3 and 7 January 1710).

By the beginning of June Byrd's wife and slaves were recovered, but his two children were ill and he was suffering from intense stomach cramps. On 3 June Byrd's son died:

> God gives and God takes away; blessed be the name of God. Mrs Harrison and Mr Anderson and his wife and some other company came to see us in our affliction. My wife was much afflicted but I submitted to His judgment better, notwithstanding I was very sensible of my loss, but God's will be done. Mr Anderson and his wife with Mrs B-k-r dined here. I ate roast mutton. In the afternoon I was griped in my belly very much but it grew better towards the night. In the afternoon it rained and was fair again in the evening.
>
> (Wright and Tinling 1941: 186–7)

In the days that followed, the pivot of Byrd's world continued to be his own intestines, while the affairs of his family and plantation revolved around him. On the 4th he had 'no more than two stools', while Jimmy brought over a walnut coffin for his son. The funeral was held on 6 June in a rainstorm, and on 7 June Byrd's stomach cramps became worse. His health was indifferent for much of the month, and on 26th Byrd took a purge which 'worked very extremely'; 'I had eight stools and my fundament was swelled with a sharp humor and very sore. I drank some water gruel. They began to reap this day'. The next day, neighbours visited 'and condoled my sore backside', and Mrs Byrd administered tobacco oil, balsam of saltpeter and hot linseed oil. While this was going on, Byrd worried about a runaway slave, the dispatch of cargo from his jetty, the education of his nephew and niece. By the 30th matters had improved; the slave had been found, the transport of the tobacco had been organized and Byrd had his good health again; 'my bum was better, thank God, and I was well again'. He ended the month with assertion; 'in the evening I said a short prayer and had good health, good thoughts, and good humor, thank God. I gave my wife a flourish' (Wright and Tinling 1941: 198).

Taken together, Byrd's public and private images of patriarchy enunciate the ambivalence of his position, the third space where the edifice of patriarchy, so carefully and symmetrically constructed, simultaneously cracks and crumbles. These ambiguities were shared by others, both in Virginia and elsewhere. They are captured in an incident in Virginia's Loudon County, some years after Byrd's death. Magistrates such as Byrd and their successors marked their status in court in the same way that they claimed patriarchal authority in the façades of their mansions and in their disputes over sumptuary status. They were seated above the courtroom floor, their ranking signified by slight variations in the design and position of the courtroom furniture. The chief justice was further elevated, and was framed by a canopy or pediment. This architecture gave some semblance of dignity in courthouses that were notorious for drinking, peddling and general debauchery (Lounsbury 1989). But in 1768 the Loudon justices discovered that

> some evil minded person ... maliciously and wickedly intending to contemn the court and the Dignity thereof have in manifest violation of the laws and contrary to the peace and good rule of government, lately set up in the courthouse in the chair of the judge ... a dead and stinking hog with a most scandalous libel in his mouth greatly reflecting on the said court and the officers thereof.
>
> (Loudon County Order Book, 9 August 1768, quoted by Lounsbury 1989)

There is a consistency that runs through the inscription of meaning, whether in Virginia or at the Cape. The garden carries invocations of fecundity and danger. The vineyard recalls sexual pleasure and defecation. The self-burial of the naked Dona Leonor signifies the engulfing power of wild nature, while hunting down the 'dark angel' in the Virginia woods invokes its mastery. The fulcrum of ambiguity is the human body itself: as the person is the nexus through which authority is inscribed on the landscape, town or household, so the person is also a primary location for ambiguity and anxiety about the viability of this authority, and the substitution of a 'dead and stinking hog' the ultimate humiliation.

The shared characteristic of the examples that have been the focus of this chapter is inconsistency. The material-culture assemblage from the well in Barrack Street is inconsistent with the probate record from the house next door. William Byrd's private diaries are inconsistent with his public persona. Otto Mentzel, celebrated by some historians and archaeologists as the Cape's reliable commentator on early colonial society, is inconsistent on points of detail throughout his text. Kolbe, often taken as an objective observer of Khoikhoi life on the eve of the devastating smallpox epidemic that would decimate their communities, is inconsistent in his portrayal of key social customs. There were inconsistencies between the patriarchal façades of houses and the images of fecundity that became a dominant design motif. There are numerous other examples. It is clear that inconsistency is a persistent feature in the historical and archaeological records.

Inconsistencies such as these are often taken as evidence of an incomplete analysis. If there is a disparity between the documentary evidence and the material-culture assemblage from a site, the archaeologist is encouraged to dig wider and deeper until greater conformity is reached. That such conformity between different sources of evidence is never achieved is ascribed to the partial nature of the historical and archaeological record, or 'noise' – extraneous factors that frustrate close and complete analysis.

My point is that the opposite may often be the case. Rather than being evidence of incomplete research, I see inconsistencies and ambiguities as the key to interpreting the colonial order. In societies dominated by anxiety about control, and forced into the nervous repetitions of Homi Bhabha's 'third space', the transcripts of colonialism can be expected to be very noisy indeed. These discords are a key to interpretation in historical archaeology, and demonstrate eloquently the imperative of taking into account both written and material sources.

Chapter 7

Emergencies of the moment

To what extent is there continuity between the nexus of words, objects and the violence of possession and dispossession of earlier global systems, and today's world? In many respects, our voyages of discovery are, of course, very different from Frobisher's and Beste's. Digital communications – the telegraph, telephone, broadcast media and now the Internet – have transformed our sense of space. Accounts of Inuit encounters, transcribed by hand and stored for weeks in a sea chest during a hazardous Atlantic, are the antithesis of packets of coded information that reassemble, seemingly instantaneously, as full-colour images from the far side of the world. Computer-mediated communications seem more than just the separation of the message from the human messenger – they offer the *sharing* of environments and experiences without physical co-presence. The 'virtual co-presence' of the Internet dissolves the boundaries of time and space, allowing the possibility of community divorced from territory and limitless connections bounded, it seems, only by the choices of the individual (Foster 1997; Lyon 1997).

But, at the same time, there is a constant harking back to the past within the present – a persistent nostalgia for a past that may often be pure invention (Appadurai 1996; Jameson 1989). 'Internet culture' often refers to premodern cosmology (Hall 1999). In *Neuromancer*, the 1984 seminal cyberpunk novel in which the concept of 'cyberspace' was coined and imagined, William Gibson alludes to a courtly, medieval world. The artificial intelligence at the centre of the plot was programmed to be dedicated to the service of 'my lady', and one of his tasks had been to 'read the book of her days' (Gibson 1984: 289). This reflects a widespread preoccupation that has been reproduced in innumerable works of contemporary fiction: 'perhaps not since the Middle Ages has the fantasy of leaving the body behind been so widely dispersed through the population, and never has it been so strongly linked with existing technologies' (Hayles 1993: 173).

Medieval theories of corporeality, transcendence and the meanings of things – still very prevalent in the times of new-world adventurers such as Beste and Frobisher – prevented easy assumptions about the unheard-of diversity of new things landed as cargoes at Europe's ports. Early modern theories of memory, for example, distinguished between storage (memoria and mnesis) and recollection (reminiscentia and anamnesis). Abstract thought was not believed possible without some kind of signifying image, and memory success depended on rich, iconic memory images, encouraging the development of complex mnemonic techniques, often with results that today appear phenomenal (Carruthers 1990). After death, the disembodied soul was not believed to require sense experiences to make knowledge present in the mind; the soul in heaven has knowledge and memory without the need of physicality (Fisher 1997).

Such theories were complicated responses to a radically new material world, and are mimicked at the new frontiers of cyberspace. Many of these excursions into the imagination are part of the narcissistic preoccupations of the affluent society. Utopian digital futures, such as Howard Rheingold's (1991, 1993) vision of a virtual world, ignore the escalating divisions in wealth across the world and almost all the economic and social consequences of globalization. However, there is also a strong case for seeing global media and the imagination as formative dimensions in the large-scale construction of identity today, and a major political force; a process that Arjun Appadurai (1996) has termed 'culturalism'. Both the contemporary dispute about the rights to Jefferson's heritage, and the global reaction to church burnings in the American South, connect the Virginia world of patriarchy and slavery and grand houses with the configurations of race and identity more than two centuries later. Culturalism, past and present, implicates the material world.

Such continuities between past and present are evident in the ways in which earlier transcripts of domination and resistance are continually reclaimed and reinterpreted in the service of the present, only to be reappropriated again in the future – an entwined discourse in which there is a consciousness of the past. Men such as William Byrd, Governor Nicholson and Thomas Jefferson deliberately used their understanding of classical architecture to convey their impressions of themselves in the world through the medium of their house façades; Byrd's library was well stocked with architectural treatises and Jefferson is celebrated for his intellect. Governor Spotswood, along with many of his contemporaries, made specific allusions to the Italian Renaissance in his design for the Williamsburg Palace garden. At the Cape, freeburghers recalled a century-old baroque architectural style in developing a tight, public identity that differentiated them from common farmers and slaves below and the Dutch East India Company above. In its turn, the sixteenth-century European baroque that was their inspiration originated in an interpretation of an earlier tradition. Van Meerhoff named the Cape landscape in reference to a remembered landscape of northern Europe – the mythological Blocxbergh, associated with old stories of Devil worship. Street names throughout the Dutch colonial world suggest a nostalgia for Dutch towns. Very often, then, material culture signified complex strings of associations that recalled and reworked history.

This continual reworking extends into the present, affecting the way in which history is understood and material culture is interpreted. The ambiguities of slavery in Jefferson's eighteenth-century world are reconfigured in civil-rights issues of the late twentieth century, and in Hollywood's discovery of Sally Hemings. Monticello and Westover, along with scores of other historic properties, are the core of a heritage industry that offers a fantasy of the past that is grounded in the tangible reality of buildings, furniture and table settings that have survived the passage of time, and which guarantee authenticity.

Such dimensions of heritage have been explored by Raphael Samuel, who writes that

> memory is historically conditioned, changing colour and shape according to the emergencies of the moment; that so far from being handed down in the timeless form of 'tradition' it is progressively altered from generation to generation. It bears the impress of experience, in however a mediated way. It is stamped with the ruling passions of its time. Like history, memory is inherently revisionist and never more chameleon than when it appears to stay the same.
>
> (Samuel 1994: 10)

In this and the next chapter, I look at some of the ways in which the theatre of memory has been played in the recent past of the Cape and the Chesapeake, and continues to be played today.

'Emergencies of the moment' are strikingly evident in South Africa's public memories of its colonial past, and are well represented by an incident in early 1985 – the year in which an upsurge of civil unrest began that was to be the last stage of apartheid rule. A member of the segregated, 'Coloured' House of Representatives announced that he had evidence that leading members of the Conservative Party – recently formed to uphold the racial exclusiveness of white Afrikaners – had slave ancestors. The statement was based on a study by a historian, Hans Heese, who had traced the genealogies of contemporary Afrikaners back to their seventeenth- and eighteenth-century roots (Heese 1984). In a South African version of the dispute about the racial purity of Thomas Jefferson's descendants, leading white families contemplated suing Heese and the newspapers that reported his work for libel, despite the undeniable weight of archival information that supported Heese's conclusions. Here, memory had literally 'changed colour' in the 'emergency of the moment' – the threat to long-entrenched white domination.

Over the next few years the celebration of colonial origins increased in proportion to the growing violence in the country's huge black townships. 1987 was the third centenary of the town of Paarl, heart of the winelands in the valleys below the Hottentots Holland mountains, a short distance from Cape Town. The pages of the Cape's leading Afrikaans newspaper, *Die Burger*, describe costumed historical plays, an enactment of the arrival of Simon van der Stel from Stellenbosch, and the burial of a time capsule containing contemporary memorabilia, to be opened in the year 2087. In his address at the ceremony, President P. W. Botha expressed his conviction that religious liberty and the Afrikaans language would make the nation safe for the next 100 years. The following year, 1988, brought a cornucopia of heritage: 150 years since the Great Trek, when Afrikaners dissatisfied with British rule left the Cape and settled the vast reaches of the southern African interior, 150 years since these Voortrekkers defeated the Zulu army at Blood River, 300 years since Huguenot refugees arrived at the Cape from France, and 500 years since Bartolomeu Dias landed at Mossel Bay, on the Cape's southern coast, as part of the Portuguese search for the sea route to the Indies.

Looking back with the knowledge that the end of white rule was less than 2 years away, two aspects of these celebrations seem striking.

First, these were overwhelmingly white affairs – costumed balls for a small affluent and racially defined minority that were organized and reported largely as if South Africa's black majority did not exist, and had not played any part in history. The Huguenot anniversary, for instance, featured a costumed landing in Table Bay from a seventeenth-century style cutter, a wagon journey to Paarl and then on, all in period costume, to Huguenot farms in the area, where there were large and bucolic family reunions. The fact of slavery was lost in a spring amnesia of blossoming fruit trees and new vine leaves.

But simultaneously, and behind this mask of festivity, the celebrations reveal inconsistencies and contradictions as they wound on through the year: Samuel's 'impress of experience' – a consciousness of the constant, sullen presence of the underclass that recalls Otto Mentzel's description of the wedding banquet over 200 years earlier. Indeed, dissent within the ranks of the ruling elite characterized these celebrations from the first days of their organization (Roberton 1988). The official mark of the Great Trek's anniversary was a replica ox wagon that would leave Cape Town on 27 August and travel 3,000 km, taking part in some 300 events at towns along the way before arriving in Pretoria on 16 December – the anniversary of the Battle of Blood River. 'Never more chameleon than when it appears to stay the same', this version of memory would celebrate authenticity and continuity – eighteenth-century cuisine, traditional music and costume, and the backdrop of gabled, eighteenth-century manor houses. But in the eyes of dissident, conservative Afrikaners – stung 2 years earlier by the suggestion that they had black blood in their veins – the government had already sold out to communist agitators and miscegenation. They organized their own festival, comprising thirteen mechanized and symbolic wagons that would take 2 months to converge on Pretoria, when 200 bearded men would ride into the city on horseback where,

in the words of their leader Professor Carel Boshoff, they would 'lay the foundations for a new movement of nationalism' (Ryan 1988).

Similarly, the celebrations of Dias's rounding of the Cape became mired in
controversy. The official ceremonies were particularly elaborate, and had
started with the construction of a replica caravel in Portugal which was to
sail to Mossel Bay – discreetly assisted by an on-board motor – where it
would be beached as the centrepiece in a museum precinct of restored
eighteenth-century homesteads. Again, there was a particular emphasis on
period costume and enactment – on culture, international connections and
the bond between Portugal and South Africa. The events, it was frequently
stressed, were 'non-political'. However, April saw a rival 'Cape Festival
1998', organized by the Cape Town municipality, and specifically dissociated
from the National Dias celebrations. For these events, the replica caravel
stopped off in Buffels Bay, on the Cape's south-eastern shore, where Dias was
commemorated in a period-costume pageant and the erection of a replica
Portuguese *padrão* (cross).

The cause of this squabble between competing troupes of costumed cele-
brants was the massive, sultry threat of racial tension and violence. Despite
the celebration of unity, harmony and civilization, South Africa was ruled
under a seemingly permanent state of emergency (the provisions of Internal
Security legislation had to be eased to allow outside gatherings of trekkers
and conquistadores, otherwise banned). Consequently, a single bizarre
incident had the force to divide the Dias quincentenary. The beach at Mossel
Bay where Dias had landed was reserved for white bathers, and a coloured
Cape Town clergyman, the Reverend Pieter Klink, was told to leave when
he took a swim with his children (Stuijt 1988). In consequence, the principals
of Mossel Bay's twelve 'coloured' schools announced that they would boycott
the celebrations and Cape Town's municipality, anxious to maintain a
façade of liberal toleration, hastily organized an alternative re-enactment
that was presented as 'non-political'. The Mossel Bay celebration went
ahead all the same, with the Khoikhoi on the beach played by enthusiasts
with boot-polish blackened faces and President Botha again offering hope for
a harmonious future. Not mentioned was the fact that when Dias had landed
on this same beach in 1488 the Khoikhoi reception had been hostile and
several men had been killed in a skirmish – heritage, as Samuel has shown,
has indeed a chameleon quality.

The dream of another century of white rule was hopeless and, with the
wisdom than comes from knowing how the story ends, the constant dressing
up and parading of 1988 has a desperate, repetitive quality. 1990 saw the
lifting of repressive legislation and 1994 the election of the African National
Congress to power and a new recycling of the representation of the past. One
small example must stand for a complex array of new meanings and images.
Wagenaer's Castle, bastion of Dutch East India Company rule and British
colonial administration, and the headquarters of the South African Defence

Figure 7.1 A new role for the Cape's Castle: Lien Botha's exhibition, *Krotoa's Room*, 1995–96 (William Fehr Collection, Castle, Cape Town).

Force's Western Province Command, was appropriated as a site for works of art that challenged the heart of this symbol of repression and violence. Karen Press's narrative poem *Krotoa's Story* (Press 1990) inspired a photographic exhibition by Lien Botha. Archival images – pictures of gables, furniture, porcelain, silverware – were layered with images of oppression (slavery, Robben Island's prison, pornographic photographs) and seen through circular apertures, like a peep show (Figure 7.1). In the artist's words, 'these fragments of visual history are juxtaposed to construct visual texts that parallel the methodology of history with the aim to open up history to other perspectives and meanings – because the room of history is ultimately also the room of the heart' (Botha 1995). The installation was given particular force by the heavy, cold stone of the Castle's walls, and by its proximity to the site of Krotoa's burial a little over 300 years earlier.

A second example of public memory – of the way in which the Cape's present is tied up in its past – is the story of District Six. Unlike the abortive celebrations of 1987 and 1998, District Six illustrates a different aspect of Raphael's

Figure 7.2 District Six, Cape Town. Aspeling Street in the early twentieth century (South African Library, Cape Town).

'theatre of memory' – the ways in which the material traces of the past can keep alive a sense of identity in the face of oppression.

When slavery at the Cape was finally abolished in 1838, government compensation had been invested in property, and streets and row houses were built outwards from the Castle and the shoreline, reaching up towards Devil's Peak. The new suburb was named in 1867, when the municipality was divided for electoral purposes, and this area became District Six, a 'doorstep dormitory' for the inner-city industry by the early years of the twentieth century (Figure 7.2). District Six derived a distinctive character from its port-side location, and as the first destination of many immigrants to South Africa:

> a child growing up there might be a progeny of a West Indian seaman and a migrant Coloured woman from the rural southwestern Cape. Its parents might be a Coloured woman raised in Harfield Village, Claremont, and a paid off Scots Fusilier who had settled in Cape Town after the South African War. It might be borne by a female migrant from St Helena married to a Lithuanian cabinet-maker. Or its father might be a Tamil Indian migrant from Natal, with a family history of

indentured plantation labour, and its mother a Muslim woman from a Kalk Bay fishing family with an unmistakably Portuguese surname.

(Nasson 1990: 63–4)

Despite a wealth of documentary evidence for the construction of social history, little is known about the urban architecture of nineteenth-century District Six. General municipal surveys mapped out streets, lanes and the block plans of houses, but there were few individual plans or drawings. As with many other nineteenth-century working-class suburbs, District Six was developed rapidly, and as a set of variations on a few standard designs (Derek Japha and Karen Strom, personal communications). Archaeological work at several houses has, however, revealed the detail of house plans; front and back rooms with narrow corridors and back yards, and frequent modifications as tenants sought to make the best of crowded circumstances (Hall 1994b; Hart and Halkett 1996).

Although the district varied from street to street, it was long overcrowded, with poor services and a mostly poor population. Residents were employed in clothing, leather working, tobacco, furniture and processed-food production, and in a sizable service sector within the suburb: retailing, shop workers, building and transport trades, self-employed tailors, carpenters, dressmakers, seamstresses, shoemakers and cabinet makers (Bickford-Smith 1990; Nasson 1990). Its cosmopolitanism led to a sense of distinction, defined by a rough, communal character. Although there were marked inequalities – landlords exploiting slum dwellers, pawnbrokers profiting from low incomes, skilled artisans holding themselves aloof from labourers – there was also 'an environ-ment marked strongly by mutual needs and sharing between families and neighbours, whatever the divisions of income, occupation or religion' (Nasson 1990: 64). Overall, District Six was marked by poverty. In the words of Richard Rive, a writer born and brought up there, 'it was a ripe, raw and rotten slum. It was drab, dingy, squalid and overcrowded' (Rive 1990: 111).

The beginning of the end of this part of District Six's history came in February 1966. Proclamation 43 set District Six aside for white ownership and occupation. The government estimated the population at about 62,000 people, three-quarters of whom were tenants, and all but about 1,000 of whom were classified 'coloured' (Horrell 1967). The intention had been to clear the area completely within 5 years, but by 1978 there were still coloured families in District Six and compensation, resettlement and demoli-tion had cost the government six times its original estimates (Hart 1990). By this time, District Six had become a rallying point for opposition to the forced removals that were taking place throughout the country. There had been protest meetings at churches and mosques, while the 1976 Soweto uprising had raised the stakes in the politics of white-minority rule. It was politically important for the government to continue, despite a clear lack of viability. When plans to house 15,000 whites in town houses and high-rise flats failed because of negative publicity, the government turned to state-funded projects, planning housing for military and police employees and, from 1979 the Cape Technikon, reserved for white students only. Part of the cleared land was sold off to private developers and a small portion was redeclared 'coloured', apparently as a sop to reformist opinion (Hart 1990; Soudien 1990).

Despite these delays and political setbacks for the government, removals were complete by early 1984, almost two decades after the original proclamation. Mosques, churches and schools remained, as well as cobbled and paved streets, curbstones and the traces of wall footings where the bulldozers had been less efficient. But seen from the Table Bay shoreline, District Six was now a jagged scar, separating Cape Town from its suburbs; in Richard Rive's words, 'South Africa's Hiroshima' (*Cape Times*, 9 January 1986).

The completion of the District Six removal programme coincided with the growing popular uprising against the government, leading to the declaration of a state of emergency in 1985. This umbrella of increasingly successful resistance affected local politics in many parts on the country. In Cape Town, the Woodstock and Walmer Estate Residents' Association (WOSAWA) was one of many 'civics' that took up local issues within a framework of national-scale opposition. WOSAWA used several issues in District Six as rallying points, including the preservation of St Mark's Church in the face of Technikon expansion and attempts to demolish the Silvertree Crèche (Soudien 1990).

In 1986 an international oil company, BP (Southern Africa), announced an initiative to rebuild District Six as South Africa's first open residential area, continuing in the government tradition of imposing policies on communities without consultation. BP's proposal – joined by a number of other companies and the Cape Town City Council – further focused opposition and stimulated the formation of the Hands Off District Six Campaign (HODS), an alliance of more than twenty organizations and a significant number of former residents of the area, which campaigned for the abolition of the Group Areas Act prior to any redevelopment (Soudien 1990).

District Six's second historical phase, then, can be seen as the period from the beginning of forced removals in 1966 until the Land Court ruling of August 1997, which gave the area back to its former residents; a victory for the position taken by WOSAWA, HODS and the District Six Restitution Front, which had successively resisted government, private and municipal attempts to control redevelopment. In distinction to the period prior to forced removals, when the area had been a poor, crowded and cosmopolitan suburb of Cape Town, the geographical configuration of this second phase was a nested set of traces on the landscape. The footprints of houses – some left exposed by demolition, a few excavated (Figure 7.3), many more masked by debris and tall grass – were contained within a grid of streets and still-standing churches, mosques and schools. Seen from still further away,

Figure 7.3 The foundations of a house in Horsley Street, District Six, after excavation
(photograph: author).

District Six was a single place within the apartheid geography of the Cape; a
physical monument to those who had been dispersed to the resettlement
townships and beyond, and to those who had successfully resisted the redevelopment of 'salted earth' at the hands of others.

This narrative of District Six – the history of its origins, growth and
economy, its destruction and the rise and success of protest against the
apartheid state – is the framework within which the complex and intertwined
transcripts of domination and resistance can be teased apart and better understood. This unravelling can be started with three threads – three of many
possible stories – sharing a common focus, but each different.

1   In September 1981 an artist heaps bricks, torn linoleum, a discarded kettle, a
     child's shoe and other remnants of the demolition on the floor of a gallery in

downtown Cape Town, a few blocks from District Six. Six shrouded chairs – 'a sign of mourning, as a sign the owners have gone away' – and a recording of the recollections of former residents, the muezzin and the battering noise of the bulldozers complete the installation. Proceeds contribute to a fund for the creation of a museum to the community and its destruction (*Argus*, Cape Town, 18 September 1981). Sue Williamson, who titles her heaped collection of debris 'The Last Supper', is a member of the Women's Movement for Peace, protesting forced removals and asserting her place in a community wider than apartheid's imposed racial divisions: 'the focus is District Six but the larger theme is what happens when people with power use it against those with no power and the wreckage these actions leave behind' (*Argus*, Cape Town, 18 September 1981).

2   Fifteen years later, a group of archaeologists make a systematic collection of artefacts from what had once been Tennant Street, close to the heart of District Six. The site had been a mid-nineteenth-century urban midden, containing a rich collection of domestic debris from nearby tenement houses. The fieldwork is the centrepiece of an educational project in which school pupils, some of them the children and grandchildren of the dispossessed community, learn about archaeology and history, and the excitement of discovery and piecing together fragments of broken tableware (Clift 1996). Collections from similar archaeological sites form displays at the newly opened District Six Museum. Overall, the archaeological project seeks a detached stance – a considered, measured history. But the involvement of children in the construction of their own heritage, making them aware of what they had not experienced directly in their own lives, brings informality and excitement: 'It's terribly sad to think that all these people's most valuable things were demolished. Everyone is looking so busy. After a while we were tired and rested. Finally, the day of suffering as archaeologists has ended and we children of unit 4 – Madikaah, Mishtaah, Donna, Fatima, Fareda, Thabiet, Leila – would like to thank all the people who made this ex-cursion possible ... What a success!!! Thanx a million and we loved it!!!' (extract from field notebook, Tennant Street, 1996; Clift 1996, figure 5).

3   The following September, the District Six Museum organizes a sculpture festival, with works scattered through the rank grass and aging debris field (Soudien and Meyer 1997). Several thousand people come to listen to the bands, eat traditional South African fare of koeksusters and boerewors and wander among the installations fashioned from broken glass, bricks, plastic and building rubble. Many have once lived here. Among them is Igshaan Jacobs, forcibly removed from Constitution Street, and an avid collector of ceramic sherds: 'this porcelain is how I relate to my history. If I could just piece together one small cup from all the pieces I've gathered I would have something to hold onto' (*Sunday Times*, Johannesburg, 28 September 1997). For Igshaan Jacobs, the collection and reconstruction of broken crockery is much more than a stimulating outing; piecing together the broken sherds

serves as a metaphor for reconstructing his own history, and the impossibility of finding the perfect teacup expresses the limitations of history; the impossibility of restoring a culture that has been crushed and dispersed across the windy resettlement areas of the Cape Flats.

These small sequences in the much larger script of District Six are claims to cultural property. Everyone involved in small examples is asserting a connection to District Six's history through action: protesting, returning and mourning, documenting, discovering. Together, these shared actions constitute 'culture', contributing to a mass of books, photographs, oral testimony, art, documents, artefacts and memories which constitute the archive of a community – heritage, 'theatres of memory' (Samuel 1994).

But, in Raphael Samuel's words, '"heritage" is a nomadic term, which travels easily . . . a term capricious enough to accommodate widely discrepant meanings' (Samuel 1994: 205). Beneath the apparent homogeny of intent in the construction of District Six's archive are complex and often conflicting interests. In 1993, Sue Williamson returned to her earlier theme with 'The Last Supper Revisited'. Now, the fragments from District Six's destruction had been encased in resin and placed to cast pools of light on a white shrouded table. Agitprop of the 1980s has become high art of the 1990s; artefact-icons were sold in individual perspex cases as a numbered edition, and the installation moved from Cape Town to the Venice Biennale. For one reviewer, this was no more than 'a large dressing table upon which is arranged the findings of our very own conscience-crazed bag lady': 'Apartheid is often seen as convenient subject matter for a quick creative buck, and a hallowed space at a dinner party or faculty shindig. Anti-apartheid sentiment has become a sure-fire blue chip in the stock exchange of contemporary social concerns. The pain of repression and dispossession belongs firstly and only to those at the receiving end – it is their subject matter, their story' (*Argus*, Cape Town, 26 May 1993). But for another reviewer, 'Last Supper Revisited' was 'an excellent demonstration of art's more subtle powers': 'The fragments – voices, a nail, pieces of masonry, scraps of fabric, lino, newsprint and suchlike – represent what's left of a living community . . . their encapsulation serves to elevate them to the status of icons . . . in their encapsulated state they should last for all time, signifying survival, recalling their origins, evoking immortal acts and prompting the conviction: never again' (*Cape Times*, Cape Town, 12 May 1993).

Parallel issues have arisen on a larger scale – in a sense, the whole of District Six has been up for sale. The 1997 Land Court had to adjudicate between two competing claims for the area. On the one side was the Cape Town City Council, which had set up the Cape Town Community Land Trust to steer the redevelopment of the area 'in the public interest', refusing individual claims by former residents in preference for a council-controlled housing project. On the other side was the District Six Restitution Front, arguing for direct restitution or financial compensation for former residents (Sandra Prosalendis, personal communication; *Mail and Guardian*, Johannesburg, 8 August 1997). Seen in this context, Igshaan Jacobs' search for a complete teacup places him precisely in a complex political play with high stakes. Most of District Six's one-time residents were informal tenants and their claim in terms of the Land Commission ruling will be made through oral testimony rather than through the documents of title deeds and leases. Igshaan Jacobs' ceramic sherds could be much more than metaphors for a fractured memory.

In these ways the raw scar of District Six was encrusted with a variety of meanings. For its former residents, it was marked ground, the geography of dispossession and dispersal. For the apartheid government, it stood for white entitlement and the principle of separate development. For reformist business and municipal interests, the land was an opportunity for investment and economic development.

For many outsiders, District Six was a slum occupied by 'habitual convicts and ex-convicts', 'drunkards', 'dagga smokers' and 'habitual loafers'. There was, it was argued, an urgent need to 'shock the public into a realization of the conditions prevailing in these areas', to make the white voter aware that 'sub-economic housing still leaves the worst slums untouched' (du Plessis 1944: 83). For others, it was a place of nostalgia with a twist of charm, an image ably summarized by Bill Nasson:

> ... exclusively a merry community, with a rich, vigorous and rowdy popular life; a higgledy-piggledy riot of buildings and architectural styles, thronged with characters with an insatiable appetite for conviviality and an insatiable thirst for alcohol; a District Six of January Coon Carnivals, of cackling flower sellers like the durable and celebrated Maria Maggies, of blaring horns from hawkers' carts during the snoek season ... a colourful, legendary place, characterised by the perpetually open front door and cuddly youth from the Globe Gang, helping frail old women across Hanover Street with their weekend shopping from Spracklens or the Parade.
>
> (Nasson 1990: 48)

One of the most successful examples of this image has been *District Six – the Musical*, written by David Kramer and Taliep Petersen, and played between 1987 and 1990 before audiences of more than 350,000 in Cape Town, Johannesburg and Port Elizabeth, as well as at the Edinburgh Festival. Its spirit is captured in the lyrics of one of its most popular songs, 'The Heart of District Six':

From Hanover Street
Comes a lovely sound

> Can you hear the music that I hear
> A rhythm and a beat
> Of the people all around
> Melodies are ringing in my ears
> And it goes klop klop
> Beating out a rhythm
> Klop klop a rhythm that is living
> It's the heart that beats in District Six.

District Six – the Musical was followed in 1991 by *Fairyland*, which opened in January 1991, following the same formula, '... a light-hearted look at the people and places that characterised District Six' and capturing 'the authenticity of the era' (*Cape Times*, Cape Town, 8 January 1991). Neither *Fairyland* or *District Six – the Musical* have plots or lyrics cast in terms of racial superiority and prejudice. Indeed, the intention of their writers is the opposite. Kramer and Petersen aim to show the people of District Six as innocent victims of an evil policy:

> We want to tell a story tonight
> About a place called District Six
> Together we lived there
> Brown black and white
> But the government changed that
> in sixty six
> All the so-called 'coloureds'
> Who had lost their rights
> Were forced to move because this area
> District Six
> Was reserved for whites.

But nostalgia and its weighty legacy tended to take the work where its authors did not intend it to go. *District Six – the Musical* opened in the last years of apartheid government, when civil unrest was a way of life, but when there was still no intimation that, within a few years, the State would concede and seek a political transition to majority rule. In its celebratory review, the *Cape Times* was quick to hope that District Six and the struggle of its people could now be consigned to history. It was 'inevitable', the reviewer supposed, that the musical 'must involve politics', but nevertheless the work was 'the definitive monument' to this now-destroyed part of Cape Town. This was because, despite the references to struggle and dispossession, the lyrics and music captured an eternal romance – they were 'ultimately about the people, their loves, their *joie de vivre* and their culture'. And, the reviewer lectured, the former residents of the District must realize that they were 'just as much to blame for the tragedy as those who callously ordered its demise' because 'people should question and not merely go along with plans, schemes and decisions made for them by the authorities' (*Cape Times*, Cape Town, 13 April 1987).

Nostalgia – a yearning for a return to the past – is very much a matter of who is remembering what. White writing and art may celebrate either a rustic idyll, in which the native shunned the city, or the merry riot of carnival untouched by politics; but victims will remember their own histories, blunting the rough edges of daily life with a romantic patina. Not surprisingly, representations of District Six's street and community life by those who once lived there are qualitatively different from outsiders staring 'from the safety of distance'. As Raphael Samuel has warned, historians have become 'accustomed to thinking of commemoration as a cheat, something which ruling classes impose on the subaltern classes'. Rather, he suggests,

> heritage might be seen as a vehicle for the pursuit of the visionary, an idiom for the expression of otherwise forbidden, or forgotten, desire. It allows utopia to occupy the enchanted space which memory gives to childhood, promising a new age which will be simpler and purer than the present. It joins the practical and the visionary, the future and the past.
>
> (Samuel 1994: 17, 294)

An expression of romance and nostalgia which, inscribed by one seeking closure on the past is reactionary and racist, can be an effective act of remembrance in the service of an 'insider'. *District Six – the Musical* illustrates this well. While appealing to those who would consign the past to a chocolate box of romantic images, it also served to keep alive the memories of one-time residents. Many went to the performances, particularly when it was restaged at the Joseph Stone theatre in the Coloured Group Area of Athlone. Many oral histories capture this same spirit of nostalgic remembrance. For example, Linda Fortune writes in her memoir:

> People who grew up and lived in District Six knew everyone who belonged in the area. So did the gangsters, who grew up there and lived there. They recognised strangers immediately, and some of them would linger about, waiting to rob an unsuspecting victim. They never bothered any of us living in District Six.
>
> (Fortune 1996: 58)

Indeed, the gangsters are cast as agents of redistribution, robbing Jewish-owned shops in what was termed 'free entertainment' by residents. For example, Shrand's shoe shop on the corner of Tyne and Hanover Streets was frequently burgled, often in broad daylight:

> No bystander ever told the truth and no one ever saw or knew anything

when questioned by policemen. If the Law asked which direction the thieves had gone, someone would always point the opposite way. Later in the week you would see children and grown-ups wearing brand new shoes that were obviously stolen. They would even dare to walk right past Shrand's shoe shop and stop to do window shopping!

(Fortune 1996: 62)

Kramer and Petersen captured this often-told image of the 'community gangster' in their song 'Sexy Boys':

> We are the Sexy Boys
> En ons is unemployed
> Die mense we annoy
> We are the Sexy Boys.

Preserving the recollections of former residents such as Linda Fortune is central to the purpose of the District Six Museum, which originated in protests against redevelopment without community participation; opposition that crystallized in the Hands Off District Six movement of the late 1980s. Opened at the end of 1994, the Museum became immensely popular with people who had been dispossessed by apartheid removals and, through its Trustees, connected the early work of WOSAWA with the eventual success of the District Six Restitution Front in winning back the land. One example is the museum's 'seniors project': 'In stitching together the torn fabric of the District Six community, the Museum has had to reach across time and space. Our efforts at building a museum would be in vain if people who were relocated to the flats could not seek assistance in visiting this exhibit, particularly those who have difficulty with transportation because of age or infirmity. Through the use of a bus made available by the National Gallery, hundreds of Senior citizens have visited the exhibition. These moving visits begin to rebuild the sense of community that was lost when the neighbourhoods were destroyed' (newsletter, District Six Museum Foundation, January 1996).

Former residents are drawn to the Museum's photographic display of life in the area. Noor Ebrahim, who took hundreds of photographs of the District from 1968 until he was evicted from his Caledon Street home, has found that photographs stimulate recollections of people, places and events, starting conversations that bring the community back to life (Noor Ebrahim, personal communication, October 1997). This is nostalgia as a yearning for the past by those who feel loss, representations that create cultural property from fragments woven into a remembrance that blunts the edges of hardship in order to keep alive a sense of community. This is a nostalgia which is uncompromisingly opposed to the cameo histories of merry carnival, raucous flower sellers and amiable drunks, but which uses many of the same images.

Figure 7.4 Heritage Day in District Six: September 1997 (photograph: author).

But such use of common images leads to ambivalence, rooted in the use of the same signs and symbols as the purveyors of repressive histories. This was evident in the September 1997 Heritage Day holiday, when several thousand people reclaimed a large part of District Six's wasteland, fanning out through the grass and rubble to look at the work of more than fifty artists (Figure 7.4). Starting with a procession led by the Alabama Malay Choir, the entertainment included a 'free musical feast', games and food stalls. The participants were mostly black, varying from the working class, to the slick middle classes, well dressed and carrying cellular phones (the ubiquitous South African symbol of success), to conservative Muslims dressed to custom, to the homeless (the new community in District Six, living in low shacks in the clumps of bushes, and the new victims of removals as the District is re-developed). Some of the musicians were young, performing recent hits, but others were older, introduced with pride as 'sons of the District', and one-time victims of the racialization of entertainment. Such were the Boogie Men, a slick foursome of middle-aged men in cream linen suits, black shirts and gold chains. There was the general smell and taste of Cape Town's popular food: breyani, boerewors rolls, solomies and Coke.

The Malay Choir and carnival, however, is at the heart of both apartheid's ethnic caricature and the softer representations of 'coloured culture' that dismiss District Six from the stage of history. On Heritage Day, this ambiguity was captured during a momentary juxtaposition. A wiry, brown-skinned man with hollow cheeks marked the event by wearing a cardboard placard with the address of the house from which he was evicted, haranguing anyone who would listen with his contempt for those who destroyed his community. His vision of retribution was thoroughly modern: 'the devil has microwaves for the people who did this'. But the bus next to which he was standing, and which had brought people from Hanover Park, Athlone and the other apartheid townships to which District Six's residents were shipped, had airbrushed across its back an idealized, softly romantic panorama of the Waterfront and Table Mountain behind – a tourist's dream in which no trace of District Six was to be seen. At the same time the Cape Flats were experiencing open warfare between gangs and vigilante groups, beyond the control of the police. A few weeks later the leader of the Sexy Boys gang – a successor to the musical's Nines, 'menacing but totally lovable' – was shot in the head as his luxury car pulled up at an intersection, assassinated as part of a dispute between the Cape's powerful drug cartels (*Cape Times*, Cape Town, 13 April 1987, 1 November 1997).

There is, then, a surplus of meaning that lies in the appropriation and reappropriation of carnival, music, recollections and the other attributes of identity, and the ambiguity that is its consequence can work against those resisting the theft and destruction of their heritage. For example, the sustained opposition to forced removals from District Six has been paralleled by an accommodationist tradition that has celebrated 'coloured culture' – the happy, timeless world of carnival and song – and sought compromise with government attempts to entrench 'separate development' in the Coloured Representative Council, Tricameral Parliament and President's Council (Prah 1997). A different example: to celebrate the 'lovable gangsters' of District Six as the kingpins in a nostalgia for the past is to risk an ambivalence in the perception of violence, drug dealing and the role of the state in using organized crime to destabilize communities and assist in control and surveillance (Scharf and Vale 1996).

Ambiguity, however, can also be turned to advantage. And here – again – is Bhabha's 'third space' at work. This can be seen in a reading of two novels of District Six: Alex la Guma's *A Walk in the Night* (1962), and Richard Rive's *Buckingham Palace, District Six* (1986). Both illustrate, in a contemporary context, the rich interplay between material culture and words that has been a persistent theme of this book.

la Guma, writing before the declaration of District Six as a white area, shows the violent consequences of South Africa's racism through an unrelenting, streetwise fiction that uses close description to build up the mosaic of daily life:

> On the floors of the tenements the grime collected quickly. A mud-died sole of a shoe scuffed across the worn, splintery boards and left tiny embankments of dirt along the sides of the minute raised ridges of wood;

or water was spilled or somebody urinated and left wet patches onto which the dust from the ceilings or the seams of clothes drifted and collected to leave dark patches as the moisture dried. A crumb fell or a drop of fat, and was ground underfoot, spread out to become a trap for the drifting dust that floated in invisible particles; the curve of a warped plank or the projections of a badly-made joint; the rosettes and bas-reliefs of Victorian plaster-work; the mortar that became damp and spongy when the rains came and then contracting and cracking with heat; all formed little traps for the dust. And in the dampness deadly life formed in decay and bacteria and mould, and in the heat and airlessness the rot appeared, too, so that things which once were whole or new withered or putrefied and the smells of their decay and putrefaction pervaded the tenements of the poor.

(la Guma 1962: 34)

There is no romance in la Guma's writing – no yearning for a golden past or another world. The only relief lies outside life, in the 'chill, comforting water' of the sea – 'the dark undulating fronds of seaweed, writhing and swaying in the shallows, like beckoning hands' – or in the future, the unborn child, the 'knot of life' in the womb (la Guma 1962: 96). District Six's marginality – poverty, and the degradation of life in the ghetto – is thrust into the face of the reader as a fist of defiance. Michael Adonis, unemployed, is criminalized as a result of his inadvertent killing of an old, drunk Irishman, and Willieboy, falsely suspected of Adonis' crime, dies at the hand of the police.

By playing, without relief, into the expected stereotype of life in District Six, la Guma simultaneously undermines it. This is evident in a second example from the same story, in which the author takes the South African obsession with race and turns it back on itself. Both Adonis and the policeman who harasses him are described in the detailed language of racial classification:

He was a well-built young man of medium height, and he had dark curly hair, slightly brittle but not quite kinky, and a complexion the colour of worn leather ... His eyes were very dark brown, the whites not quite clear, and he had a slightly protuberant upper lip. His hands were muscular, with ridges of vein, the nails broad and thick like little shells, and rimmed with black from handling machine oil and grease. The backs of his hands, like his face, were brown, but the palms were pink with tiny ridges of yellow-white calluses. Now his dark brown eyes had hardened a little with sullenness ... Michael Adonis turned towards the pub and saw the two policemen coming towards him ... the one who spoke had hard, thin, chapped lips and a faint blond down above them. He had flat cheekbones, pink-white, and thick, red-gold eyebrows and pale lashes. His chin was long and cleft and there was a small pimple beginning to form on one side of it, making a reddish dot against the pale skin . . . The backs of his hands where they dropped over the leather of the belt were broad and white, and the outlines of the veins were pale and blue under the skin, the skin covered with a field of tiny, slanting ginger-coloured hair. His fingers were thick and the knuckles big and creased and pink, the nails shiny and healthy and carefully kept.

(la Guma 1962: 2, 10–11)

This thick flow of detail turns the language of racism against itself, taking advantage of the inherent instability of the racial stereotype: 'a form of knowledge and identification that vacillates between what is always "in place", already known, and something that must be anxiously repeated', something that needs no proof, but at the same time can never be adequately proved (Bhabha 1994: 66).

Richard Rive's *Buckingham Palace, District Six* was written over 20 years later, and at a time when the last houses in la Guma's District Six had been razed, and when widespread, popular resistance to the government was gaining momentum. The book is structured around an autobiographical framework of the author's own childhood in the District, and links a series of short sketches to portray the remorseless destruction of the community, skillfully turning nostalgia and caricature into a steady determination to achieve justice.

Rive's characters have all the charm and insouciance of District Six stereo-types. Here is Pretty-Boy Vermeulen, 'born in Johannesburg of an Afrikaner father and his brown servant', and a thief with a social conscience:

He could repair any broken gadget, open any locked door and pickpocket any unsuspecting victim. He always, however, maintained a rigid code of personal honour. He stole only from those he disliked or he reckoned could afford it, and gave generously to anyone he felt needed it.

(Rive 1986: 29)

Mary Brown, daughter of a rural minister and maternal madam of the local brothel, is the heart of District Six:

One place might be like another, but one community is never like another. A community is not just a place where you live. It's not just another locality like Hanover Park or Bonteheuwel. It is much more than that. It is alive. A community is our home. It is the place where many of us were born and spent most of our lives. It is a place where, before this wicked law was passed, most of us also hoped to die. It is place some of us come home to rest in after a heavy day's work, to be with friends and neighbours. It is a place of warmth, of friendship, of love and of quarrels. Here we enjoy a feeling of togetherness. Will you find that in Hanover Park? Can you build up a community overnight?

(Rive 1986: 159)

Rive's main character is Zoot September, an amiable layabout, and certainly one of the habitual dagga smokers, drunkards and loafers deplored in apartheid's officialese. Through the story, and along with the other characters, he remains relentlessly on the margin; despite his calling as a poet, he does not follow Rive's own elevation from the District and into the class of 'educated Coloured people', and is disreputable to the end, when the last house in the row is flattened by the bulldozers. But from within this persona, Zoot September articulates first the outrage of discrimination and forced removal, and then the vision of justice. For example, after being thrown off a whites-only beach at Kalk Bay, Zoot defines a sense of community that is opposite to the romantic cliché:

> You know, it's a funny thing, but it's only in the District that I feel safe. District Six is like an island, if you follow me, an island in a sea of apartheid. The whole of District Six is one big apartheid, so we can't see it. We only see it when the white man comes and forces it on us, when he makes us see it – when the police come, and the council people and so on – or when we leave the District, when we leave our island and go into Cape Town or to Sea Point or come here to Kalk Bay. Then we again see apartheid. I know the District is dirty and poor and a slum, as the newspapers always remind us, but it's our own and we have never put up notices which say 'Slegs blankes' or 'Whites only'. They put up the notices. When the white man comes into the District with his notices he is a stranger, and when we come out of the District he makes us realise that we are strangers. It's funny but that's the way I see it.
>
> (Rive 1986: 95–6)

Later, as Mary Brown's brothel is about to be flattened, he expresses the spirit of popular resistance:

> Zoot was silent for some time, then he said slowly, 'We cannot fight this thing alone. We must join up with others who are already fighting, with those who are losing their houses and are afraid of also losing their manhood. We must join up with all the other so-called untermenschen. Only that way can be win. We lost because we tried to fight this thing alone. It's not a Buckingham Palace thing. Not only our houses are being demolished, it is not District Six that is being thrown down, but the whole country. I know what I will do. I know with whom I will work.' ... 'We are not eight. We are eight thousand, more than eight million. We are all those who suffer in this sad land.'
>
> (Rive 1986: 187–8)

District Six, then, has persisted as much more than idea. Words, music and images are rooted in the scar across the slopes of Devil's Peak – a mark of shame and dispossession that serves as a monument – a mnemonic system that makes history tangible. Such 'non-verbal' signs are not merely reducible to words – they have additional qualities, and in particular an ambiguity. This is evident in the way in which responses to everyday objects, observed or retrieved, shift between nostalgia and anger. Thus, for example, the testimony of former residents, collected through the Western Cape Oral History Project, is often framed around the importance of household possessions: proudly kept interiors contrasting with dilapidated house exteriors, poorly maintained by landlords; washstands, fireplaces, ornamental clocks, carpets, lace, brass candlesticks, cutlery (Nasson 1990). Linda Fortune, recalling childhood in District Six, remembers: 'pieces of wood from a tomato box that the bigger boys had brought home from the market in Sir Lowry Road were piled up outside on the pavement under the sash window with the wooden shutters. An empty jam tin was put on top and wilted pieces of cabbage, carrot leaves and potato peels – fetched from the kitchen where Mom was busy cleaning the vegetables – were put inside. The jam tin was then filled with water from another tin which served as a jug. In a few short minutes the food, cooked over a fire that was never lit, would be dished up with a piece of plank and 'spooned' onto toy plastic plates. Each little girl would pretend to eat and enjoy her helping of food' (Fortune 1996: 21).

The District Six Museum's most popular exhibit is a display of street signs (Figure 7.5). Suspended as long banners from the high ceiling of the one-time church, these evoke rich memories of the District's complex physical and social geography. Former residents are immediately drawn to them – 'the street names open up their whole life, how it was' (former residents Linda Fortune, Noor Ebrahim, Vincent Kolbe and Irwin Combrink, 2 October 1997). This display also represents all the ambiguities and contradictions in the violence of apartheid in its own particular history. Long assumed destroyed with the rest of the District's architectural fabric, the street signs had in fact been secretly collected and stored by one of the white demolition workers employed by the state. Seeking relief from the burden of his history, the man presented himself and his collection to the Museum shortly after it was opened, as an act of personal reparation.

This sense of the material slips easily into anger and despair. In Richard Rive's novel, Mr Anthony Wilkins, the white manager of a firm of outfitters in Long Street, owns 'a flashy Dodge, all shiny cream with black trimmings', and takes Moena Mooies as his lover, threatening her ruin. Before beating up Wilkins, Amaai and his brothers first destroy the car:

> They crossed the field in silence and found the Dodge where Zoot had indicated it would be. Then they methodically started to smash the windows and the bodywork. A crowd gathered and cheered on the destruction. The Boys paid no attention to them.

> (Rive 1986: 46)

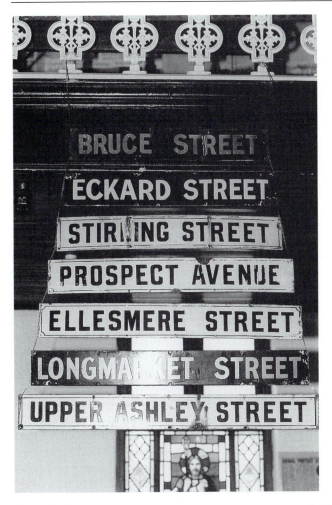

Figure 7.5 District Six street signs, displayed in the District Six Museum, Cape Town (photograph: District Six Museum).

Several years later, when the Abrahams family is finally forced to move from their house, Amaai destroys his home, which is now owned by the Department of Community Development and will be redeveloped for white occupation:

> Amaai rose and went back to the van. He searched in the boot and removed a huge, heavy spanner. Then he went to his old house and with terrible and quiet ferocity he started smashing the windows, doors and even the walls where they gave. The Boys watched without comment. Amaai worked methodically. There were wet patches on his shirt, and

sweat poured down his face. He breathed heavily but did not alter the pace of the destruction. At last he was finished. He walked back to the van and replaced the spanner in the boot. Without a word or glance at the Boys he climbed back into his seat and with a screech of tyres pulled away.

(Rive 1986: 173)

In Alex la Guma's story, the materiality of District Six is elided with the body in the description of the place where the central character lives:

Michael Adonis turned into the entrance of a tall narrow tenement where he lived. Once, long ago, it had had a certain kind of dignity, almost beauty, but now the decorative Victorian plaster around the wide doorway was chipped and broken and blackened with generations of grime. The floor of the entrance was flagged with white and black slabs in the pattern of a draught-board, but the tramp of untold feet and the accumulation of dust and grease and ash had blurred the squares so that now it had blurred the squares so that it had taken on the appearance of a kind of loathsome skin disease. A row of dustbins lined one side of the entrance and exhaled the smell of rotten fruit, stale food, stagnant water and general decay.

(la Guma 1962: 21)

'Marking the ground' in ways such as these has been important in the continuing construction of the memory of District Six. Visitors to the Museum are confronted with a large map of the District spread across the floor, and are encouraged to mark the places where they lived. Bolts of calico are draped over chairs, and former residents are asked to sign their names and recall their memories; many metres of cloth have been marked in this way since the Museum opened in late 1994. In turn, these acts of marking encourage people to talk about their lives. The Museum's staff feel that the past means much more to people when they can handle objects such as spoons and nails, collected from the area.

The same concept of marking has been extended into the landscape itself. Churches and mosques have continued in daily life, with those who are able often travelling long distances to worship in defiance of their removal from the area. In February 1996, the thirtieth anniversary of the proclamation of District Six as a white group area was commemorated by a 'memorial candle-light pilgrimage', led by priests, imams and community leaders. The pilgrimage started at St Mark's church and followed the faint traces of Hanover Street towards archaeological excavations at the corner of Roger and Stukeris Streets. After a number of speeches had been made at the site, the procession wound back to the Muir Street mosque to coincide with sunset and evening prayers. In this way, people asserted their spiritual ownership of the scarred landscape, the lines of the streets and the few, still-standing buildings.

Thus the material traces of District Six give form and shape to verbalized memory, amplifying and giving substance to the remnants of former life and the evidence of destruction. The sensory experience of this material world cannot be reduced to words alone, a commonplace observation for art, and the source of the effectiveness of the September 1997 Sculpture Festival.

Most of the Sculpture Festival's installations made use of the debris of destruction: plastic, ceramic sherds, broken glass, stone, building foundations. Although none was by an archaeologist, they were all in a sense archaeological, creating meaning from artefacts, using material things as a medium to comment on past and present. Installations included a skeletal tree spray-painted luminous red and orange, with a small cairn of gold-foil sandbags nearby – the treasure of memory – and branches touched by the sunset, or by blood. Next to this was a ship fashioned from paper and shredded plastic, with stick-figure goblins swinging in its rigging; a parody of colonial history. Cairns of Hanover Street kerbstones were taped off as a development site (or a crime scene), while further up the slope a 'garden of remembrance' had been fashioned from stones, broken glass, ceramic sherds and the other debris of daily life, dug out from just beneath the surface; ordinary artefacts re-arranged as a shrine.

One work well expressed the multiple coding of material things – the chameleon-like switching between repression and exaltation. Roderick Sauls, himself a one-time resident and subsequently a student of archaeology, celebrated the nostalgia recollection of carnival while turning it in on itself. Many have remembered District Six's carnival processions. Linda Fortune, for example, recalls lengths of satin material hung from the top of electric poles along Tyne Street on New Year's Eve: 'The shiny satin made our street look so pretty. Walking up Tyne Street from the Chapel Street end, looking straight ahead, you could see the different-coloured streamers stretching from one end of the street to the other ... Now and then a gentle breeze would make the streamers flutter to remind people that it was New Year in District Six' (Fortune 1996: 7).

Sauls expressed these memories with strips of brightly coloured cloth hanging from a tunnel-like frame, and built over the remnant of Hanover Street, the site of annual parades 30 years before. The movement of the strips of cloth mimicked the sounds and movement of the street, now lost. But within the tunnel, faded sepias of painted faces and popular lyrics were framed by slave manacles, while the poles of the structure were deeply buried and will stand until the District is redeveloped, forcing a second destruction of memory.

The material world of District Six, then, signals a radically unstable space. Objects are continually reinterpreted and reclaimed, the ground is marked and paced out, and mosques and churches used in defiance of the wasteland.

In consequence, the space that is District Six after the years of apartheid's bulldozers has remained 'lived': active, defiant, contradictory and contested. And this lived quality is founded in the material, the embodiment of 'third space' and the resistance of the margins. The cultural memory of District Six has been kept alive in the paradox of its unstable, nostalgic memory, so well captured in the closing lines of Richard Rive's *Buckingham Palace, District Six*. Zoot and a Xhosa watchman share the warmth of a fire beside the destroyed houses:

> The flame in the galley was very low and licked weakly over the glowing bits of wood. For some time Zoot stood deep in thought staring at it, then he pulled himself together and began to walk down Caledon Street. He also did not look back. The flame flickered for some time, determined to stay alive.

(Rive 1986: 198)

Chapter 8

Heart of whiteness

South Africa's reinventions of history – and the shifts in meaning that these confer on its material relics – have an extreme quality. But similar contradictions in apparently more benign public transcripts are evident when the assumption of the harmony of a balanced world-view is replaced with the expectation of the 'third space' at work. Memory and its material manifestation in heritage is reconfigured to meet contingent needs through the circulation of meanings, whether via long sea voyages in Frobisher's early explorations of Europe's periphery, replica caravels and ox wagons in apartheid South Africa's closing days, the cultural memory of the dispossessed community of District Six, or through today's digital media, where local acts of vandalism against black churches in the Chesapeake become focal points in the identity of a global black diaspora. Indeed, the new 'media age' (Poster 1990, 1995) brings immediate experience and the past into a single frame, promoting what Fredric Jameson (1989) has called 'nostalgia for the present'.

This is well illustrated by what Governor Spotswood's Williamsburg has become today – the paragon of restoration experiences – and the manner in which the Colonial Williamsburg Foundation has chosen to present itself on the World Wide Web. It has often been pointed out that Williamsburg's restoration, which began as a collaboration between the local parish priest and the tycoon John D. Rockefeller Jr in 1926, was part of the broad American reaction to communism and the perception that 'traditional values' had to be maintained and promoted (Samuel 1994; Handler and Gable 1997). But it is notable that Rockefeller's conservative vision, which could by now be respectably buried, is promoted with pride on the Web – the quintessential post-Cold War invention. Rockefeller, Williamsburg on the Web recounts, funded the restoration because of 'the lesson that it teaches of the patriotism, high purpose, and unselfish devotion of our forefathers to the common good'. The Colonial Williamsburg Foundation uses its Web site to endorse this view at the turn of the millennium, stating as its primary purpose 'that the future may learn from the past', and claiming that time spent in its reconstructed eighteenth-century world will promote 'the fundamental concepts of our republic – responsible leadership, a sense of public service, self government, and individual liberty' (Colonial Williamsburg Foundation 2000).

In this vein, Williamsburg on the Web celebrates Thomas Jefferson's association with the town. The site features a profile of 'Thomas Jefferson in Williamsburg', starting in 1760 with his student days at the College of William and Mary and continuing through until his residence in Spotswood's Governor's Palace between 1779 and 1780. The biographical sketch is soaked in informed nostalgia. Frequent visits to the Governor's Palace with student friends epitomize golden youth at its best, while romances, love of music and learning do not detract from the serious purposes of the 'common good' – a distinguished career in law and politics. Jefferson's Williamsburg was civility enshrined: 'after a dinner of oysters, wild duck, and Virginia Ham, the conversation might touch on anything from the value of western lands to the latest telescope or water prism sent from London . . .' (Colonial Williamsburg Foundation 2000). This is a public transcript in the tradition of William Byrd's formal record of his expedition to the interior, the outgoing face of the Virginia gentry and Governor Spotswood, and of Monticello and the Association of Descendants of Thomas Jefferson today. The 'Williamsburg experience' – and its digital simulacrum – invite today's Americans to immerse themselves in the healing waters of eighteenth-century civilization, and to be themselves restored by the experience (Handler and Gable 1997).

But – as always – there is the difficulty of slavery, the inconsistency in Jefferson's life and career that is awkward for the celebration of his 'patriotism and high purpose'. Williamsburg on the Web is quite explicit about the place of slavery in colonial society: 'slavery was a defining characteristic of 18th-century Virginia society. This institution, along with the racial attitudes and class structure that developed alongside and served to legitimate a slave system based on color of skin, tinctured all aspects of life in 18th century Virginia ... The horrors endured by enslaved African-Americans, whether physical or mental, were numerous.' But this very recognition establishes an inconsistency – the absent-but-present fact of slavery in Otto Mentzel's wedding feast once again. On the one hand, white Virginians were determined by their circumstances, by 'social distinction based on whether or not they were slaveholders', by economic dependence on slavery, and by 'unyielding racial prejudice' ('Introduction to Colonial African-American Life', in Colonial Williamsburg Foundation 2000). But how can those guilty of 'unyielding racial prejudice and cultural bias' be the responsible leaders, public servants and upholders of liberty celebrated by John D. Rockefeller, and still celebrated today?

Just as Mentzel was torn between the different roles of ethnographer and apologist, so the Colonial Williamsburg Foundation attempts to be both critical historian (in its own words, a 'university without walls') and custodian of conservative American values. Its Web site expresses this un-comfortable alliance. On the one hand, the site is an entertainment portal: five-star hotels, golf holidays and colonial enactments. On the other hand, it is a home page for scholarly pursuit, epitomized in the new Education Center, supporting 'a team of scholars, curators, librarians, archivists, conser-vators, researchers, and film and television producers' working 'behind the scenes, year-round, towards Colonial Williamsburg's original and ultimate goal: education' ('Colonial Williamsburg Builds A Campus For Its 'University Without Walls'', in Colonial Williamsburg Foundation 2000).

The consequence of this contradiction is a set of inconsistencies that runs through the text of the Foundation's Web site, digital equivalents to the revealing inconsistencies in early texts of colonialism, such as Byrd's accounts of his expedition to North Carolina, Sparrman's account of the Cape and van Meerhoff's diary of his expedition to the interior. Slavery in Colonial Williamsburg is presented in an account by Curtia James titled 'To Live Like a Slave'. A group of African Americans work and sleep at Carter's Grove – the Foundation's reconstructed slave quarter – where they toil in the fields, prepare food, listen to a Baptist preacher and discuss enslavement and freedom. The emphasis is on making the connection between past and present:

> Looking back, I realize I had always only perfunctorily thought of my own ancestors who dwelt on some other quarter in Georgia, withstanding trials I've never known. Perhaps their now silenced struggles are quelled in that tender, fearful place in my psyche, cowering in my heart, that I had always reserved for slavery.
>
> (James 2000)

But the stress is also on the lack of evidence. For Curtia James, these slaves are 'theoretical people': 'because evidence about them is so scant, any attempt to fully recreate their lives would be mere conjecture . . .'.

This conclusion – that slaves in the Chesapeake are more 'theoretical people' than ordinary white colonists – is inconsistent with other sources on the colonial past. Colonial Williamsburg's reconstruction of Carter's Grove was based in part on archaeological evidence from pits used for the storage of food and personal items. In the Chesapeake, cellar pits and 'root cellars' have proved a rich sources of information for interpreting aspects of slaves' ways of life (Kelso 1984, 1986; McKee 1988). In addition, there is a wide variety of additional, empirical, evidence that could be used, belying the assumption that enslaved African American's were an enculturated community with no identity of their own (Franklin 1995). Theresa Singleton (1995), in a prominent and wide-ranging review of the archaeology of slavery in North America, has shown how emphasis on the richness and value of memory and reconstructed tradition and the paucity of empirical evidence is to bracket off an 'African American experience' that is distinct and different from a so-called 'mainstream' of history.

The effect of the way in which slavery is presented at Colonial Williamsburg – both on the Web and in the layout of the heritage areas – is to separate Carter's Grove from the main 'Historic Area' and the 'slave experience' from the 'colonial experience', and to create 'an ethnic archaeology of the Other' (Singleton 1995; Handler and Gable 1997). This apartheid in representation becomes even more apparent when the Carter's Grove enactment is set against another of the Web's cameos – Mary Miley Theobald's account of 'Sampling 18th-Century Fare at Shield's Tavern'. Again, the emphasis is on participation and re-enactment, using the fragmentary evidence that comes from documents and archaeological evidence. But now there is none of the reservation about the quality of the data. Visitors to Shield's Tavern are offered 'historically accurate colonial-style dinners, with the correct table settings, table manners, and serving customs of the period in addition to the authentically prepared foods and beverages'. This authenticity has been achieved through 'an interdisciplinary approach to the study of food' that marshalled 'existing research and assistance from throughout the Foundation'. The result is 'an event that transports guests back in time', and open-ended possibilities for ever more detailed connections with the past. In Chef Swann's words, 'there is no end to what we're going to do here at Shields with 18th century food' (Theobald 2000).

In contrast to the reconstruction of the Carter's Grove Slave Quarter, Shields Tavern sells a rich, empirically authenticated experience of the past that offers limitless future possibilities for expansion. Rather than an opportunity for empathy with 'theoretical people' who cannot be brought to life through the evidence, Shield's Tavern is a time machine – the past as it really was. Mainstream, white, history is interpreted as factual, while black history is presented as close to fiction (Gable *et al.* 1993). In a detail that recalls Mentzel's exclusion of slaves from the wedding feast, the Web site reports that waiters at Shield's Tavern are always silent: 'waiters were meant neither to be seen nor heard. Much of their time was spent standing like statues, waiting for an unobtrusive signal from the hostess to proceed with the next task' (Theobald 2000).

Williamsburg on the Web is a public transcript for the new millennium – an 'archaeology of the present' that constructs present-day identities in the images of the past, sustained by the tangibility of the material world. This is an aspect of what Manuel Castells has called 'informationalism' – 'the construction of social action and politics around primary identities, either ascribed, rooted in history or geography, or newly built in an anxious search for meaning and spirituality' (Castells 1996: 22). Castells has shown that the convergence of telecommunications, broadband transmission and a quantum leap in computer performance in the early 1990s conquered time, allowing a global system working in 'real time' on a planetary scale. From this follows a simple, but radical, proposition – 'space organizes time in the network society' (Castells 1996: 376). The implications of this, and the way in which Castells's 'space of flows' organizes material referents to the past, is illustrated by a far more extreme example of the politics of identity – the decade-long series of conflicts in the Balkans which closed the millennium.

The Balkans have long stood for the backward, primitive and barbarian within Europe. Maria Todorova has argued that 'Balkanism' evolved independently from Said's Orientalism, with a Christianity that was opposed to Islam but was also non-Western:

> geographically inextricable from Europe, yet culturally constructed as 'the other', the Balkans became, in time, the object of a number of externalized political, ideological and cultural frustrations and have served as a repository of negative characteristics against which a positive and self-congratulatory image of the 'European' and 'the west' has been constructed.
>
> (Todorova 1994: 455)

One recent revival of Balkanism has been Robert Kaplan's *Balkan Ghosts* (1994), celebrated for the claim that its argument for the inevitability of tribal conflict in the Balkans strongly influenced the White House's policy in south-east Europe. Described as 'a dreadful mix of unfounded generalizations, misinformation, outdated sources, personal prejudices and bad writing' (Cooper 1993: 592), Kaplan's travelogue was, in its turn, a revisiting of Rebecca West's famous Balkan journey of 1937. Kaplan carried West's *Black Lamb and Grey Falcon* (1941) with him, and revelled in his perception of a centuries-old continuity of experience.

Here, Kaplan describes the archive of thirteenth-century paintings and frescoes in the Church of the Apostles in Peć:

> The workings of my eyes taught me the first canon of national survival: that an entire world can be created out of very little light. It took only another minute or so for the faces to emerge out of the gloom – haunted and hunger-ravaged faces from a preconscious, Serb past, evincing a spirituality and primitivism that the West knows best through the characters of Dostoyevsky. I felt as though I were inside a skull into which the collective memories of a people had been burned. Dreams took shape, hallucinations: St. Nicholas, with his purple robe and black, reminding eyes at the back of my head; St. Sava, Serbia's patron saint and founder of this very church, who descended through the watery void to proffer gifts of mercy and inspiration; the Ascended Christ, a dehumanized peasant-god beyond the last stage of physical suffering, more fearful than any conqueror or earthly ideology. Apostles and saints intermingled with

Figure 8.1 Virtual scriptoria: Visoki Decani Monastery, Kosovo (http://wwww.decani.yunet.com/edecani.html).

medieval Serbian kings and archbishops. They all appeared through a faith's distorting mirror: with elongated bodies and monstrous hands and heads. Many of the saint's eyes had been scratched out. According to a peasant belief, the plaster and dye used to depict a saint's eyes can cure blindness.

(Kaplan 1994: xx)

Ten years later, these same medieval frescoes and icons could be visited through the Web. By 1998, every monastery in the Kosovo diocese of Raska and Prizren had its Web site and gallery of images (Figure 8.1). Visoki Decani Monastery, for example, described its history (beginning in 1327) and its incomparable art and architecture. The twenty black-robed members of its brotherhood were introduced and their daily routine described: prayer from 5.00 a.m., individual obediences, kitchen duties, breadmaking, iconography, farmwork. The monks' current project was publishing, using computers, scanners and the Internet: 'in this way the brotherhood is trying to revive the ancient tradition of the monastery scriptoria where hundreds of books were written and translated' (Visoki Decani Monastery 2000).

But can a manuscript collection be reduced to a virtual scriptorium? Do the digital obediences of Visoki Decani's monks replace the experience of seeing the image of Christ ascended by the light of hundreds of candles in an atmosphere laden with beeswax? In Howard Rhinegold's world, the answer is emphatically 'yes' – there are potentially no limits to the sensory experiences of Virtual Reality. But in 1998, as the tension that would explode as the Kosovo war built up, Visoki Decani's monks were protected by young Yugoslav army conscripts who guarded the monastery from the Kosovo Liberation Army and the surrounding Muslim communities under the pall of imminent conflict. There was no digital escape from an AK-47, as the months ahead would show. As with the conflict over Ayodhya, described in Chapter 1, the treasures of the local site were of vital importance – and the violence was palpable.

Kosovo is at the heart of Serbian nationalism; mythologized as the place of defeat by the Ottoman Turks in 1389, the stain of Muslim occupation and the core of the Serbian Orthodox Church (Fine 1983, 1987; Malcolm 1998). Religious and historic places in Kosovo are the ground zero of Serbia's nationalist politics. At the same time, when war broke out between Yugoslavia and NATO in 1999, Serb nationalists were dispersed throughout the world, maintaining a fierce loyalty to the idea of 'greater Serbia'. Local identities in faraway places were formed around the idea of Serbia – its history, memories of 'home' and imagination of the past and future. Such was the Serbian Unity Congress of the USA, an 'international organization representing Serbs and friends of Serbs in the diaspora, committed to ensuring the continuation of the Serbian heritage'. In the run-up to the 1999 war, the SUC was lobbying in Washington, organizing fund-raising events and conventions and running a large Web site (Serbian Unity Congress 2000). This featured 'electronic exhibitions' of Serbian culture, including coinage (Bozinović 1998) and medieval material culture:

> This unique electronic exhibition organized by the Serbian Unity Congress presents, for the first time, the attire, jewelry and ornaments of the Serbian kings and czars in the 12th through 15th centuries. Symbolic significance, political influences and pure fashion can all be traced as they intermingle in this fascinating presentation featuring 24 pictures with careful reconstructions of masterpiece frescoes found in churches and monasteries throughout the Serbian lands.
>
> (Vuleta 1998)

The SUC's electronic galleries led directly to Slobodan Milosević's Belgrade and attempts to whitewash atrocities in Bosnia-Herzegovina that were reminiscent of Nazi propaganda (Dabić and Lukić 1997), while the very tangible situation of Visoki Decani's virtual scriptorium in Kosovo's impoverished and bitterly contested landscape pointed to the vital connection between the virtual and material worlds.

Serbian nationalism, as well as Croatian identity, stems from the distinction of religion. This has led to a continual emphasis on the differing physicality of

Catholicism and the Orthodox Church, expressed and constantly recreated through art, architecture and iconography. These perceptions of difference have been fervently held for many years. However, the generally held belief – fuelled by the tradition of Balkanism so well represented in the writing of West and Kaplan – that the war between Croatia and Serbia and the sequential Bosnian conflict were the consequence of an upwelling of ingrained ethnic character does not stand closer scrutiny. In the last census in the 'old' Yugoslavia of the 1980s, more than 25 per cent of the population were in inter-married families while a significant proportion of urban communities declined to describe themselves with the ethnic identifiers of Muslim, Orthodox or Catholic (Denitch 1994; Malcolm 1996).

In contrast to the concept of primordial inevitability, there is clear evidence that ethnic affiliations and historical referents were overtly manipulated in struggles for power in the vacuum that had existed since Josip Tito's death in 1980 (Woodward 1995).Yugoslav nationalists were championed by the West, and in particular by the International Monetary Fund, in their opposition to reformist Communists, strengthening the position of political figures such as Slobodan Milosević. Milosević – Serbia's leader through the war with Croatia and the Bosnian conflict, and subsequently President of the 'new' Yugoslavia – established his power base in 1986 as the leader of the Serbian League, manipulating Orthodox suspicion of Islam and Serbian historical pride to oppose Kosovar demands for greater autonomy (Denitch 1994).

The central importance of Kosovo to Serbian nationalism rests on the myth of the 'Field of the Blackbirds'. Serbian epic poetry and folklore record that Prince Lazar, elected leader of the Serbian nobility, was converted to piety by Elija (in the form of a grey falcon) and built an Orthodox church at Kosovo Polje on the eve of battle that was lost to the Ottoman Turks on 28 June 1389 (Malcolm 1996). Hence the doubly inscribed significance of Kosovo to Serbian nationalism: the site of the battlefield where humiliation at Muslim hands must be avenged, and the place where fourteenth-century monasteries preserve a direct line, in their art and architecture, to a proud and independent medieval kingdom. The 600th anniversary of the Battle of Kosovo Polje was marked in 1989 by the culmination of a celebration that had started a full year earlier. A funeral procession of Knez Lazar's disinterred coffin travelled through every town and village in Serbia, drawing 'huge, black-clad crowds of wailing mourners at every spot' (Kaplan 1994: 38; Malcolm 1996). This culminated in the battlefield ceremony:

> in the courtyard of the monastery at Gracanica (south of Pristina), while people queued to pay their devotions to the Prince's bones inside, stalls sold icon-style posters of Jesus Christ, Prince Lazar and Slobodan Milosević side by side. At the ceremony on the battlefield Milosević was accompanied by black-robed metropolitans of the Orthodox Church,

singers in traditional Serbian folk costumes, and members of the security
police in their traditional dress of dark suits and sunglasses . . .

(Malcolm 1996: 213)

Similarly, contemporary Croatian nationalism is constructed from a deep
history given form by sites, monuments and the material archive of the past.
A palimpsest of a rich Adriatic archaeology and architecture – Roman
Dalmatia, overlain by early Christian sites and medieval towns and villages –
supports the remembrance of tenth-century kingship. This is captured in the
life and work of Nenad Jeptanović, a Croatian born in Chile, educated at
Princeton and now returned to the Adriatic island of Brač (and living in the
same village where Bogdan Denitch spends his summer months). A paragon
of Said's contemporary organic intellectual, Jeptanović is curator of a family
mausoleum built in 1927 at the behest of Francisco Petrinović, Jeptanović's
uncle made rich by Chilean phosphates. The mausoleum's sculptures express
the essence of Croatian historical identity: the unity of Greek and Roman
influences, the principles of Catholicism and the struggle between good and
evil. Its dome is capped by a bronze sculpture of the Archangel Michael, and
its vaults house the coffins of Petrinović family members, including the
mummified corpse of Francisco himself, returned to Brač in 1961, a decade
after his death. The mausoleum is set on an ocean promontory, backed by
terraced vineyards that predate the Roman empire, a medieval village and
church and the beach where four teenage patriots were executed by Italian
soldiers half a century ago. Jeptanović uses this richly material setting as a
stage – a living archive that expresses his sense of place, history and identity.
He is obsessed with the graves that surround the mausoleum, and with
graveyard maintenance; how, after the passage of years, bones in a sarcopha-
gus are swept aside to make way for new corpses and how the bones leach
into the limestone soil. As such, he is the curator of his past written across the
landscape, and of his own grave (Jeptanović, n.d.).

For its part, Bosnia had been conquered by the Turkish army in 1463, and
subsequently many Bosnians had converted to Islam, often to improve their
social, legal and economic status within the Ottoman Empire (Malcolm
1996). Islamic communities dominated major towns such as Sarajevo and
Mostar, which thrived under Ottoman rule (although there were prosperous
Catholic, Orthodox and Jewish minorities). Changes in the system of land
tenure had a huge impact on the countryside. The earlier, military–feudal
system, in which both Christians and Muslims could be landowners, was
replaced by a system of hereditary estates, almost all owned by Muslims and
on which the majority of peasants were Christian. Through the years, the
major causes of conflict in Bosnia had not been religious, or the result
of 'ancient ethnic hatreds', but economic; the resentment of a mainly
Christian peasantry towards Muslim landlords and Muslim administrators
and merchants in the principal cities (Malcolm 1996). Within Bosnia's

cities – and in common with other parts of the former Yugoslavia – there had been increasing securalization, and by the late 1980s 30 per cent of marriages in urban districts were 'mixed': For many rural Muslims, and almost all urban ones, being Muslim consisted of a set of cultural traditions: 'Muslim names, circumcision, baklava and the celebration of Ramazan Bajram, getting a godparent to cut a one-year-old child's hair, a preference for tiny coffee cups without handles, a sympathy for spiders and various other traditional practices, the origins of which are frequently unknown to those who practice them' (Sorabji 1992: 5–6, quoted by Malcolm 1996: 222).

The open conflict that had erupted between Croatia and Serbia spread to Bosnia. Rather than being an ethnic inevitability, the destruction of Bosnia between 1992 and 1995 was a further consequence of Western support for nationalist leaders, combined with political manipulation by the Serbian Government. Following initial engagement by Serbian security forces and volunteers, serving to mobilize Bosnian Serbs, the Yugoslav army withdrew from Bosnia claiming that the conflict was an inevitable civil war based on ethnic rivalry, playing into Western belief in the theory of 'ancient hatreds'. The pattern of European intervention made the situation worse through the promotion of ethnically defined 'autonomous provinces', essentially similar to South African Bantustans (Malcolm 1996; Woodward 1995).

The reinvention of Croatian, Serbian and Muslim ethnicity by rival power blocs in the wake of Tito's multi-ethnic Yugoslavia was facilitated by the manipulation of a wealth of material symbols, records and the tangible evidence of centuries of history. The use of mass media – newspapers and, particularly, state-controlled television services – depended critically on the sensory presence of history, the visual and tactile presence of the archive in the everyday experience of the people. This is not to suggest the action of some false consciousness – a media brainwashing at the hands of an evil genius. On the contrary – the particular power of the tangible archive is to make the claims of history seem everywhere in their evidence, and incontrovertible in their logic. The political direction of 'invented tradition' may be given by a Tudjman or a Milosević, but its success depends on organic intellectuals such as Nenad Jeptanović, who will recreate their sense of identity on a daily basis in the fabric of the landscape, urban architecture and sacred books and relics in the local museum and church, reinforced by shared experiences in cafes, political meetings and Sunday sacraments.

An inevitable corollary of celebrating an identity that is rooted in the archive of manuscripts, records and architecture is the belief that competing claims, passionately denied, can only be defeated if the archive is restored to purity. From the first weeks of the conflict between Croatia and Serbia, 'ethnic cleansing' was more than driving communities into exile. In the border town of Vukovar, rival ethnic nationalisms escalated as harassment, attacks on individuals and, particularly, damage to houses. In the summer of 1991, the town was besieged by the Serbian army. Some 30,000 Croats fled into exile. The Eltz Manor House, which housed the Vukovar Municipal Museum, was destroyed and the art gallery and other museums in the town extensively damaged. Systematic shelling by Serbian artillery reduced most of the historical precinct to rubble. Many of the surviving art works, archaeological collections and archives were stolen, and are believed to be in collections in Belgrade and other parts of Serbia; some have been offered for sale in Belgrade markets (Denitch 1994; Pavić 1997). The Yugoslav army and the volunteer militia were intent on wiping away the historical traces of a Croat presence from the banks of the Danube.

Buildings and archives continued to be specific targets as the war continued. Croatia's Museum Documentation Centre, claimed such attacks as a 'scorched earth' strategy, an attack on 'the Croatian National identity' (Sulć 1997: 14). It was argued that destruction of cultural property on this scale was not just the 'collateral damage of warfare', but rather the 'assassination of culture' as defined in the 1948 Genocide Convention and other international protocols (Hodder 1996). In October 1991 the first Serbian air raids on Zagreb's upper town – the historical quarter of the city – resulted in damage to historic buildings and museums. In the same autumn, the Yugoslav navy moved along Croatia's Adriatic coast, first shelling Diocletian's Palace, a fourth-century World Heritage Site celebrated by Croatian nationalists for the association with the glories of Rome, and then moving south to the thirteenth-century city of Dubrovnik, which was to remain under siege for a year (Vinterhalter 1997).

Those who experienced this war first-hand, or who have written about it, describe a conflict far removed from the Hollywood stereotype of high-tech scientific attack on distant targets, although Hollywood has indeed been closely implicated. In the play between locality and global media, focused attacks on the archives of arcane histories have been mingled with the paraphernalia and memorabilia of transcontinental imagery. Throughout the war, both the Croatian and Serbian governments maintained a tight hold on all media, and particularly television (Maass 1996). The consequence was a material expression that encapsulated the global and the local. Many of the direct attacks on civilians and their culture were carried out by volunteer paramilitary units under the protection of the professional army. These militias were often made up of unemployed youth and other marginalized groups – 'the same alienated groups from which xenophobic skinheads and soccer gangs have been recruited in Western Europe' (Denitch 1994: 10). Serbian chetniks adopted long hair and beards, peasant caps and daggers in reference to past struggles. Serbian volunteers, organized by Belgrade gangsters, chose US style camouflage costumes and were clean shaven with the exception of moustaches, and were strongly influenced by American Vietnam movies. Croat reservists adopted Cherokee roaches and shaved heads, with black headbands, Rambo-style. French and German skinhead mercenaries were formed as a blackshirt legion (Denitch 1994). As the next

Balkan conflict began to escalate, the Kosovo Liberation Army was reported as fashioning its identity on Stalinist Albania and Mussolini's fascist black-shirts (Schork 1998). Global images – a deadly cyberpunk fantasy – had been brought to bear on the specifics of local histories: Knez Lazar's tragic piety, the Emperor Diocletian's retirement to grow cabbages in Dalmatia, the Vukovar museum's assertion of Croat history on Serbia's doorstep.

Attacks on cultural property escalated as the epicentre of conflict shifted to Bosnia-Herzegovina.

> It is as if the protagonists, unable to strangle the last living representatives of what they see as an alien culture, seem to think that with the destruction of place, an architectural cleansing, as it were, they can eradicate the people who inhabit that place ... Like the horrifying rapes of women ... these are violent efforts to remake the world in another image. Like the women of Bosnia, for many of whom the preservation of their traditional culture and the creation of home is an essential role, so too architecture creates home, represents memory, and preserves culture. Without mini-mizing the scale of human suffering, this attempt to destroy architecture, to annihilate place, like the violence against the women, is criminal warfare and cultural genocide.
>
> (Adams 1993: 389)

A young Muslim man, after his 500-year-old mosque had been destroyed, said: 'it's not that my family was burned down, but it's my foundation that burned. I was destroyed' (Hodder 1996). There were specific attacks on archives – libraries, manuscript holdings, museums and other cultural institu-tions. This applied as much in the cities – Sarajevo, Mostar – as in the towns and villages, and it has been estimated that the cadastral registers, *waqf* documents and parish records of more than 800 Muslim and Croat commu-nities have been destroyed by Serbian nationalists and that more than 1,200 religious and cultural sites have been destroyed or damaged, including mosques, the historic centres of many towns, Muslim graves and pilgrimage sites, Catholic churches, monasteries, cemeteries and Jewish religious buildings (Riedlmayer 1995).

Attacks on cultural property were carried out by nationalists on all sides. Mostar – Bosnia-Herzegovina's second city – had grown from a small village to a prosperous town under the Ottoman Empire. Its focal point – and the key to its economic prosperity – was the bridge over the gorge of the River Neretva, Stari Most ('old bridge'), built in 1566 and a UNESCO World Heritage Site. Through the 1980s the historic core of Mostar had been conserved and restored in a world-renowned project run by an inter-ethnic group of Croats, Serbs and Muslims, winning the Aga Khan Award for Architecture in 1986. Such a project was anathema to nationalists intent on eradicating all traces of other histories from Bosnia. Much of Mostar's historic precinct was destroyed by systematic shelling in November 1993 (Ozkan 1994). Stari Most, widely recognized as a symbol of Bosnian unity and culture, was blown up by the Croatian army (Woodward 1995).

In Sarajevo itself, the pattern of Serbian shelling suggests that libraries and museums were specifically targeted for destruction; surrounding buildings were often left intact. In the summer of 1992 Serb forces bombarded the National Museum. Two hundred thousand volumes were rescued under sniper fire, including the fourteenth-century Sarajevo Haggadah, brought to Sarajevo in the fifteenth century by Jews fleeing the Spanish Inquisition, and considered one of Bosnia's principal cultural treasures. The building was badly damaged by shells, and the Museum's director was killed while arranging for plastic sheeting to protect what was left of the collections (Riedlmayer 1995). In May 1992, the Serbs attacked Sarajevo's Oriental Institute with phosphorous grenades, weapons designed to maximize damage by fire. This time, the entire holdings were destroyed, including 5,263 bound manuscripts in Arabic, Persian, Turkish, Hebrew and Serbo-Croatian-Bosnian in Arabic script, as well as tens of thousands of Ottoman-era documents (Riedlmayer 1998). Serbian forces also occupied the Franciscan Seminary in Nedzarici, a western suburb of Sarajevo, looting and destroying collections of books, sculptures and paintings (Lovrenović 1994).

The attack on the National Library of Bosnia and Herzegovina came later in the summer, on the night of 25 August. Like the Oriental Institute, the National Library was known for the richness and diversity of its archive, preserving the record of centuries of Serb, Croat and Muslim interaction. Known as the Vijecnica (the name of the elaborate nineteenth-century building in which it was housed), this was a legal deposit library for the 'old' Yugoslavia, Sarajevo University's library and the major archival depot for Bosnia-Herzegovina (Kujundzić 1997). The bombardment was witnessed by Sarajevo writer Ivan Lovrenović, whose own library was destroyed the same summer by Serbian militia in an ad hoc street ritual. Hundreds of incendiary rockets were fired from Serbian artillery in the hills surrounding the city, followed by machine gun and mortar fire to deter people from rescuing the books and manuscripts: 'black, sooty, still hot butterflies – books and papers aflame, the library's treasure – were flying around and falling over distant parts of the city' (Lovrenović 1994).

The ferocity of the attack on the archives of Croatia and Bosnia-Herzegovina in the wars of the 1990s, and the way in which the politics of mobilized ethnicity was translated into actions by individuals, is captured in this description of a Serb raid on a Croat artist's studio in the Sarajevo neighbourhood of Grbavica:

> Serbian soldiers broke into his studio looking to steal money and equipment. They were incensed to discover an Islamic levha – a calligraphic inscription from the Koran – which the painter had

mounted as a wall hanging. They took it down and, cursing, butchered it. According to witnesses, they then took all the artist's paintings, drawings and sketches, lined them up against the front wall of the house and executed them with machine-gun fire until they were in shreds.

(Lovrenović 1994)

The 'Bosnia fallacy' – that 'land, language, religion, history, and blood are congruent' – leads in turn to the West and to what Arjun Appadurai has termed the 'heart of whiteness' (Appadurai 1996: 21). Here, the triumphalism of global dominance and a new economic order mask a counter-culture of ethnic conflict and hatred that has all the characteristics of the tribalism that is assumed to be quintessentially un-American and un-European. One of the consequences of essentializing ethnic conflicts in Croatia and Bosnia-Herzegovina – as well as in other parts of the world geographically distant from western Europe and North America – is the pretence that such conflicts are organic, and therefore organically impossible in the heartlands of late capitalism.

But the particular play between the global and local – the 'death of distance' that is the characteristic of the 'media age' – makes old geographical distinctions redundant. As commentators such as Bogdan Denitch have pointed out, the revival of Serbian and Croatian nationalism has been reinforced by substantial financial support from the Balkan diaspora. Aggressive nationalism in Croatia and Bosnia-Herzegovina has been sustained as much by Serbs and Croats in North America as by Belgrade and Zagreb. Croatian ethnic fervour is felt as much in West Germany – or among Chilean exiles such as the Petrinović family – as in Croatia. Seen in this way, 'Bosnia' cannot be simply bracketed off as an obscure tribal war in a distant corner of the world.

The ways in which conflicts in areas such as Bosnia-Herzegovina are connected with the rest of the world can be seen in the use of the Web to mobilize and direct global media flows around the locally manifested 'places' of ethnic identity. In 1995, besieged Sarajevo was connected to the outside world via an e-mail satellite link, and this led to the foundation of 'Domovina Net', or 'Homeland Net' in Amsterdam, providing video and audio streams on Bosnian issues, including (in 1998) real-time audio-feeds from the International War Crimes Tribunal in The Hague (Domovina Net 2000). Domovina Net was visited by an estimated 25,000 to 50,000 people each week, from all parts of the world. 'New' Yugoslavia used its official Web site – signified by the flag, coat of arms and a sound file of the National Anthem – to claim the Federal Republic's legality of existence and commitment to 'peace, security, stability, cooperation and prosperity in the region and in the World of Future' (Yugoslavia 2000). But the main emphasis of the site was to claim a sustained and deliberate media conspiracy throughout the last decade of Balkan conflicts against the legitimate national aspirations of Serbs throughout the region, and in exile throughout the world. This position was supported and extended by the US-based Serbian Unity Congress. Through its Web site, the SUC offered an extensive apology for Serb expansionism, denied claims of atrocities, and presented counter-claims for war crimes by Croats and Muslims (Serbian Unity Congress 2000). These positions were contested at other points of presence. The Croatian Institute for Culture and Information, for instance, published an online newspaper every week, addressing issues such as religion, cultural heritage, politics and Croatia's rights of self-determination, and repeating well-tried constructions of history: 'the Croats are amongst the oldest peoples in Europe. They have inhabited the territory between the Adriatic Sea and the Drava River for at least thirteen centuries. And yet it was only six years ago that they managed to establish their own independent and democratic state ...' (Croatia 2000). The government of Bosnia-Herzegovina presented its position – and the extent of criminal injustice against the rights of its citizens to self-determination – on a Web site from Washington DC (Bosnia-Herzegovina 2000).

Not surprisingly, because of technological advances in the intervening years, the Internet played a greater role during the 1999 Kosovo war. E-mail discussion lists were used extensively by both Serb and Kosovar nationalists, stretching the idealism of advocates of free opinion to the limit as strident claims and counter-claims were made. In the words of the *Economist* (15 May 1999), reporting at the height of military action, 'now we have war on the net. As NATO planes bomb the former Yugoslavia, American Government Web sites display what is destroyed. The Yugoslav Government ripostes with numbers of planes shot down, targets missed and civilians killed. Albanian Web sites chronicle the flood of Kosovar refugees. Serb ones list atrocities by Kosovar terrorists. All of this against a backdrop of interactive maps, living histories, bile-filled bulletin boards and eye-witness e-mails. This is the first web war'.

There are important distinctions between broadcast media and more recent forms of digital communication. The ways in which Serb and Croat nationalisms were shaped by state-controlled television services in the late 1980s and the first half of the 1990s are different from the use of the Web in the second half of the 1990s. For example, Peter Maass (1996) has argued that Milosević's control of Serbia's television service was the key to his ability to control the sway of public opinion by denying all reference to alternative points of view. In this respect, Web-based information is the inverse of broadcast television, and by the time war came to Kosovo, Milosević was not able to prevent at least some Serbians from seeing, and being influenced by, any site that they could find (a quality explicitly exploited by Domovina Net). But the crucial issue, of course, was access; the majority of citizens of Bosnia-Herzegovina, Croatia and Yugoslavia, battling to survive the rigours of poverty and the effects of war, were hardly likely to become cyber-surfers. Thus the attention that is being given to the Web as a medium for claims and

counter-claims of regional ethnic rights emphasizes again the ineluctable connection between global media and local place in the cultural construction of
identity. *The Economist's* 'war on the web' is the conflict of international
opinion – the global distribution of snatches of information pioneered by
CNN in the Gulf War at the beginning of the 1990s. Local opinion within
Yugoslavia was the domain of broadcast media, a point well understood by
NATO strategists, who identified Serbian television stations and transmitters
as prime targets for bombing.

The use of the Web in war was shown starkly in the escalation of conflict in
Kosovo and Albania's borderlands in the months before the NATO airstrikes
began. Albania is often presented as the savage heart of this part of Europe;
ancient mountain chiefdoms; a place where Byron found primordial inspiration; the most repressive of Cold War regimes; a place of blood feuds where
an AK-47 can be traded for a carton of cigarettes and one of the poorest
countries in the world. But Albania was presented on the Web through a
cheerful home page that was pitched at the diaspora: 'you may ask yourself,
why is this the Albanian home page, rather than an Albania home page.
Albanians cover a far larger territory than the country of Albania, and to
speak of Albania only would mean excluding half of the ethnic Albanian population' (Albania 2000). This Albanian identity was marked by means of a
classic suite of ethnic markers; a description and history of language, folk
music and folk costume; a history that is traced back to 2000 BC and the
Illyrians; and a 'virtual menu', including *patë e egër e pjekur* ('take a wild duck,
clean it well, and keep it in vinegar overnight . . .'). The claim to a 'greater
Albania' (reflecting the same ideology as 'new' Yugoslavia's claim to a
'greater Serbia') was expressed in a map that embraced Albania, Kosovo
and parts of Macedonia and Montenegro. But the most active link on the
page was to the 'Kosova Crisis Center', with news updates on the breaking
war, and a gallery of images of destroyed buildings and victims of the
fighting. To navigate the Web site was to move through graphics of historic
landscapes and buildings – a deep ethnic past – to folk culture (people in folk
costume, dancing), and then to images of buildings destroyed by Serbian
militia, twisted and mutilated bodies and close-ups of men, women and
children with limbs and faces torn away. The sponsor of this Web site was the
Albanian-American Academy, based in the US, and selling 'all kinds of
Albanian music and movies'. The Kosovo news page is linked to one of the
world's largest Web-based book stores, Amazon, for purchases of the latest
books about the region.

This example of the use of the Web in a local war is a striking illustration of
the use of material referents to claim identity in the 'space of flows'. The
political goal was a 'greater Albania' – the independence of Serbia's Kosovo
province and its realignment with neighbouring Albania, and less specific
claims to parts of Macedonia and Montenegro. To this end, long-standing
images of regional ethnicity were appropriated and revitalized in history,

language, costume, custom and food, and were related to the qualities of a fiercely beautiful, primitive landscape. This construction of an integrated Albanian culture was projected at the world and was instantly available to anyone, anywhere, who had access to the Web. Particular targets were Albanians abroad – those with remembered identities living in Western Europe or the US who were also interested in purchasing books, CDs and videos. From this digital perspective, it seemed only natural that Albanians should have the right to live within their landscape as they had for centuries, and that Serb aggression was a travesty of this natural order. The images of twisted bodies of children, headless torsos and destroyed faces of pregnant women made the claim that the Serbian militia were monsters outside this natural order, completing the nexus of local claims to place and identity, the global circulation of the essence of imagination, and violence – the digitally enhanced, visceral detail of horror.

This is the global circulation of the markers of identity at work, linked with often-violent, local manifestations. In Maurits and Wagenaer's day, violence was pushed out to the colonial periphery, contrasting the core of 'holy Christendom' with the civilizing mission at 'earth's extremest end'. An archive such as Maurits's was initially stained by the blood of those who had been dispossessed and subjugated, but collections of the exotic had been wiped clean, ordered and neatly labelled by the time they were deposited in the collections of Europe's great libraries and museums. An effect of the defeat of distance – the achievement of today's information technology – has been to cancel this displacement of violence.

The comparison of the complex discourses of colonialism in southern Africa and the eastern seaboard of North America, along with instances of the way in which the evidence for the past is articulated in the politics of the present in these and other parts of the world, has amplified the qualities of historical archaeology. It is clear that people, across the complex intersections of class, race and gender, work with far more than words. The accumulated detritus of colonialism's five centuries is more than the waste product of a history that can be understood verbally. It required authorial detachment to articulate Esteban Trueba's palatial dream. If he were to be anything like the gentry who built their mansions along Virginia's rivers, or the Cape's rural slave owners and their baroque excesses, Trueba would not have been able to put his intentions into words.

Although the study of material things is at the heart of historical archaeology, cultural materialism is not, of course, the exclusive preserve of one discipline, and understanding the early colonial world depends on work in close fields of study that include art and cultural history, architecture, literary studies and critical theory. In the final analysis, 'archaeology' is no more than one set of techniques for understanding one dimension of complex, lived experiences. The value of realizing the interconnectedness of various fields of study has been demonstrated in the chapters that have gone before, and is similarly demonstrated in interconnected studies from within different disciplinary traditions. Here, historian Simon Schama's study of forests serves as an excellent example.

Schama shows how concepts of rustic innocence, martial prowess and 'folk memory' converged by the mid-eighteenth century in a new generation of German patriots; a significant movement for the Cape, as the Dutch East India Company enlisted many Germans in its service. Allegorical painting took large oak trees as emblems of Germany and there was an accompanying 'oak fetish' in the literature of the period. As the theme gathered momentum in the nineteenth century, the forest was seen as a place of both terror and adjudication, a place for primitive redress, and an expression of the essential German character and racial purity. A logical, if bizarre, outcome was the Third Reich's strong advocacy of woodland conservation, with Hermann Göring as *Reichsforstminister*, dressed in an appropriate uniform, and outlawing vivisection (Schama 1995). Schama's continuing exegesis shows how forests acquired diametrically different meanings in England – ideals of liberty and individualism, rather than the Germanic concepts of domination and authority.

The English 'mythic memory of greenwood freedom', surviving well into the nineteenth century, was an opposite of German arboreal nationalism, if ultimately serving the same cause:

> Greenwood . . . is the upside-down world of the Renaissance court: a place where the conventions of gender and rank are *temporarily* reversed in the interest of discovering truth, love, freedom, and, above all, justice . . . This being England, the greenwood generally votes conservative. Its reversals of rank and sex are always temporary and its sentiments incurably loyal and royal. The grim slaughters of Białowieza and the Teutoburgwald are unthinkable in the sylvan habitat of Merrie England: there it is forever green, always summer. The nightingales sing, the ale is heady, and masters and men are brought together in fellowship by the lord of the jest: Robin Hood.
>
> (Schama 1995: 141, original emphasis)

Schama's point is that landscapes are culture before they are nature. Rich sets of meanings, specific to complex historical settings, are attached to things, and these sets of meanings constitute the way people see themselves in the world, and cast both their pasts and their futures.

Simon Schama's cultural history insists that the symbolic meanings of things are understood within specific trajectories that link present to past, and his study of forests begins with his own genealogical connections with Europe's past. An influential strand of contextual archaeology has taken empathy as the basis for explanation: 'experiential archaeologies which assume that past people's encounters with landscapes and architecture would have been much the same as our own' (Thomas 2000). But it is a deceit that it is possible to study the past without standing apart as an observer. Although it must now be common cause that there is always a complex relationship between the politics and perceptions of the archaeologist and the subject upon which he or she concentrates, it is surely also the case that immersion in the subjectivity of the past – searching for an empathy by treading the same paths and breathing the same air – is not enough in itself to gain a full understanding of history.

This must particularly be the case for an archaeology of colonialism which is, above all else, an archaeology of displacement and oppression. From Ceuta onwards, indigenous communities were swept aside, incorporated as the colony's underclass or simply killed en masse. Throughout the seventeenth and eighteenth centuries, the Atlantic slave trade redeployed millions of Africans in servitude. In the Netherlands' eastern possessions the Dutch East India Company transported immensely profitable cargoes in an economy that depended on various forms of unfree labour. The fine-porcelain tea services and plates, silks, spices and other rare commodities which were redistributed throughout Europe and its colonial world, and which found their way into the probate records and assemblages which are the core of archaeological interpretations, were delivered by merchants and officials who were completely dependent on servants, indentured soldiers and sailors and chattel slaves. As has been shown, this material culture was at the heart of marking identity. And in marking identity, these consumers of the wonders of the colonial world were marking their aspirations to be like those above them, and their differences from those below. They had every interest in making their slaves and servants as invisible as possible to the archaeologist. Limiting understanding to an empathetic context which has as its ideal an unity with the person who used the artefact is to run the risk of accepting uncritically the very illusions that were created through the use of the material world by those who held power.

This is well illustrated by the necessities for an archaeology of slavery – an institution that united William Byrd's Virginia, and the Cape described by Valentyn, Mentzel and Kolbe. Orlando Patterson has shown that slaves were socially non-existent:

> The essence of slavery is that the slave, in his social death, lives on the margin between community and chaos, life and death, the sacred and the secular. Already dead, he lives outside the mana of the gods and can cross the boundaries with social and supernatural impunity.
>
> (Patterson 1982: 51)

Not surprisingly, slave owners often made every effort to render their slaves materially non-existent as well, allowing them a minimum of possessions and systematically attacking any evidence of a cultural identity. Theresa Singleton has argued that plantation archaeology in North America has colluded with this exclusion by insisting on distinct ethnic markers in material culture, rather than looking at the ways in which artefacts were adopted and reconfigured by slaves determined to resist the oppression of their owners (Singleton 1995).

At the Cape, visitors not familiar with life in a slave society realized with a literary shudder that slave owners did not 'see' their chattels who worked and slept around them; an illusion that has been preserved in the contemporary presentation of the South African past, allowing modern visitors to former slave plantations to believe that colonial farmers built their houses and tended their vines with their own hands. Gayatri Spivak (1985) has noted how systems of colonial domination have, over and over again, fabricated representations of historical reality – representations that are strengthened enormously by the manipulation of the material world. The problem for historical understanding is to discover those voices which colonial authority attempted to mask – to step beyond contextual empathy and hermeneutic play and look for the life in the long shadows cast by domination. This book has set out such an approach, constructed from the theoretical insights of Michel Foucault, Gayatri Spivak and Homi Bhabha. It can be drawn together as six principal themes.

The first theme is that of the world order – the global circulation of material things and their representations in words and images. This was an essential quality of Europe's colonization of the world from its earliest years, epitomized by George Beste's account of Frobisher's voyage to Baffin Island. The value of things that were 'more for ornament than for necessarie uses' presaged the importance of the 'rich trades' characteristic of the colonial system of distribution: silk, furs and caviar; the spices, porcelain and other exotic goods which were the payload for the Dutch East India Company; the tobacco that was the making of Chesapeake patriarchs such as William Byrd and his dynasty. The establishment of such global systems of circulation resulted in entrepôts of exotica, ideas and impressions such as Prince Johan Maurits van Nassau-Siegen's entourage of botanists, astronomers and artists, the collection of 'every bird and animal that he could find' at his colonial capital of Mauritstad, and the return of the collection to The Hague. This 'museumizing imagination' (Anderson 1991: 178) was an intimate part of the politics of power, both creating and expressing a clear distinction between Europe and its colonial periphery.

As Neil McKendrick has put it, 'spurred on by social emulation and class competition, men and women surrendered eagerly to the pursuit of novelty, the hypnotic effects of fashion, and the enticements of persuasive commercial propaganda' (McKendrick 1982: 11). In this, consumers (who were at the same time wage labourers) were coupled to the dominant elites not through the persuasiveness of false consciousness, but by the desire to signify status in a competitive, class-conscious world. Josiah Wedgewood, writing in 1779 at a time when he was exporting the majority of his products (many of them to North America), understood this relationship well: '*Fashion* is infinitely superior to *merit* ... and it is plain from a thousand instances if you have a favourite child you wish the public to fondle and take notice of, you have only to make choice of proper sponcers [*sic*]' (quoted in McKendrick 1982: 100, original emphasis). If he had lived two centuries later, Wedgewood would have made a fine historical archaeologist.

Secondly, and counterbalancing global systems of circulation, was locality – the constitution of the global in the local, the relationship between widely held world-views and individual action. The archaeology of the modern world was made by the actions of individuals: William Byrd II moving between London and the Chesapeake periphery, and Zacharias Wagenaer travelling the outer reaches of the known world in a career that took him from Maurits's Brazil to the Cape, via a spell of duty in Japan; slaves transported from West Africa to the Caribbean, or from Indonesia to southern Africa. The play between widely held world-views and individual action gave local twists given to general ideas. Pieter Potter's Cape Town, and Nicholson and Spotswood's Annapolis and Williamsburg, conformed to the general pattern of geometrically designed colonial settlements, and captured local idiosyncrasies. Wagenaer's interpretation of military science was adapted to the contours of the landscape beneath Table Mountain, and Jefferson's Monticello was an individualized interpretation within a widely held system of neoclassical architecture. Martin Melck expressed Prussian nationalism in vernacular craft work, crowning with his own monogram the king's ivory and ebony eagle. Craftsmen – some, like the Cape carpenter Anton Anreith, known, and many anonymous and enslaved – gave local interpretations to general lexicons of expression.

The third theme is the multiplicity of meanings of this rich, material world. Material culture was – and is – more than an assemblage of words. 'Things' anchored meanings and allowed polyvalent interpretations, extending the meanings of verbal forms of expression, qualities that were widely recognized, whether in mnemonic memory systems and their philosophy, or in sumptuary laws promulgated by rulers jealous of their power. Historical archaeology reveals rich systems of meaning; houses full of artefacts, revealed in probate records and excavations; contemporary genre paintings and their associations of people and everyday possessions; texts such as Adam Tas's diary fragments and their inadvertent revelation of the importance of household things in daily life. In unravelling these multiple meanings, there is particular value in the comparative approach of world archaeology, looking at particular localities across global systems of circulation. In this approach, men such as William Byrd, Martin Melck and Salomon Bosch reveal the implication of the material world in the daily recreation of patriarchal control, and women such as Krotoa show the power of expression beyond words as she marked her movement between the colonial and Khoikhoi worlds at the Cape by changing clothes.

Fourthly, material culture was a site of ambiguity. Colonialism, requiring the constant exploitation of the periphery for the benefit of Europe, was fundamentally unstable. Its ambiguities of power and control give the 'language of things' a particular quality – the opulence of the newly discovered periphery set against the inevitability of death in Hans Holbein's *Ambassadors*. Here, historical archaeology has the particular facility (and defining characteristic) of setting material culture against words as parallel and contemporary sources of information about the past. Seen through the lens of ambiguity and anxiety and set against the record of contemporary materiality, verbal accounts such as Byrd's expedition records and secret journal and the responses of travel writers when confronted with the fecundity of nature give a particular insight into the way in which colonial domination and resistance were worked through on a day-by-day basis. This is the 'third space' at work – the agonistic quality of colonialism's cultural forms, forcing constant repetition, whether the attempts to 'civilize' Krotoa through dress and eating habits, or the neurotic repetition of symmetry in colonial architecture.

Fifth is the persistent connection between the past and the present. The archaeology of the modern world is built within the framework of the present, with all its obsessions, emphases and theories. Similarly, the past is constantly created and recreated as part of the politics of contemporary identities, whether nostalgic remembrances of European colonization in the closing years of South Africa's apartheid era, or in the cauldron of new nationalist politics in the Balkans.

Finally, but crucially, there is the quality of violence that lies behind the arrays of salvaged and well-scrubbed artefacts laid out in archaeological laboratories. Here, material culture can reveal the effects of 'subaltern voices' – those who cannot be seen directly, but whose 'everyday acts of resistance' are evident in the form of dominant transcripts; slaves and the threat of arson, forcing modifications in architectural styles; the unstable parody in the description of Khoikhoi ethnography, and the genocide that lay just behind the screen of ethnographic description.

Whatever the scale of analysis or time frame, the constant thread is that of individual agency of Krotoa and Van Meerhoff, of William Byrd and the 'dark angel' in Virginia's woodland, of Anders Sparrman chasing a Khoikhoi girl through the bush, only to have her turn on him with a knife, and of the symbolic assassination of an art collection in contemporary Sarajevo. The corporeal fate of three criminals – separated in time and space but subjected to the institutionalized violence that is the key to Michel Foucault's concepts of power and discourse, illustrate the point.

Estienne Barbier led a minor rebellion by a group of colonists at the Cape who were discontented with the Dutch East India Company's restrictions on their own violent exploitation of the Khoikhoi. Here is a description of his execution by his contemporary, Otto Mentzel. Barbier was

> bound upon a double wooden cross that was used for those condemned to be broken on the wheel; first his right hand and then his head were struck off with a hatchet; he was then quartered and his entrails buried under the gallows, while the head and hand were nailed to a stake which was set up in Heer Straat, a road that leads from the Castle to the interior. The four quarters were sent into the interior and fastened to stakes which were set up in the districts.
>
> (Mentzel 1919: 117)

Mentzel concluded with some irony: 'such was the melancholy end of a turbulent fellow who could, if he would, have lived in the utmost peace and contentment . . .'.

In 1632, Rembrandt had finished his painting of Dr Nicholaas Tulp dissecting the executed criminal Aris Kindt. The portrait, which now hangs in Maurits' house in The Hague, has granted Kindt, his body peeled open, a violent immorality. More than 350 years later Joseph Jernigan was executed in Texas. His body was acquired by the National Library of Medicine and cut into almost 2,000 thin sections. Now renamed Adam, Jernigan has also gained immortality, the digitized thin sections animated in a sequence that travels from the head, down through the torso, arms and legs and ends at the tip of the toes, and which is available on the Internet (Warner 1998; National Library of Medicine 2000).

Estienne Barbier, Aris Kindt and Jernigan/Adam are appropriate avatars for the historical archaeology of the modern world, in which the global circulation of people, ideas and things congeal in local identities and the often-violent action of people on the persons of others.

Bibliography

Adams, N. (1993) 'Architecture as the target', *Journal of the Society of Architectural Historians* 52: 389–90.

Albania (2000) *Alb@nian.com. The home of Albanians on the Internet*. Online. Available HTTP: http://www.albanian.com (10 January 2000).

Allende, I. (1986) *The House of the Spirits*, London: Black Swan.

Amussen, S. (1988) *An Ordered Society. Gender and Class in Early Modern England*, Oxford: Blackwell.

Anderson, B. (1991) *Imagined Communities: Reflections on the Origin and Spread of Nationalism*, London: Verso.

Anderson, E. B. (1984) *Annapolis. A Walk Through History*, Centreville: Tidewater Publishers.

Appadurai, A. (1986) 'Commodities and the politics of value', in A. Appadurai (ed.), *The Social Life of Things*, pp. 3–63, Cambridge: Cambridge University Press.

—— (1996) *Modernity at Large: Cultural Dimensions of Globalization*, Minneapolis: University of Minnesota Press.

Archaeology Contracts Office (1993) *Archaeological Investigation of the Elsenburg Herehuis*, Archaeology Contracts Office, Department of Archaeology, University of Cape Town.

Armstrong, J. C. and Worden, N. (1989) 'The slaves, 1652–1834', in R. Elphick and H. Giliomee (eds), *The Shaping of South African Society*, pp. 109–83, 2nd edn, Cape Town: Maskew Miller Longman.

Arner, R. (1975) 'Westover and the wilderness: William Byrd's images of Virginia', *Southern Literary Journal* 7(2): 105–23.

Axelson, E. (1973) *Portuguese in South-East Africa 1488–1600*, Cape Town: Struik.

Bain, R. (1987) 'William Byrd of Westover (1674–1774)', in R. Bain and J. M. Flora (eds), *Fifty Southern Writers Before 1900. A Bio-Bibliographic Sourcebook*, pp. 55–74, New York: Greenwood Press.

Baker, H. (1900) 'Introduction', in A. Trotter (ed.), *Old Colonial Houses of the Cape of Good Hope*, London: Batsford.

Barker, F. (1984) *The Tremulous Private Body. Essays on Subjection*, London: Methuen.

Benisovich, M. (1943) 'The history of the *Tenture des Indes*', *Burlington Magazine* 83(486): 216–25.

Berger, J. (1972) *Ways of Seeing*, Harmondsworth: Penguin.

Beverley, R. (1968 (1705)) *The History and Present State of Virginia*, facsimile edn, Louis B. Wright (ed.), Charlottesville: University Press of Virginia.

Beyers, C. J. (ed.) (1977) *Dictionary of South African Biography*, Vol. 3, Pretoria: Human Sciences Research Council.

Bhabha, H. (1985) 'Signs taken for wonders: questions of ambivalence and authority under a tree outside Delhi, May 1817', in F. Barker, P. Hulme, M. Iversen and D. Loxley (eds), *Europe and its Others. Proceedings of the Essex Conference on the Sociology of Literature*, pp. 89–106, Colchester: University of Essex.

Bhabha, H. K. (1994) *The Location of Culture*, London: Routledge.

Bickford-Smith, V. (1990) 'The origins and early history of District Six to 1910', in S. Jeppie and C. Soudien (eds), pp. 35–43, *The Struggle for District Six: Past and Present*, pp. 35–43, Cape Town: Buchu Books.

Bogaert, N. (1711) *Historiche Reizen Doort d'Oosterssche Deelen van Asia*, Amsterdam: Nicolas ten Hoorn.

Bosnia-Herzegovina (2000) *The Embassy of Bosnia and Herzegovina*. Online. Available HTTP://www.bosnianembassy.org (10 January 2000).

Botha, L. (1995) *Krotoa's Room – Photographic Component*, William Fehr Collection, Castle, Cape Town, exhibition pamphlet.

Boxer, C. R. (1957) *The Dutch in Brazil, 1624–1654*, Oxford: Clarendon Press.

Bozinović, R. (1998) *Serbian History Through Coinage*. Online. Available HTTP: http://www.suc.org/exhibitions/coins (10 January 2000).

Bradlow, E. (1977) 'Cape Town's labouring poor a century ago', *South African Historical Journal* 9: 19–29.

Braudel, F. (1981) *Civilization and Capitalism, 15th–18th Century, Volume 1, The Structures of Everyday life: The Limits of the Possible*, New York: Harper and Row.

—— (1982) *Civilization and Capitalism, 15th–18th Century, Volume 2, The Wheels of Commerce*, New York: Harper and Row.

—— (1984) *Civilization and Capitalism, 15th–18th Century, Volume 3, The Perspective of the World*, New York: Harper and Row.

Braunfels, W. (1988) *Urban Design in Western Europe. Regime and Architecture, 900–1900*, Chicago: University of Chicago Press.

Brenner, R. (1977) 'The origins of capitalist development: a critique of Neo-Smithian Marxism', *New Left Review* 104: 25–92.

Brewer, J. and Porter, R. (1993) 'Introduction', in J. Brewer and R. Porter (eds), *Consumption and the World of Goods*, pp. 1–18, London: Routledge.

Brink, T. (1801) *Petition to Acting Governor of the Cape of Good Hope*, Cape Archives, Cape Town, BO79: 96–108.

Brink, Y. (1992) 'Places of discourse and dialogue: a study in the material culture of the Cape during the rule of the Dutch East India Company, 1652–1795', PhD dissertation, University of Cape Town.

Byrd, W. (1924) 'Letter to Charles, Earl of Orrery', *Virginia Magazine of History and Biography* 32.

Cairns, M. (1974) *Cradle of Commerce: The Story of Block B*, Cape Town: Woolworths.

—— (1980) 'Paradise, Newlands', *Quarterly Bulletin of the South African Library* 35: 60–5.

Carruthers, M. (1990) *The Book of Memory. A Study of Memory in Medieval Culture*, Cambridge: Cambridge University Press.

Carson, C., Barka, N., Kelso, W., Stone, G. W. and Upton, D. (1981) 'Impermanent architecture in the southern American colonies', *Winterthur Portfolio* 16: 136–96.

Carter, P. (1988) *The Road to Botany Bay. An Exploration of Landscape and History*, Chicago: University of Chicago Press.

Castells, M. (1996) *The Information Age: Economy, Society and Culture, Volume 1, The Rise of the Network Society*, Oxford: Blackwell.

—— (1997) *The Information Age: Economy, Society and Culture, Volume 2, The Power of Identity*, Oxford: Blackwell.

—— (1998) *The Information Age: Economy, Society and Culture, Volume 3, End of Millennium*, Oxford: Blackwell.

Chappell, E. (1984) 'Looking at buildings', *Fresh Advices (Colonial Williamsburg)* November: i–iv.

Clift, H. (1996) *Excavation of a Spoil Heap in District Six*, Research Unit for the Archaeology of Cape Town, University of Cape Town.

Coetzee, J. M. (1982) *Dusklands*, Johannesburg: Ravan Press.

—— (1988) *White Writing. On the Culture of Letters in South Africa*, New Haven: Yale University Press.

Collinson, R. (1867) *The Three Voyages of Martin Frobisher*, New York: Burt Franklin.

Colonial Williamsburg Foundation (2000) *Williamsburg Restored*. Online. Available HTTP: http://www.history.org (10 January 2000).

Conrad, J. (1971) *Heart of Darkness*, New York: W. W. Norton.

Cooper, H. (1993) 'Review of Robert Kaplan, "Balkan Ghosts"', *Slavic Review* 52: 592–3.

Croatia (2000) *Croatian Institute for Culture and Information*. Online. Available HTTP: http://www.croatia.hr (10 January 2000).

Dabić, V. and Lukić, K. (1997) *Atmosphere of Fear and Ethnic Cleansing in Vukovar*. Online. Available HTTP: http://www.suc.org/politics/war_crimes/vukovar/vukovar7a. html (15 December 1998).

Davidoff, L. and Hall, C. (1987) *Family Fortunes. Men and Women of the English Middle Class, 1780–1850*, London: Hutchinson.

de Bosdari, C. (1953) *Cape Dutch Houses and Farms*, Cape Town: Balkema.

—— (1954) *Anton Anreith. Africa's First Sculptor*, Cape Town: Balkema.

de Kock, W. J. (ed.) (1968) *Dictionary of South African Biography*, Vol. 1, Pretoria: National Council for Social Research.

Deetz, J. (1977) *In Small Things Forgotten. The Archaeology of Early American Life*, New York: Anchor Books.

—— (1993) *Flowerdew Hundred. The Archaeology of a Virginia Plantation, 1619–1864*, Charlottesville: University Press of Virginia.

—— (1996) *In Small Things Forgotten. An Archaeology of Early American Life*, expanded and revised, New York: Anchor Books.

Denitch, B. (1994) *Ethnic Nationalism: The Tragic Death of Yugoslavia*, Minneapolis: University of Minnesota Press.

Domovina Net (2000) *Domovina Net*. Online. Available HTTP: http://www. domovina.net (10 January 2000).

Dougherty, J. (1996) *Clinton Sounds Call to Stop Church Burnings*. Online. Available HTTP: http://www.cnn.com/US/9606/08/clinton.radio/cnn (10 January 2000).

Douglas, M. and Isherwood, B. (1978) *The World of Goods. Towards an Anthropology of Consumption*, London: Allen Lane.

Duke, L. (1993) 'Jefferson: the question of a slave son', *Washington Post*, 13 April 1993.

Duncan, J. (1990) *The City as Text: The Politics of Landscape Interpretation in the Kandyan Kingdom*, Cambridge: Cambridge University Press.

du Plessis, I. D. (1944) *The Cape Malays*, Cape Town: Maskew Miller.

Elphick, R. (1985) *Khoikhoi and the Founding of White South Africa*, Johannesburg: Ravan Press.

Erickson, A. L. (1993) *Women and Property in Early Modern England*, London: Routledge.

Fine, J. V. A. (1983) *The Early Medieval Balkans*, Ann Arbor: University of Michigan Press.

—— (1987) *The Late Medieval Balkans*, Ann Arbor: University of Michigan Press.

Fisher, J. (1997) 'The postmodern paradiso: Dante, cyberpunk, and the technology of cyberspace', in D. Porter (ed.), *Internet Culture*, pp. 112–28, London: Routledge.

Fortune, L. (1996) *The House in Tyne Street: Childhood Memories of District Six*, Cape Town: Kwela.

Foster, D. (1997) 'Community and identity in the electronic village', in D. Porter (ed.), *Internet Culture*, pp. 23–37, London: Routledge.

Foster, E. A., Jobling, M. A., Taylor, P. G., Donnelly, P., de Knijff, P., Mieremet, R., Zerjal, T. and Tyler-Smith, C. (1998) 'Jefferson fathered slave's last child', *Nature* 396: 27–8.

Foucault, M. (1972) *The Archaeology of Knowledge*, London: Tavistock.

—— (1979) *Discipline and Punish. The Birth of the Prison*, New York: Vintage Books.

Fouché, L. (ed.) (1970) *The Diary of Adam Tas 1705–1706*, Cape Town: Van Riebeeck Society.

Frank, A. G. (1978) *Dependent Accumulation and Underdevelopment*, New York: Macmillan.

Franklin, M. (1995) 'Rethinking the Carter's Grove Slave Quarter reconstruction: a proposal', *Kroeber Anthropological Society Papers* 79: 147–64.

Fransen, H. (1987) 'Classicism, baroque, rococo and neoclassicism at the Cape. An investigation into stylistic modes in the architecture and applied arts at the Cape of Good Hope 1652–1820', PhD dissertation, University of Natal (Pietermaritzburg).

Fransen, H. and Cook, M. A. (1980) *The Old Buildings of the Cape*, Cape Town: Balkema.

Fraser, V. (1990) *The Architecture of Conquest. Building in the Viceroyalty of Peru, 1533–1635*, Cambridge: Cambridge University Press.

Gable, E. R., Handler, R. and Lawson, A. (1993) 'On the uses of relativism: fact, conjecture, and black and white histories at Colonial Williamsburg', *American Ethnologist* 19(4): 791–805.

Ganz, P. (1950) *The Paintings of Hans Holbein*, London: Phaidon.

Geyl, P. (1964) *History of the Low Countries; Episodes and Problems*, London: Macmillan.

Gibson, W. (1984) *Neuromancer*, London: HarperCollins.

Giddens, A. (1984) *The Constitution of Society. Outline of a Theory of Structuration*, Cambridge: Polity Press.

Glassie, H. (1975) *Folk Housing in Middle Virginia*, Knoxville: University of Tennessee Press.

Gray, S. (ed.) (1989) *The Penguin Book of Southern African Verse*, Harmondsworth: Penguin.

Greenblatt, A. (1991) *Marvelous Possessions. The Wonder of the New World*, Oxford: Clarendon Press.

Guelke, L. (1974) 'The early European settlement of South Africa, PhD dissertation, University of Toronto.

—— (1989) 'Freehold farmers and frontier settlers, 1657–1780', in R. Elphick and H. Giliomee (eds), *The Shaping of South African Society, 1652–1840*, pp. 66–108, Cape Town: Maskew Miller Longman.

Hall, M. (1987) *The Changing Past: Farmers, Kings and Traders in Southern Africa, 200–1860*, Cape Town: David Philip.

—— (1990) '"Hidden history". Iron Age archaeology in Southern Africa', in P. Robertshaw (ed.), *A History of African Archaeology*, pp. 59–77, London: James Currey.

—— (1992a) 'Small things and the mobile, conflictual fusion of power, fear and desire', in A. Yentsch and M. Beaudry (eds), *The Art and Mystery of Historical Archaeology. Essays in Honor of James Deetz*, pp. 373–99, Boca Raton: CRC Press.

—— (1992b) *People in a Changing Urban Landscape: Excavating Cape Town*, inaugural lecture, Rondebosch: University of Cape Town.

—— (1994a) 'The secret lives of houses: women and gables in the eighteenth century Cape', *Social Dynamics* 20(1): 1–48.

—— (1994b) *Horstley Street, District Six*, Research Unit for the Archaeology of Cape Town, University of Cape Town.

—— (1999) 'Virtual colonisation', *Journal of Material Culture* 41(1): 41–57.

Hall, M., Halkett, D., Huigen van Beek, P. and Klose, J. (1990a) '"A stone wall out of the earth that thundering cannon cannot destroy"? Bastion and moat at the Castle, Cape Town', *Social Dynamics* 16(1): 22–37.

Hall, M., Halkett, D., Klose, J. and Ritchie, G. (1990b) 'The Barrack Street Well: images of a Cape Town household in the nineteenth century', *South African Archaeological Bulletin* 45(152): 73–92.

Hall, M., Malan, A., Amann, S., Honeyman, L., Kiser, T. and Ritchie, G. (1993) 'The archaeology of Paradise', *South African Archaeological Society Goodwin Series* 7: 40–58.

Hall, S. (1990) 'Cultural identity and diaspora', in J. Rutherford (ed.), *Identity: Community, Culture, Difference*, pp. 222–37, London: Lawrence and Wishart.

Handler, R. and Gable, E. (1997) *The New History in an Old Museum: Creating the Past at Colonial Williamsburg*, Durham: Duke University Press.

Hart, D. (1990) 'Political manipulation of urban space: the razing of District Six, Cape Town', in S. Jeppie and C. Soudien (eds), *The Struggle for District Six: Past and Present*, pp. 117–42, Cape Town: Buchu Books.

Hart, T. and Halkett, D. (1996) *Excavations in District Six: a Residential Property at the Corner of Stukeris and Roger Streets*, Research Unit for the Archaeology of Cape Town, University of Cape Town.

Hartmann, H. (1981) 'The unhappy marriage of Marxism and Feminism: towards a more progressive union', in L. Sargent (ed.), *Women and Revolution: A Discussion of the Unhappy Marriage of Marxism and Feminism*, pp. 1–41, Boston: South End Press.

Hasseltine, W. B. and Smiley, D. L. (1960) *The South in American History*, Englewood Cliffs: Prentice-Hall.

Hayles, K. (1993) 'The seduction of cyberspace', in V. Conley (ed.), *Rethinking Technologies*, Minneapolis: University of Minnesota Press.

Heese, H. F. (1984) *Groep Sonder Grense. Die Rol en Status van die Gemengde Bevolking aan die Kaap, 1652–1795*, Cape Town: Institute for Historical Research, University of the Western Cape.

Heidelberg Project (2000) *The Heidelberg Project*. Online. Available HTTP: http://www.heidelberg.org (10 January 2000).

Hinduism Online (2000) *Hinduism Online*. Online. Available HTTP: http://www. hinduismtoday. Kauai.hi.us (10 January 2000).

Hobsbawm, E. J. (1987) *The Age of Empire 1870–1914*, London: Little, Brown and Company.

Hodder, H. F. (1996) *Bibliocide. Harvard Magazine*. Online. Available HTTP: http:// www.harvard-magazine.com/nd96/right.biblio.html (10 January 2000).

Hoge, J. (1946) 'Personalia of Germans at the Cape, 1652–1806', *Archives Year Book* 9.

Horrell, M. (ed.) (1967) *A Survey of Race Relations in South Africa*, Johannesburg: South African Institute of Race Relations.

Huizinga, J. H. (1968) *Dutch Civilization in the Seventeenth Century*, London: Collins.

Iijima, M. (1998) 'Feature: Indian temple town just wants peace', *Reuters*, 5 July 1998.

Isaac, R. (1982) *The Transformation of Virginia*, Chapel Hill: University of North Carolina Press.

Israel, J. (1989) *Dutch Primacy in World Trade, 1585–1740*, Oxford: Clarendon Press.

James, C. (2000) *To Live Like a Slave: In Reenactment at the Carter's Grove Slave Quarter, Black Interpreters Gain Insights to their Ancestral Past*. Online. Available HTTP: http:// www.history.org/other/journal/slave.htm (10 January 2000).

Jameson, F. (1989) 'Nostalgia for the present', *South Atlantic Quarterly* 88(2(Spring)): 517–37.

Jeptanović, N. (n.d.) *Mausoleum of the Family Petrinovic in Supertar, Island of Brac*, Brač, Croatia (Emineograph).

Johnson, M. (1996) *An Archaeology of Capitalism*, Oxford: Blackwell.

—— (1999) 'Reconstructing castles and refashioning identities in Renaissance England', in S. Tarlow and S. West (eds), *The Familiar Past? Archaeologies of Later Historical Britain*, pp. 69–86, London: Routledge.

Jorg, C. J. A. (1982) *Porcelain and the Dutch China Trade*, The Hague: Martinus Nijhoff.

Judges, S. (1977) 'Poverty, Living Conditions and Social Relations – Aspects of Life in Cape Town in the 1830s', Master of Arts, University of Cape Town.

Kaplan, R. D. (1994) *Balkan Ghosts: A Journey Through History*, New York: Vintage.

Kelso, W. M. (1984) *Kingsmill Plantations, 1619–1800. Archaeology of Country Life in Colonial Virginia*, Orlando: Academic Press.

—— (1986) 'The archaeology of slave life at Thomas Jefferson's Monticello: "A wolf by the ears"', *Journal of New World Archaeology* 6(4): 5–20.

Kerr, R. (1986) *Chinese Ceramics. Porcelain of Qing Dynasty 1644–1911*, London: Victoria and Albert Museum.

Kimball, F. (1966 (1922)) *Domestic Architecture of the American Colonies and of the Early Republic*, New York: Dover Publications.

Kolbe, P. (1968 (1719)) *Present State of the Cape of Good Hope*, trans. Guido Medley, New York: Johnson Reprint Corporation.

Kostof, S. (1991) *The City Shaped. Urban Patterns and Meanings through History*, London: Thames and Hudson.

Kujundzić, E. (1997) *From Ashes: the Fate of the National and University Library of Bosnia and Herzegovina*. Online. Available HTTP: http://www.geocities.com/CapitolHill/ 6777/library.htm (15 November 1998).

la Guma, A. (1962) *A Walk in the Night*, London: Heinemann.

Leech, R. (1999) 'The processional city: some issues for historical archaeology', in S. Tarlow and S. West (eds), *The Familiar Past? Archaeologies of Later Historical Britain*, pp. 19–34, London: Routledge.

Leibbrandt, H. C. V. (1896) *Precis of the Archives of the Cape of Good Hope. Journal, 1699–1732*, Cape Town: W. A. Richards and Sons.

—— (1901) *Precis of the Archives of the Cape of Good Hope. Journal, 1662–1670*, Cape Town: W. A. Richards and Sons.

Leighton, J. (1862) *Moral Emblems, with Aphorisms, Adages, and Proverbs, of all Ages and Nations, from Jacob Cats and Robert Farlie*, London: Longman, Green and Roberts.

Leone, M. (1988) 'The Georgian order as the order of merchant capitalism in Annapolis, Maryland', in M. Leone and P. Potter (eds), *The Recovery of Meaning. Historical Archaeology in the Eastern United States*, pp. 235–61, Washington: Smithsonian Institution.

Lockridge, K. (1987) *The Diary, and Life, of William Byrd of Virginia, 1674–1744*, Chapel Hill: University of North Carolina Press.

Lounsbury, C. (1989) 'The structure of justice: the courthouses of Colonial Virginia', in T. Carter and B. Herman (eds), *Perspectives in Vernacular Architecture*, Vol. 3, pp. 214–26, Colombia: University of Missouri Press.

Lovrenović, I. (1994) 'The hatred of memory: in Sarajevo, burned books and murdered pictures', *New York Times*, 28 May 1994.

Lyon, D. (1997) 'Cyberspace sociality: controversies over computer-mediated relationships', in B. Loader (ed.), *The Governance of Cyberspace; Politics, Technology and Global Restructuring*, pp. 23–37, London: Routledge.

Maass, P. (1996) *Love Thy Neighbor: A Story of War*, New York: Vintage.

McConnell, D. (1998) *Artists's Dream Nears End. Council on Course to Move or Level Heidelberg Project*. Online. Available HTTP: http://www.freep.com/news/local/qheid29.htm (29 September 1998).

Maclaren, N. (1960) *The Dutch School, 3 Volumes, National Gallery Catalogues*, London: Trustees of the National Gallery.

McKee, L. (1988) 'Plantation food supply in nineteenth century tidewater Virginia', Doctor of Philosophy, University of California (Berkeley).

McKendrick, N. (1982) 'Commercialization and the economy', in N. McKendrick, J. Brewer and J. H. Plumb (eds), *The Birth of a Consumer Society. The Commercialization of Eighteenth-Century England*, pp. 9–196, London: Europa Publications.

Malan, A. (1990) 'The archaeology of probate inventories', *Social Dynamics* 16(1): 1–10.

—— (1993) 'Households of the Cape, 1750–1850. Inventories and the Archaeological Record', Doctor of Philosophy, University of Cape Town.

Malcolm, N. (1996) *Bosnia: A Short History*, New York: New York University Press.

—— (1998) *Kosovo: A Short History*, New York: New York University Press.

Malherbe, V. C. (1990) *Krotoa, Called 'Eva': A Woman Between*, Cape Town: Centre for African Studies, University of Cape Town.

Malkani, K. R. (1998) *BJP History: Its Birth, Growth and Onward March*. Online. Available HTTP: http://www.bjp.org/history.html (15 September 1998).

Mandal, D. (1993) *Ayodhya: Archaeology After Demolition*, Hyderabad: Orient Longman.

Markell, A., Hall, M. and Schrire, C. (1995) 'The historical archaeology of Vergelegen, an early farmstead at the Cape of Good Hope', *Historical Archaeology* 29(1): 10–34.

Martin, P. (1991) *The Pleasure Gardens of Virginia. From Jamestown to Jefferson*, Princeton: Princeton University Press.

Maser, E. A. (ed.) (1971) *Cesare Ripa. Baroque and Rococo Pictorial Imagery. The 1758–60 Hertel Edition of Ripa's 'Iconologia'*, New York: Dover.

Mason, P. (1990) *Deconstructing America. Representations of the Other*, London: Routledge.

Melwani, L. (1998) *Hey, Just Who Are You Guys, Anyway?* Online. Available HTTP: http://www.hinduismtoday.kauai.hi.us/Newspaper/History/LavinaStory.html (15 December 1998).

Mentzel, O. F. (1919 (1784)) *Life at the Cape in Mid-Eighteenth Century, Being the Biography of Rudolf Siegfried Allemann, Captain of the Military Forces and Commander of the Castle in the Service of the Dutch East India Company at the Cape of Good Hope*, Trans. Margaret Greenlees, Cape Town: Van Riebeeck Society.

—— (1921 (1785)) *A Geographical and Topographical Description of the Cape of Good Hope, Part One, Edited by H. J. Mandelbrote*, Cape Town: Van Riebeeck Society.

—— (1925 (1785)) *A Geographical and Topographical Description of the Cape of Good Hope, Part Two, Edited by H. J. Mandelbrote*, Cape Town: Van Riebeeck Society.

—— (1944 (1787)) *A Geographical and Topographical Description of the Cape of Good Hope, Part Three, Edited by H. J. Mandelbrote*, Cape Town: Van Riebeeck Society.

Miglani, S. (1998) 'Hindu group plays archaeology card in temple now', *Reuters*, 24 June 1998.

Miller, D. (1987) *Material Culture and Mass Consumption*, Oxford: Blackwell.

Monticello Association (2000) *The Monticello Association*. Online. Available HTTP: http://www.monticello-assoc.org/index.html (10 January 2000).

Morgan, E. S. (1975) *American Slavery, American Freedom. The Ordeal of Colonial Virginia*, New York: W. W. Norton.

Mossop, E. E. (1927) *Old Cape Highways*, Cape Town: Maskew Miller.

Murray, B. (1997) *Clearing the Heirs. We May Soon Know if Jefferson Had Black Children*. US News Online. Available HTTP: http://www.usnews.com (22 December 1997).

Nasson, B. (1990) 'Oral history and the reconstruction of District Six', in S. Jeppie and C. Soudien (eds), *The Struggle for District Six: Past and Present*, pp. 44–66, Cape Town: Buchu Books.

National Library of Medicine (2000) *The Visible Human Project*. Online. Available HTTP: http://www.nlm.nih.gov/research/visible/visible_human.html (10 January 2000).

Obholzer, A. M., Baraitser, M. and Malherbe, W. D. (1985) *The Cape House and its Interior*, Stellenbosch: Stellenbosch Museum.

Orser, C. E. and Fagan, B. M. (1995) *Historical Archaeology*, New York: HarperCollins.

Ozkan, S. (1994) 'The destruction of Stari Most', *Development Network* 14: 5–7.

Pama, C. (1981 (1893–1895)) *Genealogies of Old South African Families, 2 Volumes, C. C. de Villiers, Revised and Edited by C. Pama*, Cape Town: Balkema.

Parker, K. (1995) 'Telling tales: early modern English voyagers and the Cape of Good Hope', *The Seventeenth Century* 10(1): 121–49.

Patterson, O. (1982) *Slavery and Social Death. A Comparative Study*, Cambridge: Harvard University Press.

Pavić, V. (1997) 'The register of war damage to museums and galleries in Croatia', in *War Damage to Museums and Galleries in Croatia*, pp. 55–166. Zagreb: Muzejski Dokumentacijski Centar.

Pearse, G. (1959) *Eighteenth Century Architecture in South Africa*, London: Batsford.

Pollack, M. D. (1991) *Turin, 1564–1680. Urban Design, Military Culture, and the Creation of the Absolutist State*, Chicago: University of Chicago Press.

Poster, M. (1990) *The Mode of Information: Poststructuralism and Social Context*, Cambridge: Polity.

—— (1995) *The Second Media Age*, Cambridge: Polity Press.

Prah, K. K. (1997) *Beyond the Colour Line: Pan-Africanist Disputations*, Johannesburg: Vivlia.

Pratt, M. L. (1992) *Imperial Eyes: Travel Writing and Transculturation*, London: Routledge.

Press, K. (1990) *Krotoa's Story*, Cape Town: Buchu Books.

Pugh, S. (1988) *Garden-Nature-Language*, Manchester: Manchester University Press.

Quétel, C. (1990) *History of Syphilis*, Cambridge: Polity Press.

Raven Hart, R. (1971) *Cape of Good Hope 1652–1702. The First Fifty Years of Dutch Colonization as Seen by Callers*, 2 volumes, Cape Town: Balkema.

Rheingold, H. (1991) *Virtual Reality*, New York: Simon and Schuster.

—— (1993) *The Virtual Community: Homesteading on the Electronic Frontier*, Reading: Addison-Wesley.

Riedlmayer, A. (1995) *Destruction of Libraries in Bosnia-Herzegovina*, Middle East Studies Association Bulletin. Online. Available HTTP: http://www.cua.edu/www/mesabul/bosnia.htm (15 December 1998).

—— (1998) *Fighting the Destruction of Memory: A Call for an Inagathering of Bosnian Manuscripts*. Online. Available HTTP: http://www.applicom.com/manu/ingather.htm (15 December 1998).

Rive, R. (1986) *Buckingham Palace, District Six*, Cape Town: David Philip.

—— (1990) 'District Six: fact and fiction', in S. Jeppie and C. Soudien (eds), *The Struggle for District Six: Past and Present*, pp. 110–16, Cape Town: Buchu Books.

Roberton, H. (1988) 'Battle for the heart of Afrikanderdom', *Cape Times*, 1 October 1988.

Robinson, A. M. L. (ed.) (1973) *The Letters of Lady Anne Barnard Written to Henry Dundas from the Cape of Good Hope 1793–1803*, Cape Town: Balkema.

Rosenau, J. (1990) *Turbulence in World Politics: A Theory of Change and Continuity*, Princeton: Princeton University Press.

Ross, R. (1983) *Cape of Torments. Slavery and Resistance in South Africa*, London: Routledge and Kegan Paul.

Ryan, C. (1988) 'Battle of the Great Treks is on again', *Star* (Johannesburg), 10 April 1988.

Samuel, R. (1994) *Theatres of Memory*, London: Verso.

Savage, G. (1963) *Porcelain Through the Ages*, Harmondsworth: Penguin.

Schama, S. (1988) *The Embarrasment of Riches. An Interpretation of Dutch Culture in the Golden Age*, Berkeley: University of California Press.

—— (1995) *Landscape and Memory*, London: HarperCollins.

Scharf, W. and C. Vale (1996) 'The Firm – organised crime comes of age during the transition to democracy', *Social Dynamics* 22(2): 30–6.

Schork, K. (1998) 'Analysis – KLA shatters Europe's placid self-image', *Reuters*, 9 July 1998.

Schutte, G. J. (ed.) (1982) *Briefwiseling van Hendrik Swellengrebel Jr oor Kaapse Sake 1778– 1792*, Cape Town: Van Riebeeck Society.

Scott, J. C. (1985) *Weapons of the Weak. Everyday Forms of Peasant Resistance*, London: Yale University Press.

—— (1990) *Domination and the Arts of Resistance. Hidden Transcripts*, New Haven: Yale University Press.

Scully, V. (1991) 'Architecture: the natural and the manmade', in S. Wrede and W. H. Adams (eds) *Denatured Visions: Landscape and Culture in the Twentieth Century*, pp. 7–18, New York: Museum of Modern Art.

Semple, R. (ed.) (1968 (1805)) *Walks and Sketches at the Cape of Good Hope*, F. R. Bradlow (ed.), Cape Town: Balkema.

Serbian Unity Congress (2000) *Serbian Unity Congress*. Online. Available HTTP: http://www.suc.org (10 January 2000).

Serton, P. (1971) 'Introduction', in P. Serton, R. Raven-Hart, W. J. De Kock and E. H. Raidt (eds), *Françoise Valentyn. Description of the Cape of Good Hope with the Matters Concerning it. Part I*, Cape Town: Van Riebeeck Society.

Shackel, P. (1993) *Personal Discipline and Material Culture: An Archaeology of Annapolis, Maryland, 1695–1870*, Knoxville: University of Tennessee Press.

Shell, R. C.-H. (1994) *Children of Bondage. A Social History of the Slave Society at the Cape of Good Hope, 1652–1838*, Johannesburg: Witwatersrand University Press.

Singleton, T. A. (1995) 'The archaeology of slavery in North America', *Annual Review of Anthropology* 24: 119–40.

Smith, R. (1938) 'The Brazilian landscapes of Frans Post', *Arts Quarterly* 1 (4): 238–67.

Smuts, F. (ed.) (1979) *Stellenbosch Three Centuries*, Stellenbosch: Town Council of Stellenbosch.

Sorabji, C. (1992) *Bosnia's Muslims: Challenging Past and Present Misconceptions*, London.

Soudien, C. (1990) 'District Six: from protest to protest', in S. Jeppie and C. Soudien (eds), *The Struggle for District Six: Past and Present*, pp. 143–83, Cape Town: Buchu Books.

Soudien, C. and R. Meyer (1997) *The District Six Public Sculpture Project*, Cape Town: District Six Museum Foundation.

Sparrman, A. (1975 (1772–1776)) *A Voyage to the Cape of Good Hope*, V. S. Forbes (eds), Cape Town: Van Riebeeck Society.

Spivak, G. C. (1985) 'The Rani of Sirmur', in F. Barker, P. Hulme, M. Iversen and D. Loxley (eds), *Europe and its Others. Proceedings of the Essex Conference on the Sociology of Literature*, pp. 128–51, Colchester: University of Essex.

Spohr, O. H. (1967) *Zacharias Wagner. Second Commander of the Cape*, Cape Town: A. A. Balkema.

Stallybrass, P. and A. White (1986) *The Politics and Poetics of Transgression*, Ithaca: Cornell University Press.

Stavorinus, J. S. (1969 (1798)) *Voyages to the East Indies*, 3 volumes, London: Dawsons.

Stoler, A. L. (1991) 'Carnal knowledge and imperial power: gender, race, and morality in colonial Asia', in M. Di Leonardo (ed.), *Gender at the Crossroads of Knowledge. Feminist Anthropology in the Postmodern Era*, pp. 51–101, Berkeley: University of California Press.

Stuijt, A. (1988) 'Quick dip at "quiet" beach leads to festival boycott furore', *Weekend Argus* (Cape Town), 9 January 1988.

Sulć, B. (1997) 'Museums in war', in *War Damage to Museums and Galleries in Croatia*, pp. 11–18, Zagreb: Muzejski Dokumentacijski Centar.

Taylor, J. G. (1983) *The Social World of Batavia. European and Eurasian in Dutch Asia*, Madison: University of Wisconsin Press.

Taylor, P. J. (1981) 'Political geography and the world economy', in A. Burnett and

P. J. Taylor (eds), *Political Studies from Spatial Perspectives. Anglo-American Essays on Political Geography*, pp. 157–72, Chichester: John Wiley and Sons.

TBWT (1997) *TBWT Launches Sankofa University on the Web*. Online. Available HTTP: http://www.tbwt.com/misc/tbwtpress1.asp (10 January 2000).

—— (2000) *The Black World Today*. Online. Available HTTP: http://www.tbwt.com (10 January 2000).

Theal, G. M. (1964 (1927)) *History of South Africa before 1795, Volume 3, Foundation of the Cape Colony by the Dutch*, Cape Town: Struik.

Theobald, M. M. (2000) *Sampling 18th-Century Fare at Shields Tavern*. Online. Available HTTP: http://www.history.org/other/journal/tavern.htm (10 January 2000).

Thom, H. B. (ed.) (1952) *Journal of Jan van Riebeeck, Volume I, 1651–1655*, Cape Town: Balkema.

—— (ed.) (1954) *Journal of Jan van Riebeeck, Volume II, 1656–1658*, Cape Town: Balkema.

—— (ed.) (1958) *Journal of Jan van Riebeeck, Volume III, 1659–1662*, Cape Town: Balkema.

Thomas, J. (2000) 'Reconfiguring the social, reconfiguring the material', in M. Schiffer (ed.), *Social Theory in Archaeology*, Salt Lake City: University of Utah Press.

Thomsen, T. (1938) *Albert Eckhout; ein Niederlandischer Maler und sein Gonner Moritz der Brasiliander*, Copenhagen: Munksgaard.

Thunberg, C. P. (1986 (1772–1775)) *Travels at the Cape of Good Hope*, V. S. Forbes (ed.), Cape Town: Van Riebeeck Society.

Tilley, C. (1989) 'Interpreting material culture', in I. Hodder (ed.), *The Meanings of Things. Material Culture and Symbolic Expression*, pp. 185–94, London: Harper Collins.

Tilley, C. (1994) *A Phenomenology of Landscape: Places, Paths and Monuments*, Oxford: Berg.

Todorov, T. (1984) *The Conquest of America: The Question of the Other*, trans. Richard Howard, New York: Harper and Row.

Todorova, M. (1994) 'The Balkans: from discovery to invention', *Slavic Review* 53(2): 453–82.

Valentyn, F. (1971 (1726)) *Description of the Cape of Good Hope with the Matters Concerning it. Part I*, R. Serton, R. Raven Hart, W. J. de Kock and E. Raidt (eds), Cape Town: Van Riebeeck Society.

—— (1973 (1726)) *Description of the Cape of Good Hope with the Matters Concerning it. Part II*, E. Raidt (ed.), Cape Town: Van Riebeeck Society.

Vinterhalter, J. (1997) 'Protection in museums – the first wartime task. Six years later', in *War Damage to Museums and Galleries in Croatia*, pp. 19–38, Zagreb: Muzejski Dokumentacijski Centar.

Visoki Decani Monastery (2000) *Visoki Decani Monastery*. Online. Available HTTP: http://www.decani.yunet.com/edecani.html (10 January 2000).

Vlach, J. M. (1986) 'The shotgun house: an African architectural legacy', in D. Upton and M. Vlach (eds) *Common Places: Readings in American Vernacular Architecture*, pp. 58–78, Athens: University of Georgia Press.

VOC (1754–86) *Kaapse Plakkaatboek* 3: 12–15.

Volker, T. (1959) *The Japanese Porcelain Trade of the Dutch East India Company after 1683*, Leiden: E. J. Brill.

—— (1971) *Porcelain and the Dutch East India Company as Recorded in the Dagh-Registers of*

Batavia Castle, Those of Hirado and Deshima and the Other Contemporary Papers 1602–1682, Leiden: E. J. Brill.

Vuleta, T. (1998) *Medieval Serbian Royal Ornaments*. Online. Available HTTP: http://www.suc.org/culture/history/Medieval_Ornaments (10 January 2000).

Wallerstein, I. (1974) *The Modern World System: Capitalist Agriculture and the Origins of the European World Economy in the Sixteenth Century*, New York: Academic Press.

—— (1980) *The Modern World System II. Mercantilism and the Consolidation of the European World Economy, 1600–1750*, London: Academic Press.

Warner, M. (1998) 'Is there another place from which the dickhead's self can speak?', *London Review of Books*, 1 October 1998.

Wenger, M. (1980) 'Westover: William Byrd's mansion reconsidered', Master of Architectural History, University of Virginia.

West, R. (1941) *Black Lamb and Grey Falcon*, New York: Viking Press.

Woodward, C. S. (1974) *Oriental Ceramics at the Cape of Good Hope 1652–1795*, Cape Town: Balkema.

Woodward, S. (1995) *Balkan Tragedy, Chaos and Dissolution after the Cold War*, Washington: The Brookings Institution.

Wright, L. B. (ed.) (1966) *The Prose Works of William Byrd of Westover. Narratives of a Colonial Virginian*, Cambridge: Belknap Press of Harvard University Press.

Wright, L. B. and M. Tinling (eds) (1941) *The Secret Diary of William Byrd of Westover, 1709–1712*, Richmond: Dietz Press.

Yentsch, A. (1994) *A Chesapeake Family and their Slaves. A Study in Historical Archaeology*, Cambridge: Cambridge University Press.

Young, R. (1990) *White Mythologies. Writing History and the West*, London: Routledge.

Yugoslavia (2000) *Federal Republic of Yugoslavia. Official Web Site*. Online. Available HTTP: http://www.gov.yu (10 January 2000).

Index